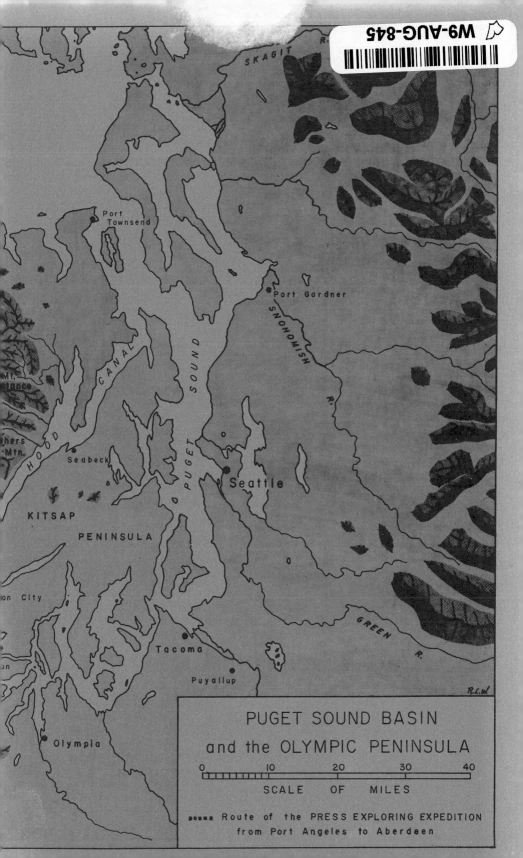

SKAGIT R.

Port
Townsend

Port Gardner

SNOHOMISH

CANAL

R.

PUGET SOUND

Mt.
...iance

HOOD

...hers
...Mtn.

Seabeck

Seattle

KITSAP

PENINSULA

...on City

GREEN

R.

Tacoma

Puyallup

R.L.W.

Olympia

PUGET SOUND BASIN
and the OLYMPIC PENINSULA

0   10   20   30   40

SCALE   OF   MILES

▪▪▪▪▪ Route of the PRESS EXPLORING EXPEDITION
from Port Angeles to Aberdeen

Across the Olympic Mountains

THE PRESS EXPEDITION, 1889–90

Across the
Olympic Mountains

THE PRESS EXPEDITION, 1889-90

by Robert L. Wood

Published by
THE MOUNTAINEERS
and the
UNIVERSITY OF WASHINGTON PRESS
SEATTLE AND LONDON

All maps in this book were drawn by the author

Copyright © 1967 by the University of Washington Press
Library of Congress Catalog Card Number 67–13110
Printed in the United States of America

To the memory
of those who lived
the Press Expedition

James H. Christie
Charles A. Barnes
John W. Sims
John H. Crumback
Christopher Hayes
Dr. Harris B. Runnalls

explorers with
"abundance of grit and manly vim."

PREFACE

The original, detailed account of the Press Exploring Expedition appeared in the July 16, 1890, edition of the Seattle *Press*, the newspaper that sponsored the expedition. For a half century afterward nothing was written about this group, the first to cross the Olympic Mountains. Within the last twenty-five years, however, a number of sketchy, abbreviated accounts of the expedition have appeared, in the form of brief magazine and newspaper articles or portions of chapters in books dealing with the Pacific Northwest. Because of their brevity, these accounts have necessarily touched only the highlights of the exploration.

So far as I am aware, no one has attempted to present the complete account since its original publication more than three quarters of a century ago. In retelling the story, I have been favored with the perspective made possible by the passage of time, and by an intimate knowledge of Olympic geography. But passing time also obscures, and what was common information a few decades ago may be unknown today. Thus, writing this book presented some interesting problems.

The expedition was more than just the men, their dogs, mules, and supplies, or the country traversed. It was what they did, the things they saw and heard, from the inception of the adventure until its conclusion. In relating the story, unwilling to sacrifice factual accuracy, I have not permitted myself to indulge the temptation to soar into flights of hyperbole. I have attempted to write for the general reader a straightforward account of the Press Exploring Expedition. Scholars who may be interested in greater detail should consult the original account as published by the Seattle *Press* in 1890.

Most of what is known about the Press Exploring Expedition is found in that original account, which consisted of some general editorial comments, plus the lengthy narratives of James H. Christie, the expedition's leader, and Charles A. Barnes, the historian. Christie's story was termed a diary in some places, a journal in others; Barnes's account was referred to as a narrative. Each man gave a day-by-day account of the group's activities. However purists might wish to classify these accounts — as diaries, journals, or narratives — is immaterial. It is quite clear that the men kept notes while the expedition was in progress; it is equally apparent that upon returning to civilization they embellished their accounts. How closely the story as printed in the *Press* conformed to their field notes is a matter of speculation, as the notes were probably destroyed years ago.

There are slight variations between the two stories. These differences cannot be reconciled, nor can anyone now determine which of the two is the more correct in a given instance. Usually the points of disagreement are slight and relatively unimportant. Christie's diary appears to be more reliable as far as actual dates, whereas Barnes's longer, rambling narrative, with its greater detail, is written in more interesting language. Christie apparently spent fewer hours polishing his story in Seattle after the expedition's return than did Barnes. His shorter narrative is terse, and he often tends to understate. All the errors in the printed story should not necessarily be attributed to either man; some of them were obvious printer's mistakes.

I have attempted in this book to interpret the Press Exploring Expedition within the light of present-day knowledge of Olympic Peninsula geography, but to retain the spirit of the time in which the event occurred. To do so, I have made liberal use of direct quotations from the narratives of the two men, interspersing these among explanatory material. The quotations chosen were those judged to have particular appeal, either from the factual standpoint or because of the quaint mode of expression. Much of the original newspaper account is dull, uninteresting, and poorly phrased. Therefore, I have written a condensed version of these parts — either in my own words or paraphrasing the original — to serve as a framework to link together the matter quoted verbatim. I was constantly confronted with the necessity to decide in a particular situation whether to quote directly from one account, excluding what the other man said entirely, or to combine the two stories and rewrite in my own words.

In a number of instances I had to make "educated inferences," relying upon my personal knowledge of Olympic topography. I have stated such inferences as fact only where I was convinced of their truth beyond a reasonable doubt. (For example, careful study of maps and the text led me to the inevitable conclusion that Barnes's Mount Bennett was Mount Olympus.)

Because direct quotations from the journals of Barnes and Christie occur frequently in the text, the ordinary method of citation by means of footnotes or end notes would be cumbersome, and I therefore adopted a simpler means of identification: Each long quotation, set apart from the remainder of the text, is followed by the name Barnes or Christie in brackets — indicating that the quotation is from the narrative of the gentleman named — unless the identity of the writer is made evident by the text. On the other hand, minor quotations — such as a phrase or clause — incorporated into my own writing, have not been identified as to source, but merely enclosed within quotation marks. Scholars sufficiently interested in identifying these should refer to the original account. The quotations about the expedition in chapters I and II are all taken from the July 16, 1890, issue of the Seattle *Press*.

A word about the maps. The endpaper map shows the expedition's route across the peninsula; the various route maps show their path across segments of the mountains. Collateral explorations, such as Barnes's trip up Belle River and ascent of Mount Seattle, are not indicated, mainly because there is considerable uncertainty as to the exact route of these side trips.

In writing this story of the Press Exploring Expedition, I am indebted not only to the original narrators, James H. Christie and Charles A. Barnes, but to others as well:

I am particularly grateful to Harvey H. Manning, who encouraged me to undertake this project and refused to allow me to procrastinate. In addition, Mr. Manning offered many suggestions as the manuscript proceeded through various stages. I owe a great deal to Robert Hitchman, who, as Ruby el Hult has stated, "gives so much of himself to other people's projects." Mr. Hitchman not only was helpful in running down elusive information, but he also made available Christie's unpublished scrapbook and permitted reproduction of the few remaining expedition photographs. Mrs. Pierre Barnes, a gracious lady, offered invaluable assistance. She told me the details of Charles Barnes's life, and provided the splendid "before" and "after" group photographs of the expedition, heretofore unpublished. Shirley I. Fager told me of the life of her grandfather, Dr. Harris B. Runnalls, and made available his extensive collection of personal letters and documents. Mary Buell and Gladys Arnold related details of the life of their father and stepfather, John W. Sims, and provided photographs. Also, my mother, Beulah C. Wood, painstakingly read the manuscript and offered numerous suggestions, particularly regarding the use of quoted material. Others who looked at the text with a critical eye include Jesse Epstein, Robert Keller, Mrs. June Maguire, and Frank O. Shaw.

A number of persons helped collect photographs. In addition to Mrs. Barnes and Mr. Hitchman, Mrs. Anna M. Ibbotson, Acting Librarian at the Washington State Historical Museum, was particularly helpful in providing prints of Asahel Curtis' fine photographs of the Olympic country. These she sifted from the more than ten thousand Curtis negatives in the files of the Washington State Historical Society. Others who helped with photographs were Robert W. Kaune, Jr., of the National Park Service; Loomis Miller; and Gordon Wendels and Bert Kellogg, who provided the pictures of old Port Angeles.

I should also like to acknowledge the assistance given me by Trevor Kincaid; Bettie Dunbar; Pauline Jackson; Edmond S. Meany, Jr.; Richard C. Berner and Robert Monroe of the University of Washington Library; Jerry Russell, news editor of the

Bremerton *Sun*; Earl L. Phillips, State Climatologist; and Professor Franklin P. Badgley, Department of Atmospheric Sciences, University of Washington.

ROBERT L. WOOD

Seattle, Washington
August, 1966

CONTENTS

ILLUSTRATIONS

Photographs

Maps

Across the Olympic Mountains

THE PRESS EXPEDITION, 1889–90

INTRODUCTION

THE PACIFIC slope of North America came under the surveillance of civilized man at a comparatively late date. After European settlers had established themselves firmly on the eastern seaboard, fought the American revolution, and founded a vigorous new nation, the great western expansion began — a reaching out to new frontiers. The exploration and settlement of the American West was not, however, one vast, integrated sweep across the plains and mountain ranges (although in perspective it may appear so); rather, it was a mosaic resulting from numerous investigations — large and small — on one of the world's great continents.

The seafarers came first. During the seventeenth and eighteenth centuries, ships from several nations ranged along the Pacific coast. Some of their captains were searching for the Northwest Passage, others seeking the wealth of virgin lands. Then, during the nineteenth century, the sea explorers were replaced by those who traveled on land — men who moved across the plains and into the vast area west of the Continental Divide. In this era of great expeditions sponsored and outfitted by the United States government, explorers became famous almost overnight. Zebulon Pike gave his name to a mountain overlooking the plains, John Charles Frémont roamed the deserts of the Southwest, and Meriwether Lewis and William Clark trekked across the plains and Rockies and on into the Oregon country. Climaxing it all, the government sent four surveying parties into the western territories — the ex-

3

peditions of Clarence King, Dr. Ferdinand V. Hayden, Lieutenant George M. Wheeler, and Major John W. Powell.

The flood tide of exploration (followed by settlement), which began on the eastern coast of North America, accelerated as it moved westward. During the latter half of the nineteenth century, it swiftly crossed the plains and mountains lying between the Mississippi and the Pacific. By 1890 the flood was starting to recede (except for one arm reaching northward into the wilds of Alaska and Canada), and the American frontier was closed.

Floods follow the pathways lacking resistance, and in so doing inevitably skirt inaccessible areas. Thus, the land explorations left many pockets — isolated islands of unexplored country, untouched by the vanguard of the flood pushed relentlessly forward.

The Olympic Peninsula was one of these. Before the admittance of Alaska and Hawaii into the union, the peninsula constituted the northwestern corner of the nation. The seafarers had, of course, skirted its northern coast as they made their way into Puget Sound via the Strait of Juan de Fuca, and the land explorers swarmed around it but failed to penetrate beyond the outermost edges. Once shunned by England, the peninsula was a no-man's land, and, because it was ignored, it remained unknown.

Thus, the stage was set near the end of the nineteenth century for a little drama — one more comic than tragic, although meant to be a serious undertaking. During the winter and spring months of 1889–90, a group known as the Press Exploring Expedition — or, more simply, the Press Party — crossed the then unknown Olympic Mountains which form the heart of the peninsula. The activities of this exploring party were scarcely more than a minor eddy in the backwash left by the flood of exploration and settlement. The Press Party bore little resemblance to the military expeditions that had earlier explored the West; it was more like the "mopping up" operations conducted by a platoon of infantry after the major battle has been fought. The expedition — originally, six men, four dogs, and two mules — was on a small scale compared to the large parties outfitted at government expense. Political overtones connected with the national expansion westward did not apply to the Press Expedition, although it was purportedly organized to open the country for settlement. Locally conceived and executed, the party's exploration of the Olympic Mountains was pure adventure — adventure filled with humor and pathos, gaiety, near tragedy, comedy, sorrow, and happiness, as men with limited resources struggled against a hostile, unknown environment.

The story of the Press Exploring Expedition occupies a unique niche in the history of America, but has remained largely unknown, much like the "terra incognita" that served as the stage for its drama.

Chapter I

TERRA INCOGNITA

THE YEAR was 1889 — the height of the Victorian Age and the eve of the decade commonly called the "Gay Nineties," which saw the closing of the American frontier. The Pacific Northwest was coming of age. Six years earlier, the Puget Sound region had been linked by transcontinental railroad to the East, and the direct result was an influx of settlers. Then, on November 11, 1889, Washington became the forty-second state admitted to the union. A few months later, the eleventh census of the United States revealed the new state to have a population of 349,390 — a 365 per-cent increase in ten years. In one decade Seattle had grown from a town of thirty-five hundred to a city with more than forty thousand inhabitants, and Tacoma had increased from one thousand souls to thirty-six thousand. Other communities enjoyed comparable growth.

Boom conditions prevailed, for this was new country — land endowed with resources on a scale large enough to attract fortune seeker, adventurer, and homesteader alike. Lumbermen and prospectors swarmed over the Puget Sound basin, the loggers appraising the vast stands of giant timber with an eye to exploitation (as they quickly denuded the slopes next to salt water), the prospectors searching for sudden wealth in the mountain streams. But the land was not yet crowded. Aside from the footpads and boomers who drifted into the towns, most of the inhabitants were practical, hard working settlers, many skilled in the use of firearms since childhood.

6

The era probably seemed fast moving to those who lived it, but was relaxed and leisurely by comparison with today's pace. Gas lights were used for illumination, and Thomas Edison's "talking machine" was a popular conversation piece. Gingerbread design and solid construction characterized the architecture of the day, and an eight-room house could be purchased in Seattle for less than two thousand dollars. Gentlemen's suits of excellent quality sold for fifteen dollars, children's outfits for half as much, and the stores were filled with the latest fashions to please the ladies — long skirts, high button shoes, and ostrich-plume hats.

During this time newspapers ran advertisements for pills and tonics guaranteed to cure any ailment — physical or mental — afflicting the human race, and physicians and surgeons carried listings in the classified columns. Other advertisers were steamship and railroad companies, bankers, clothing merchandisers, and the manufacturers of baking powder and the newest rage, Saratoga chips.

In some respects, however, the conditions were not very different from those of today. Real estate men were busy developing and subdividing land (indicative of the economic boom), and stories of lust and violence, accounts of murder trials, and the activities of opium smugglers filled the newspapers. Labor and management wrangled, with certain groups of workmen threatening to strike for higher wages. Simultaneously, relief programs on behalf of the needy were being instituted by the ladies of society, for government-sponsored welfare programs were many years in the future.

The summer of 1889 had been memorable. The business district of Seattle was destroyed by fire, and similar holocausts had also devastated the hearts of three other Washington cities — Ellensburg, Vancouver, and Spokane. In Seattle, where rapid rebuilding was under way, an electric railway system was being extended to Green Lake; on the Olympic Peninsula promoters were campaigning for a railroad to Port Townsend; while in Olympia delegates convened to draft a constitution for the state.

The eighties and nineties were, indeed, a time of uninhibited growth in the Pacific Northwest, and exploitation and settlement were widespread. Every town was flourishing, and real estate men promoted hamlets that to this day are little more than villages as the "Pittsburgh of the Pacific." Kirkland, a small settlement on the eastern shore of Lake Washington, was blatantly proclaimed "the coming iron metropolis of the world," and the same future was prophesied for Snoqualmie Falls. Unconfirmed but persistent rumors insinuated that a New York businessman had come to the west coast "for the purpose of locating a railroad to Alaska."

The automobile had not yet changed the American way of life, however, and the first airplane flight by the Wright brothers was more than a decade away. The few existing roads were muddy, rut-streaked paths edged by towering trees, and people traveled on the water whenever possible. Steamships busily plied the waters of Puget Sound and the Strait of Juan de Fuca, carrying passengers, freight, and livestock. The railroads had come, however, and their arrival stimulated rapid development and exploitation of the region's natural resources.

To the west of Seattle however, across Puget Sound, lay a virtually unknown region — the Olympic Peninsula, sixty-five hundred square miles of wild land covered with forests of giant fir, spruce, and cedar. In the center of the peninsula and surrounded by these forests towered snow-mantled mountains, glittering in the sunshine or withdrawing behind dark, wind-driven clouds.

The Olympic Mountains had been first observed by white men more than a century earlier. On August 10, 1774, Captain Juan Perez, sailing under the Spanish flag, named the loftiest peak "El Cerro de la Santa Rosalia." In the next few years, men from other sea exploring expeditions noted these mountains — particularly sailors under the command of the Spanish explorers Bruno Heceta and Juan de la Bodega y Quadra. Then, on July 4, 1788, an Englishman, Captain John Meares, sighted Santa Rosalia. Impressed, he called the massive white peak Mount Olympus, after the home of the Greek deities, declaring it to be a suitable dwelling place for the New World's gods, and the name has endured for nearly two hundred years.

Olympus was an elusive mountain, however. For more than a hundred years after white men first observed the peak, it had re-

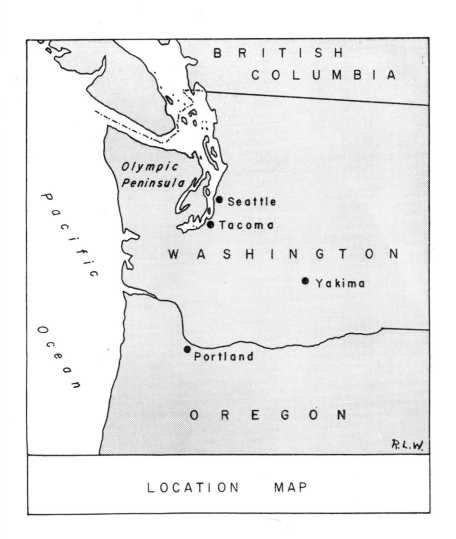

LOCATION   MAP

mained inviolate, nor had the surrounding canyons, mountains, and ridges been explored. The Olympics were clearly visible from the three seaward sides of the peninsula—the Pacific, the Strait of Juan de Fuca, and Puget Sound—but their appearance was different as viewed from each side. This puzzle aroused speculation as to what the mountains enclosed. Yet they remained inaccessible. So mysterious was the interior of the peninsula, in fact, that in 1888 Eugene Semple, the governor of Washington Territory, was inspired to write and forward to the Secretary of the Interior a colorful report about the region. According to the Seattle *Press*, a contemporary newspaper, this poetic and striking description deserved to have a wider circulation than it enjoyed as a public document filed away among the government archives.

> On the western side of Washington territory, facing the restless ocean and defying its angry waves with a rockbound coast, stands the Olympic range of mountains. To the east of them is that magnificent spread of inland waters, comprising Hood's canal and Puget Sound, that has been called the Mediterranean of the Pacific. These mountains, during nearly all the year, present a continuous array of snow-clad peaks for a hundred miles southward from the Strait of San Juan de Fuca, which washes their northern end. They stand on the peninsula all in line, like soldiers up for inspection, while the mightier summits of Rainier and Baker in the Cascade range, in majestic isolation, appear in front, like officers of high rank reviewing the parade. The space between Hood's canal and the ocean is almost entirely occupied by the Olympic range and its foothills. The mountains seem to rise from the edge of the water, on both sides, in steep ascent to the line of perpetual snow, as though nature had designed to shut up this spot for her safe retreat forever. Here she is intrenched behind frowning walls of basalt, in front of which is Hood's canal, deep, silent, dark and eternal, constituting the moat. Down in its unfathomable water lurks the giant squid, and on its shores the cinnamon bear and the cougar wander in the solitude of the primeval forest. It is a land of mystery, awe-inspiring in its mighty constituents and wonder-making in its unknown expanse of canyon and ridge.

The mountains were plainly discernible from the Governor's office, and Semple confessed that he often paused by his window to look at them. In the winter, however, they were frequently obscured by lead-colored rain clouds, sometimes for weeks or months at a time. Occasionally, though, the clouds drifted away, and the long chain of peaks — clear-cut and dazzling white from freshly fallen snow — seemed very near. At a distance of fifty miles their angles were distinct and their forests defined almost tree by tree. This apparent nearness, inconsistent with their inaccessibility, heightened the sense of mystery that shrouded the mountains.

As spring followed winter, the peaks shone forth more often, bright and serene, one day appearing languid in the sunshine, the next presenting a savage aspect while storm clouds swirled about the cliffs; then, on the third, sunshine and cloud shadows would alternate across the precipitous slopes. During the summer the mountains became friendlier in appearance, and formed in the evening a sharply outlined silhouette against the redness of the western sky. Still later, during the balmy, often hazy days of Indian summer, the mountains appeared to recede until their outlines became dim and uncertain. But it was the storms, with ominous clouds and high winds, that most impressed the Governor; then he could well believe that restless evil spirits dwelled within the mysterious depths of the mountains.

> Looking at the Olympic range from the eastern shore of Puget Sound, one can easily perceive how superstitious ideas could be fostered by them, in the minds of Indians and trappers who have to contend with the elements as well as with fanged and muscled beasts of prey that glare in their path and menace their advance. Red men and white men have gone all around this section, as bushmen go all around a jungle in which a man-eating tiger is concealed, but the interior is incognito. In tradition alone has man penetrated its fastnesses and trod the aisles of its continuous woods. Superstition lends its aid to the natural obstacles in preserving the integrity of this grand wilderness. The Indians have traditions in regard to happenings therein, ages ago, which were so terrible that the memory of them has endured until this day, with a vividness that controls the actions of men.

In those remote times, as Semple interpreted the mythology of the aborigines, a valley existed in the heart of the Olympic Mountains, above the canyon on the upper Wynooski River.[1] The wide and level valley was bordered by mountains on every side, through which tumultuous rivers had cut steep-walled canyons. Most of the valley was open land, "matted with grass and sweet with

[1] Apparently an old spelling of Wynooche.

flowers, while the edge of the river and foot of the hills were fringed with deciduous trees." Although the tribes of the Northwest fought each other with murderous intent, in this sylvan valley no conflict ever raged, for the place was held sacred as a neutral ground. Once each year the warriors of the various tribes congregated in the valley — there, in friendly rivalry, to trade whatever articles of commerce they possessed and to play games and otherwise participate in feats of strength and skill, "in contests requiring courage and endurance akin to the Olympic games of the ancient Greeks, with which heroic people they may have been contemporary."

> No account exists of any violation of the neutrality; but a great catastrophe occurred long, long ago, during the continuance of one of their festivals, from which only a few of the assembled Indians escaped. According to the accounts of the Indians, the great Seatco, chief of all evil spirits — a giant who could trample whole war parties under his feet, and who could traverse the air, the land and the water at will; whose stature was above the tallest fir trees, whose voice was louder than the roar of the ocean, and whose aspect was more terrible than that of the fiercest wild beast; who came and went upon the wings of the wind, who could tear up the forest by the roots, heap the rocks into mountains, and change the course of rivers with his breath, became offended at them and caused the earth and waters to swallow them up — all but a few, who were spared that they might carry the story of his wrath to their tribes and warn them that they were banished from the happy valley forever.

Semple theorized that an earthquake had opened chasms in the mountains and blocked the exits of the streams, "thus spreading death among the peaceful delegations." In the eons since the catastrophe, however, the river had again eroded a passageway through the rocks, and the upper valley of the Wynooski had resumed its aspect of tranquil beauty. But legend dies slowly, and the dreadful warning of the great chief of the evil spirits was passed on by word of mouth through countless generations. The happy valley became a forbidden place, entry into it taboo, and since that time the lake in the valley had not reflected the image of an Indian. Even the white hunter and trapper — having acquired from the Indian not only "his methods of taking game and his woodcraft," but his superstitions as well — had avoided the place. Thus, the elk and deer still roamed there undisturbed, at peace with their environment.

Governor Semple concluded his report on a somewhat wistful note:

> The next person to stand upon the scene of the ancient convulsion will be the all-conquering "average man" of the Anglo-Saxon race, who will tear up the matted grass and the sweet flowers with his plow, and deprecate the proximity of the snow-clad peaks because they threaten his crops with early frosts and harbor the coyote that tears his sheep.

Semple's report at least temporarily spurred interest in exploration of the Olympic Mountains. Then, on October 23, 1889, a story in the Seattle *Press*[2] — the result of a conversation between a reporter and Semple's successor, Elisha P. Ferry — called for an expedition of discovery. During the interview Governor Ferry had "expressed himself very forcibly about the advisability of having the area between the Olympic mountains and the Pacific ocean explored." The article was subsequently copied by newspapers in all parts of the United States, and "especially in all the papers of the new state of Washington, the idea of exploring such an area of unknown lands within the confines of the commonwealth being especially forcible to them."

The story announced that here, indeed, was an opportunity for an intrepid explorer. In the northwestern corner of Washington was a section some twenty-five hundred square miles in extent, enclosed by the Olympic Mountains, which had "never, to the positive knowledge of old residents of the territory, been trodden by the foot of man, white or Indian."

The newspapers of the time were filled with accounts of Sir Henry Morton Stanley's exploits on the dark continent, and the *Press* reporter could not restrain himself from making comparisons. "Washington has her great unknown land like the interior of Africa," the story proclaimed. The mountains — which rose six to eight thousand feet above the sea from low, comparatively level country on all sides of the peninsula — shut in a vast unexplored area. According to the writer, the Indians had never penetrated

---

[2] The *Press* was a forerunner of the present-day Seattle *Times*. In 1889 the paper's office was located at 214 Columbia Street.

this land, because their traditions held that a fierce tribe, which none of the coastal Indians dared molest, inhabited it. The reporter acknowledged, however, that such a band could probably not dwell in this mountain country without its presence becoming known by white men.[3] Still, no one had ascertained that the tribe did not exist, and white men had received only vague accounts of anyone ever having passed through the region. Furthermore, investigation of the claims of travelers invariably proved that they had traversed only the outer edges of the unknown land.

> The most generally accepted theory in regard to this country is that it consists of great valleys stretching from the inward slopes of the mountains to a great central basin. This theory is supported by the fact that, although the country around has abundant rain, and clouds constantly hang over the mountain tops, all the streams flowing toward the four points on the compass are insignificant, and rise only on the outward slopes of the range, none appearing to drain the great area shut in by the mountains. This fact appears to support the theory that the streams flowing from the inner slopes of the mountains feed a great interior lake. But what drains this lake? It must have an outlet somewhere, and as all of the streams pouring from the mountains rise on their outward slopes, it must have a subterranean outlet into the ocean, the straits or the Sound. There are great discoveries in store for some of Washington's explorers.

The *Press* article went on to relate that a gentleman from Olympia claimed to have traversed from Hood Canal to the "summit of the eastern range," from where he could see "great valleys stretching toward the west." Also, a group of railroad prospectors asserted that they had explored the interior, but they were unable to give an account of it and apparently had only skirted the outer slopes. The story also mentioned the attempt, in 1881–82, by a party of soldiers from the Twenty-first Infantry — under Lieutenant Colonel Alexander Chambers, who commanded at Fort Townsend — to penetrate the mountains back of the fort and construct a trail. After six months of weary labor, the soldiers succeeded in cutting a route to and across both branches of the Dungeness River, but in reaching the last range of foothills "the way seemed so difficult and the undertaking so impracticable that the attempt was aban-

[3] This story was, of course, inconsistent with the legends related by Governor Semple.

doned." Since that time the trail had been known only to military authorities and perhaps a few hunters and woodsmen.

Numerous attempts had been made, according to the article, to organize parties to explore the Olympic Mountains, but these invariably failed, "the courage of the projectors oozing out at the last moment" when they were faced with the reality of having to force their way over inhospitable terrain: steep mountain spurs, precipices, and narrow canyons walled in by jutting cliffs, the whole cloaked with dense, jungle-like forests, windfalls, and almost impenetrable underbrush.

The writer in the *Press* summarized the situation as it existed in 1889 by stating that here, indeed, was "a fine opportunity for some of the hardy citizens of the Sound to acquire fame by unveiling the mystery which wraps the land encircled by the snow capped Olympic range."

After the article appeared, the *Press* received a steady flow of inquiries, largely from persons wanting to organize or join an exploring expedition. Some of the men claimed to have been "all over" the unknown area, but confessed, when questioned closely, that they had not been in "the immense district lying between the Quiniault and the Quillayute rivers and the Olympics and ocean. They had been along the edges, but not one had been over the summit of the mountains into the region named."

Finally, however, the proprietor of the Seattle *Press* received a letter which aroused more than ordinary interest. The letter — sent from North Yakima on November 6, 1889, and signed by one J. H. Christie — indicated that the writer was interested in exploring the Olympics for the purpose of opening up the unknown wilderness adjacent to Seattle.

> From your article upon the Olympics [Christie wrote] I judge that we are both interested in the unveiling of the mystery which at present exists regarding the Olympic country. My interest, aroused by the fact that the mountains have not as yet been penetrated by white men and an ambition to accomplish what others may have failed in, backed by an inherent love of adventure, caused me to form the resolution to penetrate the depths of the unknown range. It is now my intention to act upon this resolution by entering the mountains this next month.

To explore the unknown Olympics in the winter must have sounded rash in the extreme, but Christie appeared to be eminently well qualified for the undertaking — if one accepted, without reservations, his own statement of his experiences.

> It is no ambitious, untried youth who now writes you, but a man tried in all the vicissitudes of mountain, forest and plain life, schooled in the great plain of the northwest territories during the Sioux and Nez Perce wars, having met with most of the reverses that fell to the lot of frontiersmen during the years between 1871 and 1878.

Since then, Christie stated, he had spent most of the time in the mountains hunting, prospecting, and exploring, the trips varying in length from one to three years, in regions "beyond the limits of civilization." In fact, in that time he had ranged from the eastern boundary of Quebec to Hudson Bay, and in the Northwest Territories from the forty-ninth parallel to the Arctic Circle — through the various ranges of the Rocky Mountains from the American border "to the unnamed mountains in the far north in the Peace, Laird [Liard] and Mackenzie river districts on the eastern boundary of Alaska."

Christie expressed regret — not too modestly, however — that he could not afford to outfit an expedition as completely as would be desired "to guarantee a possibly lengthened stay in the mountains." This difficulty could be overcome, he was certain, if "a few of the public men of the country" would underwrite the expenses of sending Christie and his companions into the mountains. Surely there were gentlemen of means — mill men, miners, and others — who were interested in developing the Olympic country, either publicly or privately.

"Why not," Christie concluded his letter, "let the PRESS give its countenance and support to an expedition for the clearing up of mystery lying at the very door of Seattle?"

Chapter II

THE PRESS EXPLORING EXPEDITION

JAMES H. Christie had returned to the United States in the spring of 1889, after traveling three years in the Arctic region of north-western Canada.[1] During that time he had explored the Liard, Peace, and Mackenzie rivers and claimed to have discovered the Peace River coal fields. An adventurous man, he was presently en route to Africa, but had stopped for a short visit with friends in North Yakima. Here he met Christopher O'Connell Hayes, a young cowboy from the range lands east of the Cascades, who called to his attention the article in the *Press* wherein Governor Ferry had expressed a desire that the Olympics be explored.

Almost without giving it second thought, Christie decided that he would explore these mountains immediately and unveil the mystery, provided that he could obtain the necessary financial support. Therefore his letter to the *Press*, to which he apparently received a favorable reply. Accompanied by Hayes and two others — John H. Crumback and John W. Sims — Christie reached Seattle during the last week in November, just when the winter rainy season was getting well under way. With him also were two "bear dogs of quality" named Bud and Tweed, and Sims's black dog, Daisy. In Seattle the group was met by Edmond Meany, of the *Press* staff, who introduced them to William E. Bailey, the newspaper's proprietor.

[1] Christie was a Canadian citizen, and after the Olympic exploration spent most of his life in British Columbia.

17

James H. Christie after his three-year exploration in Alaska, 1886–88
(Courtesy Robert Hitchman)

Apparently Bailey was impressed by the tall, hard-muscled Scot and his husky companions, sufficiently so that he decided to sponsor the expedition. Preliminary arrangements were quickly completed, and on December 3 S. R. Frazier, the newspaper's editor, suggested to Christie that a photographer accompany the group. Christie immediately thought of his friend, Captain Charles A. Barnes, late of the United States Revenue Marine. And a letter had been received from a Puyallup doctor, Harris Boyle Runnalls, who wished to accompany the expedition as surgeon. His application was promptly accepted. Although numerous other letters arrived from men who desired to join the group, apparently attracted by the sensational nature of the undertaking, the expedition was limited to six men.

When the question of personnel was settled, the *Press* equipped the group with everything required "to make a complete and careful exploration of the country and to provision the party for six months, and on December 8 the party left Seattle for Port Angeles, where all preparations were completed to ascend the mountains by way of the Elwha pass."

As originally constituted, the Press Exploring Expedition consisted of six men, four dogs, and fifteen hundred pounds of provisions. Later two mules were acquired to assist in packing supplies. Nothing is known about the dogs except that their names were Daisy, Tweed, Bud, and Dike, but considerably more has been recorded about the men.

James Halbold Christie,[2] the expedition leader, was born in Moray County, Scotland, in 1854. Christie was educated in the Edinburgh high school for a military life, but never finished the term. However, he "made this good by a subsequent service in Quebec in 1870." According to the *Press*, Christie was in the employ of the Canadian government for six years, including service during the Riel rebellion, and he also "fought Indians, hunted and prospected 'as far north as water will run,' and a bare record of the thrilling incidents in his life would make a most wonderful story."

[2] The *Press* gave Christie's middle name as Helibol, but according to a letter to Robert Hitchman of Seattle from the Canadian government, the correct spelling was Halbold.

In the opinion of the *Press*, he was "the best man in the Northwest to undertake an exploration requiring such skill and experience."

Captain Charles Adams Barnes, the topographer of the party, was born in Illinois in 1859. At the age of twenty he was appointed cadet in the United States Revenue Marine, and after four years commissioned a lieutenant. He was almost continuously on duty at sea from his entry in the service. In 1887 he resigned from the service to engage in business in California, but shortly afterward moved to Seattle and had subsequently been "engaged in several business undertakings." Barnes had also explored mountains in Arizona, Oregon, and Washington. The *Press* felt that the knowledge he had obtained on both land and sea fully qualified the Captain for the task of photographing and mapping the country the party was to explore.

John Henry Crumback—who became the expedition cook—was thirty-three years old, having been born in Ontario in 1856. He had gone west and at various times had been occupied as a cowboy, hunter, prospector, and Indian fighter in the Northwest Territories. He, too, had participated in the Riel rebellion (1884), serving in T. B. Strange's contingent from Calgary.

John William Sims was a husky, dark-haired Englishman, born July 10, 1861, in Essex. He joined the British army at age fifteen and remained in the service slightly more than six years. He served in the South African uprisings under Sir Henry Evelyn Wood and, later, Sir Garnet Wolseley. Since the conclusion of his military duty, Sims had been occupied at "hunting, trapping, prospecting, and trading."

At twenty-two, Christopher O'Connell Hayes was the youngest member of the party. He was a grandson of the famed Irish patriot and liberator, Daniel O'Connell. Prior to joining the Press Expedition, Hayes had made his living as a cowboy in the Yakima Valley.

The sixth member of the group, Dr. Harris Boyle Runnalls, was to be the expedition's natural historian. Born in Penzance, England, in 1854, Runnalls graduated in 1880 from the Royal College of Surgeons, and practiced at several hospitals in England before coming to the United States in 1888. Before the Press Expedition lost contact with civilization, Runnalls was called home

Capt. Charles Adams Barnes
(Courtesy Mrs. Pierre Barnes)

John William Sims in British Army
uniform (Courtesy Mrs. Mary Buell)

Dr. Harris Boyle Runnalls
(Courtesy Mrs. Shirley I. Fager)

when his wife became seriously ill. He was unable to return and complete the trip, "much to the regret of himself and of the *Press.*"

Sufficient funds were provided by the *Press* to equip the expedition "with everything necessary for making a complete exploration of the Olympic mountains," and no expense was spared in outfitting the party "with everything that could conduce to its convenience or its chances of success." The men planned to depend primarily upon game as their means of subsistence, but ample quantities of flour, bacon, beans, coffee, and other provisions were furnished to sustain them until they reached the game country — and afterward to supplement the supply of fresh meat.

> These provisions amounted to about 1500 pounds. Winchester rifles, plenty of ammunition, a tent, canvas sheets, blankets, fishing tackle, axes, a whip saw for cutting out logs, a few carpenter tools, the necessary tools for mineral prospecting, rope, snowshoes, a small but well selected assortment of cooking and other utensils, comprised a part of the general outfit. [Barnes]

The men were also supplied with a camera, enough film for 250 exposures, and the necessary instruments for making topographical surveys and scientific observations. In addition, they took along fifty pounds of "colored fire" "for the purpose of illuminating, if possible, some peak visible from Seattle." [3]

The *Press* declared that it had organized the expedition primarily "for the purpose of exploring the hitherto unknown mountain region lying between Puget Sound and the Pacific ocean, and extending from the straits of Juan de Fuca to Lake Quiniault." This entire region — with the exception of a narrow coastal belt which had been settled for years — was still terra incognita. It was known to abound in large game, however, for the valleys that led into the unexplored area teemed with herds of elk, with cougars, bear, and deer. In fact, hunters had gone into the Quillayute region adjacent to the Pacific and returned with loads of elk antlers

---

[3] Prior to leaving Seattle, Christie arranged that Edmond Meany would go to a lookout point in Seattle on an appointed evening and watch for the colored fire to be released from one of the peaks. This Meany did, but he saw nothing. The reason why will become apparent later.

and hides. Also, bear and cougar skins were commonly found in all the Indian huts at the mouth of the Quillayute. According to some of the hunters, the unexplored region consisted of rolling prairies on a huge plateau, while others asserted that bands of Indians claimed the land as their own and demanded compensation from all who desired to enter. Reportedly, one hunter who attempted to ascend the Quillayute was compelled to pay a tribute of tobacco and cloth to some Indians before he entered their domain.

> One legend being handed down by the wise old Indians is to the effect that that region was once thickly peopled by a race of large, powerful Indians, who were adept as workers of iron and in carving, and who possessed fine horses and cattle. They prospered until a war called away the strong men, and in the severe winter that followed the bears and wild animals came down from the mountains and destroyed the camps, scattered the cattle and made desolate the homes of the red men. The plains were then deserted and the Indians now hold a superstitious dread of the whole district.

The *Press* went on to recount the experience of Joseph P. O'Neil, an Army lieutenant stationed at Fort Townsend, who had explored the northeastern Olympics in the summer of 1885. According to O'Neil, the Indians believed that a god — in the form of a huge bird resembling an eagle or raven — made its home in these mountains and would "inflict a terrible punishment on those who by entering them desecrates its home." [4] When O'Neil's Indian guide learned where they were going, he panicked, and neither the promise of big pay nor the threat of being shot was sufficient to detain him. Reluctantly he camped with the white men at the foot of the mountains, but "during the night folded his tent and quietly stole away."

Aside from the primitive legends of Indians and the exaggerated stories of hunters, however, nothing was known of the interior of the Olympic Peninsula. The government charts then in existence contained

---

[4] This was, of course, a variation of the thunderbird myth found among so many North American tribes.

but one or two elevations out of the whole range, while there was absolutely no definite description of the kind of land, the possibility of minerals, stone or coal, the quantity and quality of timber found there or the feasibility of colonizing the region.

Another purpose of the expedition was to procure accurate scientific information. The newspaper also declared that the start was being made in the winter "in order to be over the first ranges and into the central valleys ready for work when spring should open." This was probably window dressing for the public, to cover up the real reason — although the staff of the *Press* and the expedition members themselves may have believed the truth of the statement. The more compelling reason lay in the probability that whoever wished to receive the honor of the first crossing of the Olympic Mountains would have to make the journey during the winter of 1889–90, for he who waited until the following summer was likely to be a "Johnny-come-lately." Interest in exploring the mysterious Olympics had flared to a high pitch, and considerable rivalry spurred the various groups planning trips into the area in the summer of 1890.

Lieutenant O'Neil, dissatisfied with the extent of his investigation of the northern Olympics in 1885, was planning another military expedition — this time across the southern part of the mountains. In the summer of 1889 Judge James Wickersham of Tacoma had penetrated some twenty miles up the Skokomish Valley, and he too was planning a much more extensive trip toward the headwaters of some of the Olympic rivers. He would operate under the auspices of the Buckley *Banner*, which declared that Wickersham's group would

> travel north from Lake Cushman to the straits of De Fuca, right through the heart of the Olympics, skirting the base of both Mt. Olympus and Mt. Constance, through a country that no man has ever before trod as far as can be ascertained from the old settlers and Indians of the mountains.

The most serious threat to the Press Party's plans, however, came from a father-and-son team — C. A. Gilman, former lieutenant governor of Minnesota, and his son — who had been privately exploring the Olympic Peninsula and had covered an amazing expanse of territory in a short time. While the Press Exploring Expedition was being organized, the Gilmans left Grays Harbor on October 17, 1889, for the Quinault Indian Reservation. The autumn rains had been falling steadily, and winter was about to settle over the mountains. Undaunted, the Gilmans sought a guide, but the Indians "shook their heads ominously, and muttered in their own peculiar, emotionless way something about the high waters and deep snows, sure to be encountered." Nevertheless, they finally found an Indian who was willing to "expose himself to the terrors of snow and ice and water," and on October 20 the party of five set out for Lake Quinault — "the two Gilmans, the Indian and his klootchman and their baby." Their guide went as far as the confluence of the north and east forks of the Quinault, then the Gilmans proceeded alone up the East Fork Quinault to its headwaters. Here they climbed several high peaks in the vicinity of Mount Anderson, but "the skies were so thick with fog that nothing could be seen." Finally, however, the two men ascended a high mountain on a clear day, and the climbers could not only see Mount Olympus and Mount Constance, but almost discern Seattle. The Gilmans then returned to civilization by the same route, although they probably could have continued and crossed the mountains to Hood Canal. They arrived back in Grays Harbor on November 27, the day before Thanksgiving.

The tramping Gilmans had not had enough, however. They wished also to "traverse the unknown land between the mountains and the ocean." On December 11 — three days after the Press Party had departed from Seattle — the Gilmans started up the Pysht River from the Strait of Juan de Fuca. After an uneventful but long journey southward — most of the way through vast forests — on December 28 they reached the Quinault River at a point about fourteen miles above its mouth. They arrived in Grays Harbor on January 4, 1890.

The Gilman explorations, the projected O'Neil and Wickersham trips, and the likelihood that other groups were contemplating journeys into the region probably accounted for the haste with which the Press Exploring Expedition was organized and sent into the mountains at the onset of winter. Otherwise, the party would not have been the first to cross the mountains and report on the interior of the Olympic Peninsula. The *Press* declared, however, that "there was to be no rush to get through, and the work they were to do was to be done thoroughly."

The men received much unsolicited advice: people warned them against undertaking the trip during the winter months, forecast failure, and tried to dissuade them from going. But, as the *Press* stated, "they did not know the mettle of the explorers. Those men had endured all kinds of tortures and hardships while traveling in the mountains, and some of them in the Arctic regions."

The *Press* itself expressed great confidence in the expedition and claimed that the people of the Pacific Northwest could rest assured "that these men would bring them a complete record of the unknown country within the Olympics." It then summed up that confidence by stating: "All these men have endured hardship and privation at different times in their lives, and are hardy and rugged in their physical make up. They have abundance of grit and manly vim."

They did indeed, and in the coming months they would need every ounce of their grit and manly vim to compensate for their lack of knowledge about these unknown mountains — a primitive wilderness with no trails. Nor could they know that they had chosen what was to be one of the Olympic Peninsula's severest winters during which to make their exploration.

Chapter III

DECEMBER, 1889: LOWER ELWHA

THE FIRST week of December was a busy one for the Press Exploring Expedition. On December 4 the men moved their provisions — which included tents, covers, and canvas sheets — to Edmond S. Meany's ranch,[1] where it would be easier to assemble and pack the stores with some degree of organization. Christie secured additional supplies, such as ammunition, rubber boots, oilskin, blankets, and fishing tackle — the last item Christie considered a necessity in order that he could enjoy his favorite sport.

Christie spent that evening briefing Captain Barnes on the work and plans of the expedition. Then, on Thursday, December 5, the men assembled at the ranch to pack the supplies, and Christie completed purchase of the stores, wired St. Paul, Minnesota, for snowshoes, and tried unsuccessfully to find some dogs. That afternoon the expedition members posed for a group portrait. (See p. 29.)

Thus, by December 7, 1889, all the necessary arrangements had been completed, and everything stood in readiness. At the last minute a gentleman advised the group "to pack nothing but pemmican and a liberal sprinkling of flour," but this suggestion was ignored. Then during the last interview with Bailey, Frazier, and

---

[1] The ranch — which had a single dwelling plus a workshop or woodshed — consisted of about one acre of land on Ninth Avenue N.E. and Tenth Avenue N.E. (now Roosevelt Way), midway between Fortieth and Forty-first. This location — near the northern terminus of the University Bridge today — was a long way from the center of Seattle in 1890.

Meany, the party received its final official instructions before departing for the mountains.

According to Barnes the expedition left Seattle by steamer on December 7, 1889, headed for Port Angeles, but Christie gives the date as Sunday, December 8. "We made our way toward the Yesler wharf," Christie's diary entry states, "causing a good deal of remarks from the passersby on account of our show of arms and dogs." Boarding the steamer *Ferndale*, the party met Mr. Hodges, of the *Press* staff, together with friends who had come down to the waterfront to see them leave. "This meant an adjournment to a quiet corner of the cabin, and the expression of many opinions accompanied with promises made, the fulfillment of which will keep us all hustling. The last whistle warned our friends ashore and we had commenced our trip."

By sunrise the next morning the expedition was at Port Townsend, forty miles northwest of Seattle. James H. Christie was not, however, favorably impressed by the quality of transportation on the inland waterways of the Pacific Northwest. "After a night on board of a Puget Sound steamer," he wrote, "we wondered when the most beautiful body of water in the world would have passable boats on it."

While Christie superintended the transfer of the group's baggage to the Port Angeles boat, the other members of the expedition looked after the dogs. All hands then joined the search for a restaurant, "fondly looking forward to the breakfast table," following which they boarded the steamer *Evangel*,

> and a more disreputable tub never carried a passenger. The pleasure of our journey was by no means enhanced by our being seated opposite a full grown girl chewing gum much like a cow chews her cud. Dinner was served on the boat much as well bred hogs are fed. We were all thankful when we pulled alongside the wharf and found ourself at Angeles, under the shadow of the mountains we had undertaken to explore. [Christie]

In 1889 Port Angeles was a small sawmill town located on the site of an old Indian village. Its ramshackle wooden buildings — strung along a "street" which paralleled the Strait of Juan de Fuca — faced the sheltered harbor, where foghorns sounded and tall-masted sailing ships lay at anchor. Near the saloons the caulked

The Press Expedition photographed in Seattle, Dec. 6, 1889. Left to right: Sims, Runnalls, Barnes, Christie, Crumback, Hayes (Courtesy Mrs. Pierre Barnes)

The Press explorers photographed in Aberdeen, Wash., May 21, 1890. Left to right: Sims, Barnes, Crumback (kneeling), Christie, and Hayes (Courtesy Mrs. Pierre Barnes and Mrs. Mary Buell)

View of Port Angeles from the harbor, about 1890
(Courtesy Gordon Windels and Bert Kellogg)

boots of loggers thumped heavily on boardwalks, but the street itself was largely mud churned up by wagon teams.

While in Port Angeles, the expedition members called on several of the town's leading citizens in the hope of gaining information about the country ahead. They were introduced to Norman R. Smith, the second mayor of Port Angeles, whose father had been instrumental in setting aside the townsite as a military and naval reserve in 1861. At one time Smith had helped survey for a road from Clallam Bay to the Quillayute country, and he claimed that he "[had] traveled all through the Olympic country, knows the trend of every mountain range, the source of every stream, has located the paradise which Indian tradition says exists within the charmed circle of mountain peaks seen from the Sound and strait of Juan de Fuca."

Relying on advice from Port Angeles citizens, Christie decided to build a flatboat on the Elwha for transporting supplies, and "to ascend as far as practicable in that manner" by poling upstream. Further inquiries revealed, however, that it would be impractical to build the boat at the mouth of the river, for Christie had been assured by an "ancient inhabitant" that four miles upstream was a dangerous and impassable canyon. This development was disappointing and would mean delay if the expedition should be compelled to pack everything to a point above the canyon. However, Christie elected to build the boat at a point above this first canyon, and direct the expedition into the mountains from there.

The citizens of Port Angeles provided no tangible information about what lay beyond the foothills and first ranges. Christie found this disconcerting, and thus recorded in his journal:

> The ideas regarding the interior of the country I find are rather misty, and from the thousand and one advices received I cannot get one sensible idea.
>
> From the mass of rubbish that has been fully poured out for the education of our party, it is rather wonderful to hear that this section has been successfully explored, yet strange to say, I can get no information on which I can rely regarding the country beyond the mouth of Indian creek, about eight miles inland. Evidently some of our oldtime settlers are jealous of our attempting to enlighten their darkness regarding the surroundings of their birthplace.

Wagon teams hauled the expedition's outfit from Port Angeles to Philip Meagher's ranch at the terminus of the county road, five or six miles to the west. The party gratefully accepted an offer to use an unoccupied farm house on the property while they prepared for their advance into the mountains. The farm was well stocked with hay — which would feed the pack mules the expedition was hopeful of acquiring — and also boasted "a vegetable garden, a cow, a wood pile," luxuries that amply attested to the hospitality of Meagher and the comfort of his guests. In addition, a trail led from the ranch nearly to the Elwha, and over this path the expedition would have to pack its supplies.

> The trail was rough and circuitous, over hills, gulches and canyons. Great trees lay across it so that for pack animals it was impassable, and even for a man it was little better than no trail at all. From the trail to the nearest point the river is distant about three-quarters of a mile, and across this interval a trail had to be cut through dense underbrush and fallen timber. Repairing and clearing the old trail and making the new one occupied a week, and for the most part it was ax work. [Barnes]

On the morning of December 11, the men were awakened by Crumback calling them to breakfast. He had baked beans and bacon "in the approved fashion" in a Dutch oven. Together with bread baked in the same oven and flanked by some superb coffee, it was "a feast indeed," Christie commented, compared with the food that had been supplied them at the majority of the restaurants they had visited of late.

After breakfast Christie sent Runnalls and Sims toward the river to find the best possible route to the head of the canyon, Hayes arranged the stores in camp, and Crumback baked several days' supply of bread. Then Christie ordered lumber for the boat from Wariner Smith (brother of Norman R. Smith) at his nearby sawmill. When he returned to the ranch, Christie was met by Dr. Runnalls and Sims, who "reported a rather hard outlook . . . practically no trail towards the head of the canyon, distant some two and one-half miles." These findings did not agree with the information Christie had received in Port Angeles that the canyon was only a half mile from Meagher's ranch.

That evening Christie inspected part of the trail, and the next

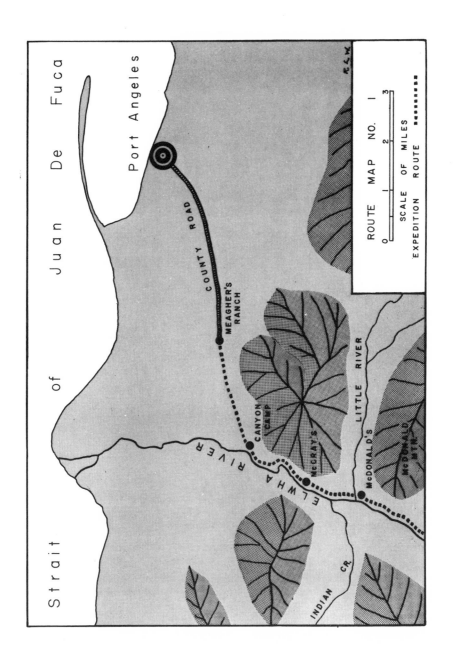

Strait of Juan De Fuca

Port Angeles

COUNTY ROAD

MEAGHER'S RANCH

CANYON CAMP

ELWHA RIVER

McCRAY'S

INDIAN CR.

LITTLE RIVER

McDONALD'S

McDONALD MTN.

ROUTE MAP NO. 1

SCALE OF MILES

0   1   2   3

EXPEDITION ROUTE ▪▪▪▪▪▪▪▪

day he sent the men forward to make improvements, "as it was in a most horrible condition, mud holes at every step and the first mile through a veritable bogwater to the knees." He then left for Port Angeles to meet Barnes and Edmond Meany, who were arriving on the steamer *Evangel* from Port Townsend, and found them accompanied by Dike, a big black dog that Barnes had "captured." Meany had come from Seattle to visit the expedition's camp on the lower Elwha.

> After the transaction of business we made tracks for camp, bidding Angeles good-bye. We made good time over a very indifferent road, reaching Smith's mill as the darkness began to be felt. Barnes fired his rifle as a signal for Meany and myself, who had dropped behind, to hurry up. The flash and report rather startled the black dog, who disappeared in the darkness, much as black cats are supposed to. And no amount of calling would bring him back. A mile of mud holes and water being got over in the darkness, we reached the boys and supper, wet to the waist. [Christie]

December 13 was a Friday, but the men — aroused at daylight by Christie — ignored the superstition attendant to that day, and after a "truly backwoods breakfast, which was soon disposed of," the party began packing toward the head of the canyon. Meany accompanied them "to try a cast or two on the Elwha," while Crumback remained in camp to cook. Later in the day Meany returned, having had no luck fishing, and expressed the thought that the expedition had "rather a hard road to travel." On Saturday he started back to Seattle to await the expedition's arrival after crossing the mountains, and to watch for the display of colored fire to be released from one of the high peaks facing Puget Sound.

Captain Barnes traveled with Meany as far as Port Angeles. It had been decided that pack animals were needed, and Barnes was supposed "to hunt up two pack mules." But he had difficulty in obtaining them,

> every person in the country round about having available animals, imagining that they had the expedition in a tight place, raised the price of their beasts several hundred per cent. For the meanest cayuse, that was worth at an honest valuation $25, $60 or $70 would be asked, and good animals were held in proportion. Even the Indians were posted and wanted fabulous prices for some broken down quadrupeds. [Barnes]

Christie had already tried, through Wariner Smith, to purchase two pack animals from Indians living at the mouth of the Elwha. When Christie met to negotiate with them, the Indians demanded one hundred dollars "for a couple of plugs." Half that amount, Christie declared, would have been "a magnificent price," and he refused to buy. Barnes was successful, however, in procuring two mules from a settler who lived in the foothills of the mountains, about twelve miles south of Dungeness. The settler was "found to be a worthy and hospitable man, got a fair price for his mules, and the *Press* two useful additions to its exploring staff." On Tuesday, December 17, the mules "arrived safely in camp after a hotly contested drive of two days, and were warmly welcomed by the whole party."

While Barnes had been searching for mules, the others had improved the settlers' trail, which Christie considered "a disgrace to any community." December 15 was the expedition's first Sunday in the wilderness, and the men welcomed the opportunity for a rest. They passed the time "in divers ways, hunting, washing, cleaning guns, etc." Then on Monday the second week commenced "with good healthy exercise, packing," and for the next few days the men worked on the trail and carried supplies toward the head of the canyon. During this time Christie finally arranged to have the lumber for the boat hauled from the mill. On Wednesday, Christie and Sims went to the sawmill to make pack saddles, while Runnalls, Crumback, and Hayes further improved the trail, working in the rain. By now the men were beginning to realize that if any work was to be done, they would have to disregard the weather. That day they completed the trail to their satisfaction, and the next morning, Thursday, December 19, began packing.

The mules — Jennie and Dollie — after several shrewd kicks, delivered with accuracy and precision from practice born of experience, and several unexpected attempts to bite, submitted to be "cinched up" to the tune of 250 pounds each, Mr. Christie, a veteran and connoisseur in these matters, reeving the diamond hitch with most artistic grace. Each man seized his 60 pounds, the dogs bounded ahead and moving camp to the river had begun.

In half a mile was reached a swamp, upon which had been bestowed a world of pains in trying to make it passable for the mules. Brush, bark, rotten wood, everything that came handy had been tumbled into the trail, and there was some hope that the mules could get through it. But a dozen steps demonstrated the futility of the hope, and soon the wretched mules were floundering about in the bottomless morass. [Barnes]

The men unloaded the packs and after considerable tugging, pulling, and prying freed the mules from the mud and reloaded them. The animals struggled but a few yards further, however, before miring once again, and the unpacking was repeated. A third trial

with a lighter load produced similar results, this time the mules adding plaintive protests to the general tumult. Jennie in mud to the tail, beans, pork, snowshoes, frying pans, tobacco, and other bric-a-brac scattered about in profusion, joined her voice to Dollie, who, in her attempt to jump a log, got only half way, and hung there between wind and water, filling the air with lamentations. Christie and Barnes, their custodians, hatless and coatless, mud to their thighs, were struggling about, tugging at bridles, slacking cinches and calling for assistance temporal, and, it has since been affirmed about camp, spiritual. The splashing and plunging, the shouting and braying of man and beast was a spectacle for men and philosophers. [Barnes]

The other members of the party, who had gone on ahead, heard the outcry and came back. With their assistance,

The animals were extricated, the bric-a-brac fished out, the mules recinched, and the caravan once more proceeded. But the swamp was attempted no more with the animals. Everything was packed on the backs of the human members of the party from the ranch through the swamp, and the mules packed there. [Barnes]

Still the men were impressed by the mules, and Barnes thought it extraordinary how the sure-footed animals could negotiate so poor a trail. Whenever they came to a fallen tree — even one three or four feet in diameter — the mules would rear up, then lift themselves and their 250-pound packs over it as lightly as a deer. The danger of straining the animals' backs, however, necessitated lightening their load whenever possible, or else cutting the log out, which was actually better and involved no more work because they passed over the trail frequently.

A precipitous-sided canyon, two hundred feet deep, tried the mules' mettle. The trail ran down one side and then up the other in zigzag fashion. Soaked with water and cut up by constant use, it became so slippery with mud that both men and mules had to walk carefully in order to avoid sliding into the chasm below.

That evening, December 19, the expedition established its first actual campsite beyond the luxuries of Meagher's ranch, and Christie confessed the next morning to having spent "a rather uncomfortable night." After breakfast he and Barnes loaded the mules, "whilst the other boys packed across the swamps, and after a hard day's work we were all happy to see the Dutch oven full of delicious baked beans, to which ample justice was done ere we sought our spruce-bough bed."

The succeeding three days were also spent packing supplies to Canyon Camp, as they called the site — a little bench on the precipitous banks of the Elwha — where they had elected to remain while building their boat. Located about one hundred feet above the water, "it was a wretched place to camp, but we had to camp as near as possible to the only good place on which to build our boat. There was a flat sand bank below. The distance over which to carry water, the scarcity of seasoned timber for camp fire, involved much extra work."

Although, from a practical standpoint, the expedition had scarcely begun, Christie noted in his diary that the supply of whisky was "well nigh exhausted, which is a good job." Then he added, apparently as an afterthought, "The party gaining their second wind: do not find packing quite so heavy."

By the evening of December 23 the entire outfit, except for the lumber, had been packed across the swamp and on to Canyon Camp, and the lumber itself had been moved from Meagher's ranch over the swamp.

That night a heavy snow storm began, and the men could hear trees falling around their camp, "keeping all hands awake and their eyes fixed upon the ridge pole of the tent." One spruce crashed down so near to the camp that they were quite uncomfortable. By daybreak a foot of snow covered the ground, and the trail was crisscrossed by a regular network of fallen timber.

So . . . we went to work to get rid of another monster fir tree, six feet through at the base, which overhung the camp in a threatening manner. It struck another great tree in its fall, and for a few moments the whole forest seemed to be going down like a lot of ten pins. When the crash ended and the snow settled enough to see the result, we found four lying about the camp, one of them so close to the tent as to bury the side ropes, but fortunately nothing was damaged. This gave us magnificent back-logs, and we sawed up much of the remainder and kept a monster fire going day and night. [Barnes]

Christmas Eve it commenced snowing again and continued until about midnight. "But Christmas morning broke cold and clear," and when the men arose, they found not only a white landscape but also "things around camp in rather an uncomfortable condition, frozen stiff." Nevertheless, they made an early start with the mules, expecting to find the trail blocked by timber brought down by the weight of the snow. They were not disappointed, but most of the trees lying across the pathway were small ones, eight inches or less in diameter. During the morning they chopped out these trees, then in the afternoon commenced packing the lumber for the boat, and "the boys were entertained by the Doctor rendering some very difficult passages of high and ancient English. Apt quotations, all appertaining to the subject of driving mules." By four o'clock the men and mules had dragged it all — six hundred feet of lumber, for the most part boards thirty-two feet long — to the gulch above the canyon. It had been an arduous day, so they quit and returned to camp, "six as hungry men as there is in the state, this night of Our Lord, doing ample justice to our Christmas dinner of bacon and beans."

The heavy green lumber being dragged along the crooked, tortuous trail was sometimes so bent and twisted as to resemble the letter S. Because both pack saddles had been broken during the struggle through the swamp on the first day, the men could not use the mules to help pull the boards from the gulch to the Elwha. The lumber, when it finally arrived in Canyon Camp on the evening of the second day (December 26), "was as smooth as if planed and the edges worn round." Without the snow, they could never have transported it so quickly. The men had put in as hard a day's work as one thoroughly under the whip, but the party take hard work, giving promise of staying powers, which will be called upon ere we reach Quinaiult. The deep slush snow making the work of handling long, green, heavy lumber very disagreeable work indeed. [Christie]

They had selected a low bench of sand at the foot of a bluff immediately below their camp as the place to construct the boat. "A piece of ugly rapids" at the launching point was an unavoidable inconvenience, for this part of the Elwha afforded few level banks. All the timbers had been packed to this site by December 27, and the outlook was more encouraging.

First the men cleared the twelve-inch-deep snow from the ground, then Sims was given the dimensions, and the boat was "laid on the stocks." They soon found that the green lumber was "in a rather tough fix for boat building." From long exposure on the trail, it was "sodden with water, and frozen hard and stiff," the thirty-foot boards being "thickened by one half inch of ice." Thus, they had first to thaw out the lumber, which caused "a good deal of work for the boys in providing fires." The services of two to three men were required to cut and pack in fuel, tend the fire, and turn the lumber.

> The weather was so cold that the thawing process was slow work, and after hours of cooking, and a plank became limber, it would freeze again before we could get it on the boat. The proper curvature was given them at the stem and stern by heaving them in with a lever arrangement. [Barnes]

For several days the men worked on the boat, Christie himself building the steering oar and boat poles.

> Our stores furnished us with oakum and pitch for calking her. The former we spun the evening before using. We calked her as well as the wet and unseasoned condition of the wood permitted, but we awaited the result after launching with great anxiety, which the sequel well justified. We were four days building — four days of frosty fingers and frozen wood — constantly interrupted by flurries of snow. [Barnes]

The boat, when completed, was thirty feet long, had a five-foot beam, and was about two feet deep. She was "flat bottomed, rounding up gradually at the bow and stern." Her sides were built with an outfall of six inches, being "one foot wider at the top or gunwale than the bottom or floor." She was decked forward and aft "to afford a footing for the bowman and steersman." A ten-inch-wide "covering board" extended along the side, connecting the two decks, and gave footing to the polemen. The "hold" or storage space was approximately twenty feet long by five feet wide.

> Strips of 2 x 4 scantling and sawed knees, constituted the frame work of the little vessel, upon which we bolted the planking of inch cedar. We added a capstan for heaving her over heavy rapids, and a 50-fathom tow line. Good spruce poles and an 18-foot steering oar comprised her furniture. [Barnes]

When the boat was nearing completion, Dr. Runnalls and Barnes rode the mules to Port Angeles to invite Wariner Smith to attend the christening and launching. "We had a royal dinner provided for the occasion of the boat, expecting Mr. Smith to be present at the ceremony. Business deprived us of the pleasure of his company, but he sent on a box of good cigars, which we fully appreciated." Later Runnalls took the mules to Macdonald's claim, four miles upstream, "to be left until called for," as Canyon Camp offered nothing in the way of food for them.[2]

The boat was finished on Monday, December 30, ready for launching the following day. Then the men packed and lowered all the heavy stores over the bluff and stowed everything below.

The day of launching was destined to be the most memorable one thus far for the Press Exploring Expedition. The weather failed to cooperate, and it snowed all day. The men struck camp, however, and packed the remaining supplies to the launching site; a few last touches were applied to the boat, and by 3:00 P.M. everything was in readiness. It was a tense moment. While the boys stood by, Barnes took photographs and the boat was "launched on the waters of the Elwha." She slid easily "over the ways into the boiling water of the rapids" and upon striking the

---

[2] It is not clear why the expedition did not simply pack their supplies by mule to Macdonald's and thus avoid the canyon altogether, but perhaps the distance was too great to pack the lumber and the men thought it would be easier to use the boat.

water was christened the *Gertie*. According to Christie the boat "took to water kindly," and by means of a line handled from shore was steered so that she swept into smooth, deep water below the rapids. "The boys stretched the tow line and we brought her up through her first rapid light. The party in camp took hold and pulled her up stream and across on her trial trip. We tied up and made our first camp on our actual journey."

It was considered about camp to be the most successful launch ever made, despite the fact "no burst of music or libations of wine" celebrated the occasion, and

> [they] proceeded to make it as successful as the resources of the camp would permit. Pea soup, boiled ham, baked beans, corn bread and prune pie garnished the board, the roaring fire battled with the falling snow, and in deep potations [*sic*] of Java best, the "Gertie" entered upon her career.
>
> This duty performed, the signal for breaking camp was given. In a moment all was bustle. The tent was struck, bags and boxes swung over the cliff by ropes, and Gertie was freighted with her cargo. But alas! as her upper seams came below water she began to take in water like a thirsty fish. [Barnes]

Christie's comment was laconic. "I am sorry to find that she takes in a little too much water," he recorded in his diary, "which will compel a recaulking. Thus ends our labor for 1889."

Chapter IV

JANUARY, 1890: *GERTIE*

ON JANUARY 1, 1890, the Press Exploring Expedition had been under way nearly a month, but had still not advanced beyond the edge of civilization. The party had been delayed for several reasons: the necessity of rebuilding the trail to Canyon Camp, of procuring and transporting the lumber, and, finally, of constructing the *Gertie* during adverse weather. Thus, the men were still on the Elwha at a point where the Olympic foothills approach the Strait of Juan de Fuca, a few miles above the river's mouth. As soon as the boat could be recaulked and relaunched, however, the expedition would be in a position to proceed southward into unexplored territory. But the progress was to be very slow. In fact, for several miles upriver from Canyon Camp the men did not really traverse unknown terrain, for there were a few homesteads situated on choice sites along the river. Each of these in turn was to be mistaken by the expedition members for the furthest outpost of civilized man.

Because the men had worked on Christmas, breaking trail and packing lumber, New Year's Day was actually their first holiday in the wilderness. To pass the time, Christie fished the Elwha while the others went hunting, but none was successful. Snow fell incessantly, and Christie became somewhat concerned, wondering when it would slacken or cease. By the next morning the camp was deeply buried, and the men were forced to dig out from under drifts. The snowfall continued all day, with few indications of a break in the weather, and because work on the trail was impossible, the men remained in camp. By the morning of January 3, the snow depth on the level measured three and a half feet.

The *Gertie,* however, rather than the snow, posed the expedition's chief problem at the moment. After she sank on her initial launching, Barnes commented that "it was determined to haul her out and give her green boards a thorough drying and try her again. We would drive oakum into her until her sides ached, and boil tar till the government interfered to save its timber, but Gertie must be tight."

That morning the men chopped ice from the boat, then crossed the river and broke a trail through breast-high snow. Here, during the forenoon, they saw their first buck deer in the Olympic Mountains and gave chase; but they quickly lost their enthusiasm because of the deep snow. In the afternoon the men pulled the boat up on a bar above a swift rapid, which they then crossed over, using "some rather hard language, as the water was uncomfortably cold."

Saturday, the fourth, was "devilish cold," but all hands worked, nevertheless, mostly shoveling and tramping snow to prepare a landing place for the *Gertie.*

> The place selected for hauling out and recaulking the boat was a little bench about 10 feet above the river. To reach it we found it was necessary to haul the boat over a low bank of gravel 150 feet, then over a narrow arm of the river strewn with boulders, and up this bank to her resting place. The ground was covered with snow to a depth of four feet, bright, sparkling, glorious to look at, but to work in quite the reverse. [Barnes]

First they plowed a passage through the snow making a lane about twelve feet wide, then cleared the small bench of a thick growth of young alder and maple. Skids or ways thirty feet in length were laid across a little water course and up the bank to the bench. That afternoon, after "a long pull and heavy lift," the six men succeeded in landing the boat once again and hove her over the skids to her berth on the bench above. Exhausted by their endeavors, the men deferred raising the boat until the next day, when they lifted her four feet by building under and around. The "despicable weather" continued cold, and it snowed most of the time.

We turned her over and built fires under her and, in order to keep off the falling snow, with which we had constantly to battle, as well as the avalanches which descended from the overhanging firs, spread awning over her fore and aft. We moved camp to the riverside adjoining her, and for several days and nights we kept her hot. The ice dropped away, the sap stewed out. By day we cut and packed in wood, by night and day we smoked her by the watch. Through the long hours of the night the heavy masses of foliage above swing gently in the firelight. The heaps of snow around us, reaching up the great bluff on one side and sloping gradually away on the other to the river below, were lighted up by the ruddy glow. The swift-flowing flood of dark water and the towering wall of darker foliage beyond, bounded the circle of light, at the center of which was a poor PRESS explorer stoking fires, his eyes full of smoke, filling himself ever and anon with coffee — with the Gertie meanwhile getting as light as a cork. [Barnes]

On the fifth Christie commented that the river had risen about twelve inches, and there was "another disagreement between the boys, which made things lively in camp for awhile." The next day Christie hunted in the hills back of the camp, but without luck. He noted that the snow there was approximately five feet deep.

For more than a week most of the time was spent working on the boat or chopping and packing firewood. On January 11, however, the caulking was finished and the *Gertie* was ready for the pitch pot. The next day the boat was once again packed to the river and launched. With recaulking the *Gertie* was a definite success. "This time she behaved in a manner worthy of her name, and, we may say, creditable to her builders," Barnes reported, while Christie remarked that their labor had not been futile, for though the *Gertie's* sides were bare of paint, "she floated like a duck, and dry as a whistle."

The weather was clear and cold on Monday, the thirteenth. The men ate their breakfast at daylight and immediately began preparations for making the expedition's long-delayed trip up the Elwha River. They packed the entire outfit (from camp and cache) to a point above the first rapids, applied a few finishing touches to the *Gertie*, and by 11:00 A.M. everyone was ready to start. Christie took the bow pole, acting as bowman, Barnes handled the steering oar, and the others — Runnalls, Crumback, Sims, and Hayes —

were assigned to the towline, which ran along the left bank of the river. "In this order," wrote Christie, "we commenced our journey up the Elwha."

The *Gertie* went over the rapids, "like a Dutchman on a holiday," as Crumback remarked. Although the boat was empty, she was found to be a strenuous drag nevertheless. They pulled her to the cache above the rapids, paused long enough to eat a hasty lunch, then started loading. That afternoon they towed the *Gertie* and her full cargo about a mile to the evening's campsite. The river wound about a bluff, with deep water on one side and, on the other, a gently sloping shore covered by boulders hidden beneath deep snow. The fall of the river was great and the current strong, with rocks churning the water to foam, although in places the stream was deep and swift, "like a mill race." The towrope was manned alternately first on one side of the river and then the other, "where footholds could best be secured."

> During the afternoon Mr. Christie, stepping off the deck, took an involuntary header. He reported that the water was cold. All hands were nearly or quite as badly off, for every boot being leaky, the first step in the water filled them full. The boys on the rope are in over the tops about half the time, however, so it does not matter so much, a leak or two. Near the end of the day's trip the boat swung on a rock by the force of the current, and Mr. Christie and I had to jump overboard to save her. [Barnes]

At 3:00 P.M., after four hours struggling with the boat, the expedition "hauled along shore to camp, all hands suffering," and settled down for the night at a large drift pile. "Devilish cold," Christie reported, "and the party rather in a frozen-out condition." They cleared away the snow from a pile of drift timber and started a fire on its lee side. Soon many great logs joined in the conflagration, and the men were warm and comfortable again by the time supper was ready. "The Elwha is quite a different stream I find from the Elwha of common report," Christie concluded philosophically after the day's efforts, while Barnes ended the day with a poetic entry in his journal: "Night clear and cold, and the boys are rolling themselves in their blankets under the blue vault of heaven."

On Tuesday the weather was cloudy and slightly warmer. "We have made to-day not more than a quarter of a mile," Barnes recorded, "but every foot was worked for and honestly won." That day they passed two series of heavy rapids and cut out a big log lying across the stream. The log, which was only two feet in diameter, lay partly under the water, and they spent an hour and a half clearing it away. Just above a picturesque salmon pool they ran into "a stretch of white water that tried the temper of the boys as well as the strength of the tow-line." This passage was "quite difficult, the water being white for 150 yards and full of boulders," and they were forced to portage the cargo. The snow presented the greatest difficulty, making it impossible to find good footholds along the river's banks. The towing on the shore was ticklish enough when good footholds could be had, and the presence of two to three feet of snow rendered the situation "anything but pleasant." The huge boulders were completely covered with snow, and frequently a man would sink out of sight between them. Barnes thus summed up the day:

> We had to-day a short but swift and difficult fall of rapids to drag through. We made three attempts to get over by towing, but the snow furnished such poor foothold that it was found impracticable to get her over that way. Finally the doctor was sent ahead to take a turn about a tree with the tow line while the rest of us plunged to our belts into the water filled with floating ice and snow, and gradually, foot by foot, we dragged her over. It was terribly cold. The air registered 16 degrees when we looked at the thermometer after it was over.
>
> As we managed to get out of the freezing water the air changed our garments to ice in a moment. At one time we thought Crumback was going to faint, and all of us were of a livid blue for some time after it was over, until we got circulation started again. The sensation of having feet and legs as ours were is a very peculiar one. They were utterly devoid of sensation; so much so that we could scarcely preserve our balance to stand upright. We might have stuck a pin an inch into our legs without feeling it.

They managed to pull the *Gertie* over the rapids, however, into smooth water, where they made the ice-caked boat fast at a landing place selected for hauling her out the following day. At four o'clock in the afternoon they tied the boat up, and, after we had recovered a bit, supper was over and the boys were gathered about the glowing fire, all care was laid aside, and many was the joke that passed and pitiable was the state of the man who could not find something to laugh about in the day's adventures. It seems marvelous that some one, if not all, were not crippled for life with rheumatism, or laid up with some of the affections [*sic*] guaranteed by works on hygiene and common sense. Not a man suffered from so much as a common cold, and with the exception of passing cramps in the legs, not one has suffered any of the consequences of his rashness. [Barnes]

That night the expedition established camp on a terrace some fifteen feet above the river's left bank, at the foot of a second series of rapids about two hundred yards above the landing.

The next morning — Wednesday, January 15 — was cold and clear, but snow fell in the afternoon and evening. Christie described the day as "cold, wet and disagreeable," while Barnes called it "a day of rapids and wet clothes." At ten o'clock they stretched the towline, loaded the boat with a half cargo, and started over the rapids. Halfway through the *Gertie* swung on a rock and was partially swamped, the water "swirling and boiling all around."

It was all hands overboard in water to the waist, and cold. By much exertion we saved her entire cargo and passed it ashore, safe but wet — all our sugar, coffee, flour, tea, somewhat the worse for a quarter of an hour under water. When lightened we hove her stern up with the windlass, bailed her clear of water and completed the passage of the rapids. Then we made portage of the cargo around the rapids, 200 yards, loaded the boat and poled up stream as far as we could make headway in that manner. [Barnes]

The struggle in the white water and with the portages, plus three hours' work making camp behind a large pile of driftwood, exhausted the men. But after "a comfortable supper of pork and beans — those dear old standbys" they forgot "the miseries of the day," and fatigue put them to sleep, though their only bed was "the soft side of a gravel bar." In this miserable state of affairs, they still found reason to be hopeful, and Barnes ended his diary for the day with a wish: "Oh, for a day's hunt and some fresh meat. We will soon be among the elk and deer."

Elwha River as photographed by Asahel Curtis, about 1907
(Courtesy Washington State Historical Society)

Thursday, January 16, dawned clear and cold, but it became warmer in the afternoon. During the entire forenoon everyone was busily engaged drying the cargo and camp outfit, which had been soaked in the near shipwreck the day before.

> The boys appreciated the occasion of rest, on account of the poor sleep of the night. We have sore bones this morning. After shoveling and melting out the snow last night for a bed place, the floor was found to be boulders the size of a man's head. No boughs available. Blankets made thin mattresses — hence, sore bones. [Barnes]

While resting, the men made portage of the cargo from the next rapids, which were shoal but "otherwise not formidable." They expended considerable energy, however, forcing the boat over boulders in the river bed. Then, at the head of the rapids, a tree seven feet in diameter lay across the Elwha. Fortunately, they were able to slide the *Gertie* beneath it, and the cargo was reloaded just above this point.

> About 200 yards above the log we nearly had another shipwreck. The boat swung around in the strong current, striking a rock broadside. We recovered ourselves purely by the grit of Crumback, who managed to hold on to the towline after it had thrown everybody else off. Dr. Runnalls was dragged over the rocks about 15 feet, bruising him badly. [Barnes]

Half a mile further on, the expedition reached the pool below McCray's ranch, where they camped for the night. Here they were hailed from the river's bank by a Mr. Lutz, who was clearing and slashing on the claim while McCray was absent. They accepted Lutz's offer of lodging, and packed their camp utensils up the steep bluff to the cabin, two hundred feet above the river. During the night it snowed, but "in his comfortable log cabin we are taking turns at his rocking chair and tasting the luxury of potatoes, and are about to roll ourselves up in our blankets on the floor of the first house we have slept in for six weeks."

Snow was still falling the next morning — Friday, the seventeenth — but it changed to rain in the afternoon. At 11:00 A.M. the party loaded the *Gertie* and again started upstream.

> We cut away a fallen tree from the channel and made several hundred yards in smooth but swift running water, which required heavy hauling.

A quarter of a mile up stream we passed heavy rapids. We tried the boat first with half cargo, but midway up became unable to force her further, but running her into the opposite shore, lightened her entirely and then got over with comparative ease. The portage this time was very laborious, being nearly all wading for 200 yards over round, smooth, slippery stones. These rapids have a fall of ten feet in a distance of 100 yards. Gertie is behaving well now, is comparatively water light [tight?] and has stood many severe strains without injury. [Barnes]

Above these rapids the river broadened to about two hundred feet and broke into shallow rapids, the water tumbling among loose boulders, where a man could wade across with ease. The party hauled in immediately below the rapids and discharged the cargo on the left bank. It was almost dark, and the men were wet to the waist and exhausted. On a shelf sixty feet above the river they built a good fire and established their camp for the night.[1]

Saturday was clear and cold, but everyone felt well when they arose, the result of a good night's sleep. They made an early start, first clearing a channel — seven feet wide and fifteen inches deep — among the boulders in the rapids. For the better part of the day, they portaged the cargo, then hauled the boat through, the men wading. The towline crew went back to work, and after negotiating swift water and several minor rapids — as well as much "sludge ice" — the men arrived at about four o'clock at the mouth of Indian Creek, a large tributary which entered the Elwha from the west.[2]

The expedition camped immediately opposite a large jam of logs obstructing the river at the mouth of the creek. The settlers in Indian Valley used the logs as a bridge, for they had no other means of crossing the river. Since cutting through the logs would involve immense labor, Christie resorted to clever strategy. He sent word to the settlers in the vicinity, requesting that they ap-

---

[1] Christie's journal states that they had "a comfortable cabin for the night," apparently a reference to the McCray ranch. Whether the expedition spent one or two nights in the cabin is not clear.

[2] Today U. S. Highway 101 crosses the Elwha just above this point. It is impossible to explore the area below Indian Creek, where the struggles with the boat occurred, for it now lies beneath the waters of a reservoir known as Lake Aldwell.

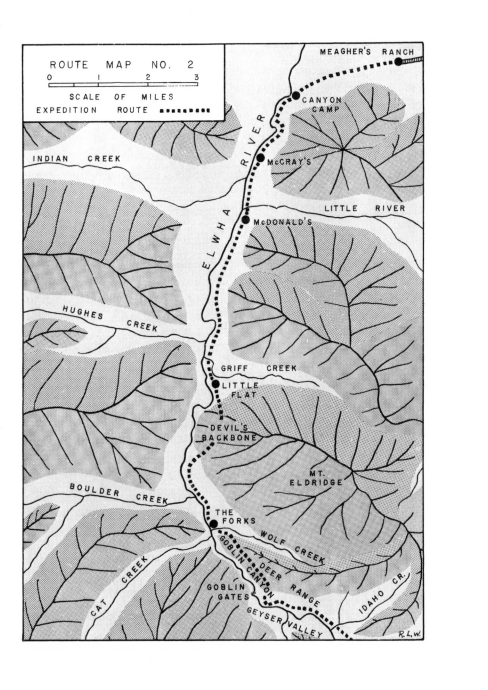

ROUTE MAP NO. 2

0   1   2   3

SCALE   OF   MILES

EXPEDITION   ROUTE

MEAGHER'S RANCH

CANYON CAMP

McCRAY'S

INDIAN   CREEK

McDONALD'S

LITTLE   RIVER

ELWHA   RIVER

HUGHES   CREEK

GRIFF   CREEK

LITTLE FLAT

DEVIL'S BACKBONE

BOULDER   CREEK

MT. ELDRIDGE

THE FORKS

WOLF   CREEK

CAT CREEK

GOBLIN CANYON

DEER RANGE

GOBLIN GATES

IDAHO CR.

GEYSER VALLEY

R. L. W.

pear at noon on Monday and help the party to portage the *Gertie* over the log jam and thus save their bridge; otherwise he would be compelled to cut it away. In the meantime the men unloaded the *Gertie*, hauled her with difficulty through the rapids, and made her fast above them. Then the men prepared their camp for the night. The evening was cold and chilly, and at dark it commenced snowing. "We are sitting very close to the fire," Barnes ended his journal entry for that day.

Sunday, the nineteenth, brought another heavy snowfall, and the men rested. William D. Macdonald, who had a claim upriver where the mules were quartered, visited their campsite and gave them "much useful information regarding the river." During the afternoon several of the men went hunting, having noted numerous cougar tracks nearby.

On Monday five settlers and two Indians assisted the expedition in crossing the log jam, which protruded six to seven feet out of the water. Inclined skids were placed on each side, and the thirteen men hauled the *Gertie* over without difficulty. She was, as Christie remarked, "one more step towards Olympus."

For the next several days the experience of the expedition was a repetition of the preceding week. Considerable snow fell, and much time was spent in the bone chilling water. However, progress upriver into the mountainous interior of the Olympic Peninsula was steady, if painfully slow. On the twenty-first the expedition moved toward Macdonald's ranch, but was compelled to make cache on the bar at the foot of a long, shallow rapid, "being unable to pull cargo owing to the wonderful low state of the river."

Now, for the first time — three weeks after the *Gertie*'s initial launching — Christie expressed doubt about this manner of transporting the supplies into the mountains. "I am afraid that I will be compelled to give up the boat," he wrote in his diary, "and take to the trail, as the depth of snow on the bank, through which the boys must plow their way, makes progress devilish slow, tedious and disagreeable."

On January 22 the expedition broke camp and placed all their outfit on the boat. They tried the rapids again, but were compelled to unload and cache half the cargo. Thus lightened, the *Gertie* could be hauled through white water to Macdonald's ranch, where the cargo was stored in his cabin. "After a change of clothing we found ourselves very comfortable," Christie observed, "squatting around McDonald's [*sic*] fireplace after seven hours' hard work in snow water to the waist."

Christie had now determined to abandon the *Gertie.* "I intend to pull the boat out as soon as we can bring up the balance of the stores, as men cannot stand any such work as we have been compelled to undergo, through the unprecedented heavy fall of snow and the low stage of water in the river."

The next morning was cold and cloudy, and the expedition members ran the *Gertie* back down to the cache during the forenoon and "loaded her up for her last trip." By 11:00 A.M. the boat was shoved into the current, with the towline taut.

> As she swung out from shore it was to begin our most severe experience with her. The rapids here are not heavy but so shoal and strewn with boulders, and the channel for the most part so far from shore, that we were soon compelled to relinquish the use of the towline and to resort to wading. We were in the water continually for two hours, at one time to our armpits. [Barnes]

The water level of the river was lower, however, than on the previous day, and thus necessitated "a good deal of hard work, in having to walk the boat up to McDonald's [*sic*], zigzaging up and across the river." At times the men on one side of the boat would be up to their chins in water, while those on the opposite side would not be in above their ankles.

> The thermometer showed several degrees of frost, and the clothing of the party would freeze as soon as any wet surface was exposed to the air above water. Several hours of this work chilled the men through and they gained but a small taste of future blessing. [Christie]

By the time they arrived at Macdonald's clearing — "the outpost of civilization as well as the head of practicable navigation with a boat" — they were suffering terribly and were "a sick-looking lot." The condition of the river — which was lower than Macdonald had ever seen it — was, they thought, the major cause of their difficulties. But once inside the comfortable cabin they quickly recovered, and "the nonchalance with which the party accepts their present hardships bodes well for the future." Hot coffee, blankets, and a roaring fire in the old Scotsman's fireplace made the men feel "as though cold water had never been."

They had had enough of the *Gertie*, however, after struggling in the icy water of the Elwha for almost two weeks, during which time they had succeeded in moving their supplies upriver approximately four miles. On Friday, January 24, the boat was stripped and stowed in a comfortable berth, "her future sphere of usefulness to be determined according to the will of Wariner Smith, whose property she becomes per agreement."

Although forced by circumstances to abandon the *Gertie*, the Press explorers had no thoughts of terminating their journey into the Olympics. It probably never occurred to them to turn back, to admit defeat. If conditions prevented their transporting the provisions into the mountains by way of the river, they could build land vehicles and carry their supplies up the valley in that manner. Therefore, while Captain Barnes worked on a chart, Christie sent the others out "to hunt up a suitable tree" from which to construct toboggans.

Macdonald's claim, where the expedition abandoned the boat, was situated "on the south branch of the little river[3] on the east side of the Elwha." Macdonald's Butte, a precipitous mountain spur forming a part of what is known today as the Elwha River Range, rose abruptly from the eastern line of the claim and towered above the ranch. While the boys were looking for toboggan material, Christie left camp, determined to reach the summit in order to gain some information regarding the country to the south, and also with the hope that he might possibly shoot a deer and procure fresh meat, which would be greatly appreciated in camp.

Christie proceeded up the "valley of the little river" about two miles, wearing a pair of snowshoes three sizes too small. He then

[3] Christie does not capitalize the word "little" in his diary. It is, therefore, not clear whether at that time the stream was called Little River, its present-day name, or whether he was merely using the term in the general sense. Probably the descriptive appellation later became the proper name. The stream is a tributary of the Elwha, flowing in from the east.

left the river and began ascending the mountain, whose slopes seemed to lie at "a very easy angle." He found, however, that the last five hundred feet were rather steep for snowshoes. The summit ridge was buried beneath ten feet of snow, "packed hard and drifted to an immense depth in many places." On his way up the mountainside, Christie observed many fresh tracks, but he saw no animals until he reached the top. From there he noted a band of five deer "across a deep gorge, dividing the Butte from the base of Mount Angeles to the southeast, but altogether too far to attempt a shot." He followed the ridge crest westward and after good snowshoeing for "a short mile" reached the highest point of the mountain. It overlooked Macdonald's claim and "commanded a magnificent view north, west and south."

At this point, more than two thousand feet above the sea, Christie was captivated by the view. He usually expressed himself succinctly, but on this occasion described the scene in eloquent terms. Northward in the distance loomed the dark bulk of Vancouver Island. At its southern tip the Race Rocks lighthouse lay serenely in the Strait of Juan de Fuca, whose waters were "lost in the far distant east and west." All about were lowlands and foothills sheltered by high peaks and covered with stands of splendid timber awaiting the saws and axes of the lumberman.

To the west Lake Sutherland shone "amidst the dark green forests which encircled its pure waters, the homes of myriads of salmon trout, the great gray and mountain trout: a veritable paradise for any disciple of the gentle art of angling." From the lake the Indian Creek Valley extended eastward toward the Elwha, and "showed a lovely stretch of level country" which, Christie predicted, would some day become "a farming and fruit country, second to none of the famous valleys of vast California." The Sutherland Range bordered and protected this "garden spot" on the south, where ridge after ridge rose skyward, finally "merging into the foot hills of Olympus towering to the south flanked by many other white capped summits on either hand." Extending eastward and westward across the expedition's line of advance, he noted, were "rugged and grand ranges . . . through which we must soon force our way, ere we can hope to master the mystery which we have determined to solve."

Christie marked his path by blazing some of the trees as he went along. On the trunk of each tree selected he made three axe cuts — one above another — and this manner of blazing became the trademark of the Press Exploring Expedition. (Today, more than three quarters of a century later, wanderers in the forests occasionally stumble upon old trees bearing this unmistakable mark of the expedition. The blazes can be discerned in many places along the expedition's route, but they are most numerous along the Elwha trail between Antelope and Idaho creeks. Unfortunately, some present-day enthusiasts have occasionally perpetrated a hoax by blazing trees in Press Party style, and the searcher should be wary that he is not misled by one of these.)

While on Macdonald's Butte, Christie took bearings for Captain Barnes of Race Rocks and a mountain he thought was Olympus.[4] He then sought a gradual slope westward toward the Elwha, and followed a well-beaten deer track for some distance along the edge of the summit cliffs where the wind had blown the snow away. He found a cleft in the face of the cliff that evidently was used as a regular trail by the deer herds which inhabited the lower ranges, but the deep snow had driven all game to the lowlands.

> Sliding and plunging to my neck in the soft snow I reached a bench about half way down the butte, feeling much like a half drowned rat. With little prospect of getting a shot, I hurried on toward McDonald's [*sic*] as the sun disappeared. The twilight warned me to make tracks, and no sooner had I covered my rifle than a fine fat-looking doe sprang from the brush some 50 yards below, disappearing ere I had a chance to uncover my gun, but gave me a snap shot 200 yards below. Unfortunately the shot took effect too far back, and although [the animal was] evidently hard hit, I was forced to give up the trail and seek camp, which I reached about 7 o'clock, to enjoy true bliss in the shape of a hearty meal and the pleasure of a comfortable pipe.

[4] Throughout the expedition this peak was "Olympus" to the party, none of the men ever detecting their error. A decade later Theodore F. Rixon — who, together with Arthur Dodwell, made the original survey of the Olympic Forest Reserve — named the peak Mount Carrie, in honor of his wife Carolina.

That night snow began to fall heavily and steadily, and it continued for three days. The flakes were "as large as an after-dinner coffee cup," and sometimes so filled the air the men could scarcely see ten yards beyond the cabin window. Because the temperature remained mild, the depth of snow increased but slightly, and three days later "barely five feet [remained] upon the ground." Nevertheless, for nearly two weeks the expedition was detained at Macdonald's.

On Monday, the twenty-seventh, Dr. Runnalls left to visit his wife, who was ill, having been "attacked by some odd new feature." Christie expressed the hope the doctor would find her "quite recovered." Runnalls expected to return in about ten days and overtake the expedition on February 4.

The day the doctor left, the snow changed to rain, and "all hands cheered themselves with the notion of a night frost, hard snow and good travel." After weeks of cold, snowy weather, they would welcome the change, and even Christie commented that he was "perfectly satisfied of the fact now that it does rain here at times."

But the expected night frost did not occur. Intermittent rain, or flurries of snow with thawing temperatures, kept the snow so soft and rotten that the equipment and supplies of the expedition could not possibly be transported. Thus, by the end of January — nearly two months after the expedition had begun — the men had not penetrated beyond the outer perimeter of the mountains. They were still low in the valley of the Elwha, not yet past the stump ranches of homesteaders. This was actually fortunate, though, for their struggles with the *Gertie,* and the attendant delays because of bad weather — however disagreeable the experiences may have been — had kept them out of the precipitous interior of the mountains during the coldest winter weather. Had the group reached the heart of the mountains then, they would probably have found survival difficult, considering the severity of the winter.

Chapter V

FEBRUARY, 1890: BACKPACKING

The stormy weather that temporarily stranded the explorers at Macdonald's continued well into February, adding to the troubles which had plagued the Press Exploring Expedition.

> For the last seven days we have been kept here as close prisoners. Practically unable to move any, owing to the extraordinary amount of rain and snow. Water fairly falling in sheets, as a rule, giving place to very heavy snow storms toward evening. There has scarcely been a single hour for the last week without a shower bath that went to the skin. Oil clothing seems to be of no use, and we have discarded it as useless. Cooped up in rather close quarters the party feels much like caged bears, but we must stand it, as the devil himself would not much relish a continued plowing through soft sodden snow to the waist, and a miniature creek coursing down his spinal column.

Thus did James H. Christie, writing in his diary on February 3, describe the beginning of the second month of 1890. Nevertheless, on Saturday, February 1, the men — discontented because of their enforced idleness — turned out "and broke a trail up stream as far as Wariner Smith's claim, chopping out and improving the trail . . . returning to McDonald's [sic] at night soaked through; the boys swearing that the rain had gone clear through hide and hair."

The expedition had planned to use the mules for packing above Macdonald's, but the extraordinary depth of the snow interfered, and for the next stage of their journey the men decided to build sledges and travois. Their plan seemed reasonable — if the snow

58

should melt, the mules would pack the outfit; if it froze and a crust formed, the sledges and travois would be utilized; and, if the snow remained soft, then—as a reluctant last resort—the men would wear snowshoes and backpack the supplies upriver.

To relieve the monotony while the expedition was delayed at Macdonald's, Christie instructed the others on methods of building various forms of sleighs in use among different tribes living in the far North. The men found no timber suitable, however, for toboggans. Christie considered "go devils" or "carry-alls"—variants of the old-time travois—to be the best substitutes. These vehicles—simpler in construction than toboggans—consisted of "but two long poles bent at one end, so as to form arms held together by two cross bars," providing there a platform where the load could be strapped.

> When all other modes fail, then remains for the boys the never-failing pack rope . . . as each individual can suit his own taste and ideas regarding mode of transporting his load there is plenty of room for choice, but, judging from the weather of the past few months and the rotten state of the snow, I have little faith in anything beyond the pack rope. [Christie]

According to Barnes, each man built his vehicle "after the fashion which suited him best." Christie decided upon a sledge as his means of transport. He procured from a neighboring slough "two good pieces of vine maple," which grew plentifully all through the valley but was "not fit for anything in God's earth but to test the patience and temper of the hunter and voyager." From these he fashioned sledge runners three inches wide and bent upward at each end. The deck and stanchions he constructed of cedar. When completed, the sledge was five feet long and twenty inches wide, "and had a tongue by which to drag it." Christie named his creation the *Carry-all*, "a tribute to its supposed strength and capacity."

Barnes chose a travois. He described it as being simple in construction, resembling

> a wheelbarrow on runners. . . . The runners are bent into the form of a bow. A stout stick is lashed in place of the cord. The runners being placed side by side a suitable distance apart, the deck is built upon the cord-

sticks. The runners extend forward four or five feet and form shafts, between which a man takes his place. Such fiery speed was expected of this product that it was christened the "go-devil."

Sims and Crumback pooled their labor to build a large, strong travois or sled which they could manage jointly. This *go-cart* was supposedly capable of carrying a double load.

Last [1] of all was the *buggy*, which Hayes made from vine maple. This "nondescript contrivance" deserved its name, being "light and airy, seemingly constructed for pleasure rather than for heavy hauling." It resembled a travois more than a sledge, but was even more like a toboggan than a travois. "It defied all attempts at classification," Barnes declared, "and must be regarded as a new invention, too fearful for description."

On Monday night, February 3, the skies cleared, and the long-awaited formation of heavy frost occurred. Early Tuesday morning there was "a thin crust on the snow . . . and as the sun rose over the eastern tree tops and painted the old man's cabin a rosy hue, the expedition was astir."

Sims and Crumback emerged first with their indescribable go-cart, which was warranted to carry three hundred pounds. They were followed by Christie and the Carry-all, a "double-ended product of human ingenuity . . . expected to surpass all estimates of its strength and endurance." Next came the go-devil, "light, airy and graceful." Finally Hayes exhibited to "an astonished camp" his buggy, completed "after many experiments and alterations."

> The train halted at the cache to load up. Three hundred pounds went aboard the "go cart." Crumback seized the traces, Sims [who was] behind prepared to hold her back lest she should go too fast. A start was made. By using a stout sapling for a crowbar they got her several feet. Her load was reduced to 100 pounds, and by dint of great pulling and hard pushing the "go cart" made a quarter of a mile. When last seen Sims was jumping with both feet up and down upon the wreck of the ill-fated "go cart" and

[1] Before he departed to visit his sick wife, Dr. Runnalls selected a travois as his vehicle, but it is not clear whether he completed it before leaving; or, in fact, ever started its actual construction. Although he had been expected to return about February 4, he did not rejoin the expedition and the diaries are henceforth silent concerning his activities.

Crumback was calling for an ax wherewith effectually to end its short but troubled career.

Meanwhile Mr. Christie tossed upon the "Carryall" bag after bag of flour and beans. A hand-pull [hard pull?] and all but 100 pounds of this burden came off and she forged ahead. Two lengths and the "Carryall" turned over on her side. This was the forerunner of many upsets, until finally at a distance of one half mile from the cache she went to join the angels. Her bones lie by the trail side, and the night wind mourns her untimely end. [Barnes]

While these disasters were occurring, Barnes loaded the go-devil with 150 pounds, and with this cargo he expected to use force in order to keep the vehicle from going too fast. He soon discovered, however, that 50 pounds could be hauled easier than 150, and lightened the load accordingly. He also found the stern rope designed for easing the go-devil downhill to be superfluous and might better have been employed as a towrope with a good span of mules ahead. However, with the reduced load, the go-devil did manage to cover a half mile.

Hayes's buggy remained by the cache. "It is its glory," Barnes noted, "that it did not fail — it never started. Hayes, like a prudent man, profited by our experience and packed his load on his back."

Barnes blamed the fiasco on the fact that the snow was too soft. The thin crust that had formed during the night proved to be deceptive, for it softened to slush "before the sun was two hours high." When the vehicles were weighted with cargo, the runners sank in the slush to the deck.

They were, of course, disappointed. First the *Gertie* had proved to be an impractical means of transporting the supplies into the mountains. Now the land vehicles, which had been painstakingly constructed, were found to be even less useful. They had no alternative but to resort to backpacking, a time-honored method of transporting supplies in mountainous country. By using snow-shoes, they could make some progress, albeit slow, through rotten snow three feet deep.

We rigged up the pack straps, and each man shouldering his fifty pounds, the actual start was made. With fifty-pound packs even the snow shoes sank six or eight inches into the snow. By nightfall we had packed 800 pounds a mile and a half into the canyon. This over a trail that was not only rough but deep [steep?]. The expedition returned that night to the ranch, quite tired from the first day's packing. It was the first of many days of similar labor. It was hard, but it was honest. [Barnes]

They packed that day to Smith's claim, beyond the alleged frontier of the white man. Rain fell all day, but that night brought another frost, which made the snowshoe trail quite firm, and the men were able to wear moccasins instead of snowshoes while back-packing. They made three trips to the cache, established the day before, halfway to Smith's claim.

Although the trail was good and packed hard by trampling a misstep over the side meant a plunge of five feet into soft snow. We used moccasins because our boots cut the trail and broke the crust. Moccasins, however, are little better than bare feet, so far as protection is concerned, and most of us began to suffer from "mal de moccasin," or foot lameness, from the unevenness and hardness of the icy trail. [Barnes]

At the end of the second trip they substituted boots for the moccasins and on the third trip managed to hobble over the trail.

But we were pretty well crippled up by night. The trail this day went through a bad country for packing. It wound about the base of a hog-back mountain, steep and broken. Sometimes one had to scramble up on all fours, then slide down a distance on the slack of his pantaloons, a means of locomotion hardly more satisfactory than the toboggans. [Barnes]

The going was easy enough, Barnes declared, without a pack, but with one there was no predicting what the outcome would be. He was certain that, had they not been carefully reared in childhood, they would have used "hasty expressions" on occasion.

As I was plodding along one day thinking that if I was accomplishing nothing else I was at least hardening my muscle and acquiring sore feet, I was suddenly shocked by hearing sundry strong expressions loudly and forcibly delivered. Upon looking about I found them to proceed from beneath the upturned roots of a great spruce tree. Sims had carelessly stepped outside the trail and in an instant had gone down and out of sight into a deep cavity formed between the snow and the roots. His cries were so appealing that I assisted him and his pack, which consisted mainly of bacon, to solid footing again, and he excused himself for his outrageous language and promised not to do so again, or until the necessity arose. [Barnes]

Because the expedition had been provisioned with a comparatively large quantity of stores — two thousand pounds[2] — the material had to be carried up the valley in successive stages. If each man carried 50 pounds, they could move a total of 250 pounds each trip. Thus, at least eight round trips were required to transport the entire outfit from one cache location to another.

On the sixth the men packed supplies from Macdonald's up to the cache. That evening they took their bedding and kitchen kit on to Smith's and, finding the cabin unoccupied, took possession and made themselves as comfortable as possible. The "breezy and well ventilated cabin," built of logs with one- to three-inch spaces between, had never been caulked. The inside boasted only a loose sheeting of cedar shakes, but it afforded some protection from the inhospitable weather.

Another heavy frost that night enabled the men to start out the next morning on snowshoes, as they prepared to continue relaying supplies from Macdonald's to Smith's.

> Long before noon, however, the crust softened and then packing became very laborious. But by hard work we got everything to the cabin. As we were bringing up the last loads we were overtaken by four Indians from the mouth of the river, on the way up to kill elk. We had them at supper with us. The band of elk the Indians were after was a band which we ourselves had planned to go for tomorrow, but this knocks all our plans in the head in all probability. We have been without fresh meat since leaving Port Angeles, and our poor dogs are almost starved. With a crowd of Indians chasing the elk we have precious little chance of overtaking them. We are getting into the game country now, however, and should get plenty of it from now on. [Barnes]

On the morning of February 10, Christie, Sims, and Hayes reconnoitered upriver toward The Forks, a place that had been mentioned to them often while they were in Port Angeles. Crumback remained in camp to cook, and Barnes went downstream to Macdonald's to plot some river courses for the map he was making of the Olympics. "The morning was crisp and sparkling," he re-

[2] The expedition left Seattle with about fifteen hundred pounds of supplies, but additional items were evidently procured at Port Angeles.

ported, "the snow was hard and in perfect condition for snow-shoes." On his return to camp, he followed the trail along Macdonald's bottomlands for nearly half a mile before taking to the rugged hillside. From there to the camp, steep sidehills, "dazzling white with snow," alternated with small patches of level land. Heavy growths of fir covered the hillsides, but the river bottoms were overgrown with alder, maple, and cedar. Barnes noted that the soil on the bottomlands — which occurred occasionally on both sides of the river — was excellent and would be easy to clear for farming. He was also duly impressed by the great cedars growing near the river. Some of them measured thirty feet around — giants which he estimated had been growing for probably two thousand years. He cut a chip from one tree, and a count of the rings of annual growth revealed thirty-five to the inch.[3] On his return to camp he found Crumback baking "some beautiful white loaves" of yeast-raised bread. "We are using bark from the red fir trees for cooking. This kind of bark, which is in thickness from two to eight inches, is full of pitch and makes a fire not unlike bituminous coal. It burns freely and with a bright blaze, with much heat."

Meanwhile, the reconnoitering party — which had taken along enough food for two days — traveled upstream to a point that afforded a splendid view of the river and valley. Below them the men could see, on a small slashing, "the cabin of Dr. Lull, another absentee squatter." Although they had reached two cabins beyond the supposed limit of settlement, the explorers did not seem embarrassed that they had as yet failed to traverse truly unknown territory.

> The curl of blue smoke rising over the tree tops about a mile beyond the shanty told us where the Indians were camped. Following along the face of the bluff we soon reached the Indian camp, though ere we had arrived at any satisfactory conclusion, we found the Indians in camp preparing their morning meal, with a quantity of fresh elk meat hung around on the trees. [Christie]

[3] Old trees grow slowly, and toward the outer part of the trunk the rings of annual growth may be extremely close together. The cedars were undoubtedly old, but Barnes probably doubled their age. At the Olympic National Park boundary on the Elwha, the present-day road into the park passes several huge cedars which may be remnants of the grove that Barnes saw.

Because of language difficulties — Christie could not speak Chinook and the Indians' English was scarcely better — little information was obtained other than the fact that, except for a short distance beyond their present camp, the Indians were "utterly ignorant of the country." They did tell Christie, however, that their fathers recalled a time when a member of the Quinault tribe had crossed the mountains and remained for some time with the Clallams.

Leaving the hunters' camp, the reconnaissance party struck out toward a bluff where, according to the Indians, they would find an old trail. They followed this trail to the foot of a mountain spur called by the downriver settlers the "Devil's Backbone." The path ascended the face of this bluff at a steep angle — Christie estimated it to be seventy-five degrees — which gave them "several good reasons to smoke" when they found convenient places to rest. As the trail wound along the mountainside, Christie noted that several areas would be "rather unsafe for any nervous youths to travel" — places which the expedition would be "compelled to improve a good deal" before their supplies could be packed across. From various points their eyes caught "an odd glimpse of the mad water in the canyon."

On gaining the upper end of the gorge, the men climbed out to a high viewpoint above the Elwha, roaring and tumbling through the narrow chasm at their feet. The entire river poured through three small channels, "the widest not over seven feet between the rocks, an effective barrier to canoeing on the Elwha."[4] The trail led for some distance through comparatively level country, crossed two small creeks, then entered a river bottom covered with heavy growths of maple. Near its center stood an old Indian smokehouse. Here the party decided to camp for the night.

Because several hours of daylight remained, the men cached their packs and "took to the hills in hopes of getting a shot." After an hour's tramp they discovered fresh elk signs leading to the river, where, as expected, they found the elk herd, the animals quietly feeding. Because the sun had disappeared, the hunters left the elk undisturbed for the night and hastened back to their camp

[4] Probably the Glines Canyon damsite.

at the smokehouse, hopeful of obtaining fresh meat by noon the next day.

When it was light enough to see the next morning, the men quickly prepared for the hunt. While Sims heated the beans and made coffee, the others rustled about, hanging up the packs and carefully checking the rifles. No one lingered over the coffee, and the men left camp as soon as they had eaten.

At first they followed the river bank through a growth of young trees. Then for half a mile the hunters proceeded along the edge of a bank, which afforded good level snowshoeing. Upon reaching a rocky point on the river, they discovered fresh signs of elk and followed the spoor to where the animals had moved onto a long gravel bar. The devious route then led them across a wide slough, into a sparsely timbered area. Here the openness of the country compelled the men to seek cover in a strip of young trees along the river. They worked their way through these, and after crossing two small creeks saw evidence that a herd of perhaps half a hundred elk had "plowed a deep, broad trail" up an abrupt mountainside.

The party was now in the vicinity of The Forks. Up the face of the mountain they followed the well-beaten trail, climbing six hundred feet, and at the top they were "glad enough to rest for wind" on a broad, level bench. Only partially timbered, it showed evidence of having been swept by fire in the distant past.

After resting a few minutes, the men were on the trail again. They moved upstream for a half mile, then entered a heavily timbered bluff, beyond which the elk spoor "showed plain and broad straight up the face of the bench to the east." Carefully surveying the country ahead, the men pressed on, and after some hard scrambling and a close examination of the ground "were rather disappointed at seeing no game in sight."

They continued to follow the trail, however, and soon it turned sharply to the left and entered a low, swampy area. The men could hear the bulls tramping the gravel and rubbing against the trees. Cautiously they backtracked out of the swamp, then divided their forces. Sims and Hayes stationed themselves near the foot of the mountainside, while Christie moved toward the edge of the bench away from the swamp.

After stalking carefully for ten minutes, Christie reached a desired vantage point and crept quietly around the roots of an upturned tree. As he looked, his eyes were

> greeted with a sight that had warmed the heart of the coolest nimrod that had ever made moccasin tracks in a mountain side. Immediately fronting me stood one of the monarchs of the mountains — a stag royal with as fine a head as ever graced the trophied hall of any highland chief — some one hundred yards distant, with his nose well into the wind as if scenting danger to his harem. Grazing quietly around, scattered through the short brush of the swamp were some 50 or 75 elk, the young and graceful yearling, the more homely cows, now heavy with calf, with several royal heads of various ages. [Christie]

With all the pride of the hunter, Christie could only stand and gaze at the picture before him, reminded forcibly of "the no uncommon sights" he had observed in mountains on both sides of the American boundary.

> Suddenly the simultaneous report of two rifles dispelled my dream as it suddenly awoke the band of elk to a sense of danger. As they gathered in a complete mass from the brush, the great stag whom I had been admiring paused for a few seconds as if uncertain [from] which direction the sounds had come. [Christie]

As the animals stampeded, dashing away through the swamp, Christie noticed a young bull. He felt a strong temptation to take just one shot, but inexplicably "allowed him to trot off in peace." The animals had hardly disappeared from the swamp "when another shot from the boys put their game out of pain" and gave the expedition a good supply of fresh meat. Christie then joined Sims and Hayes, but before cutting up the elk the men "indulged in a pipe." They selected a few choice cuts, "made tracks for camp," and enjoyed their first meal of fresh elk meat, "the forerunner of hopes of more to come."

That night a hard rain thoroughly drenched the three as they lay curled up around their fire. Consequently, by morning they were disposed to hurry back to the downriver camp; they quickly drank their coffee and departed. Blazing the trail during the return delayed the reconnaissance party until well on toward night, when they reached Smith's claim. A "supper of elk tenderloin steak, liver and bacon, with incomparable coffee, flanked by Crumback's bread," repaid them well for the day's discomfort. The party had not dined on fresh meat for two months.

The next four days — February 13 to 16 — were spent at Smith's claim. The men rested, waiting for better weather before proceeding deeper into the mountains. The weather was variable — flurries of snow, rain, and generally thawing temperatures by day, with light frost at night. On the thirteenth, they packed several loads and made cache in a valley on the river two miles above.

While packing on Saturday, the fifteenth, Christie came across the fresh trail of a cougar. From the enormous size of the footprints, he concluded that they belonged to Johnnie, "a large cougar of whom the settlers in the valley would fain be rid of." Anxious to secure the mountain lion's pelt, Christie followed the trail on the sidehill for three hours, until he reached the creek flowing between Mount Angeles and Macdonald's ranch.

> This I was unable to cross as his catship, the cougar, had to clear a good ten feet to the opposite rock. I concluded not to follow. Returning to camp I crossed a fresh cut undoubtedly made by the same animal, but there is no signs of cougar to be met with further.

On the seventeenth and eighteenth the expedition took advantage of slightly harder night frosts and finished packing the entire outfit to a little flat or vine maple swamp near the river, where they made camp. The thin crust of ice broke often under the men's weight, and they would sink to the waist in the deep, soft snow. This packing was the most difficult yet, and "the angels in heaven," according to Barnes, "shed many a tear before little flat camp was reached."

One of the expedition's purposes was to explore for mineral wealth in the mountains, and on several occasions Christie had tried panning in the Elwha. He tried again at the new camp, but had the same experience as in his previous attempts — there was no color. Evidently gold was not to be found in the Olympic Mountains.

Half a mile above the vine maple swamp the river flowed through a deep canyon, washing the base of a steep mountainside.

Across this spur or ridge — the Devil's Backbone — the men would be forced to cut a trail. On the nineteenth, Christie, Sims, and Hayes went ahead, "to overcome the engineering difficulties and to make a passable trail if possible."

Crumback and Barnes — who had remained in camp — heard barking nearby, but paid no attention, supposing the dogs had seen a squirrel.

> As we sat, Jack stirring the fire, and I preparing to go out, we were suddenly startled by a magnificent elk, who came into view followed by Tweed and Daisy, barking and nipping his heels as he ran. Distracted by the dogs, the animal did not appear to notice the camp, but trotted across a little open space within thirty yards of where we were sitting. Jack and I jumped up and the way we looked for guns would surely have found one if there had been no elk in sight. By the time we had dragged a rifle out from under the stack of flour and beans, the elk had disappeared in the bush. [Barnes]

Barnes gave chase and caught sight of the elk again just before it disappeared in the timber on the opposite side of the river. He forded across and followed its trail for two miles, but the animal had been thoroughly alarmed, and the chase proved fruitless. "On my return to camp I found that the reputation of Jack and I as sportsmen was none the better for the elk passing camp without [our] getting a shot. There was great fun in camp."

On Thursday, February 20, the camp and cache were moved a half mile to the foot of the Devil's Backbone. At the base of this jutting spur the men built their fire against a great cedar that lay upon the ground. Because the log was dry, the fire was soon blazing brightly, and the tired explorers rolled up in their blankets and spent a comfortable night. Then, during the next two days, they packed the entire outfit across the Devil's Backbone.

The expedition was now beyond the last settler's cabin, and would soon reach the farthest point yet explored by the homesteaders who lived along the lower Elwha.

For three miles below the Devil's Backbone the trail had meandered through timbered bottomlands that sloped gently from the Elwha to the base of the mountainside. Some of these flats were covered with alder and maple, so that the land could be easily cleared by settlers. The bottomland was not continuous, however,

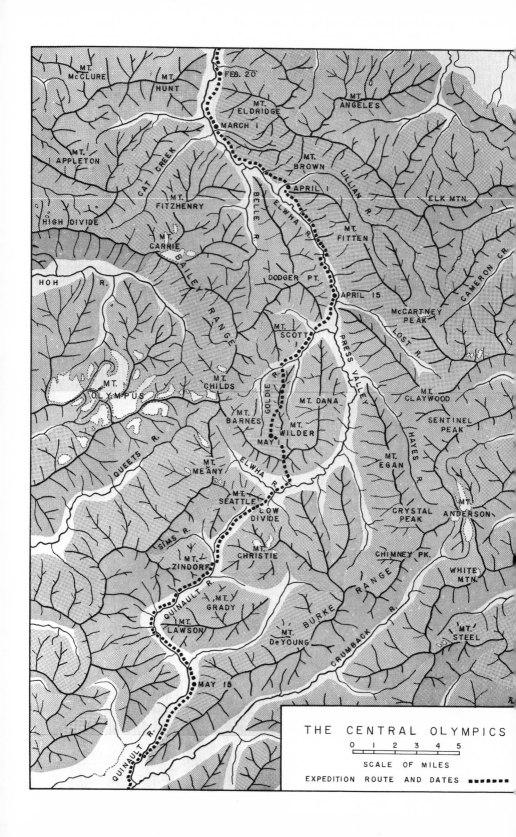

THE CENTRAL OLYMPICS

SCALE OF MILES

0 1 2 3 4 5

EXPEDITION ROUTE AND DATES ▪▪▪▪▪▪▪

for "several small tongues or spurs from the mountain" broke it into segments, each of which was large enough "to make an excellent claim."

They had no trouble packing over the trail made on the nineteenth. In several places, however, the mountainside was steep enough to necessitate the cutting of little shelves. They also removed brush and a few logs to improve the trail.

> While making the first trip we were treated to the sight of a deer chase by the dogs. The dogs started a deer some distance below us and all four gave chase. He struck down the river, and at a distance of about half a mile from us he emerged from the trees upon the river bank and plunged into the stream, followed by two of the dogs, Bud and Dike. The current was very strong at that place and full of rapids, and we became rather anxious as they were all — deer and dogs — swept down by the current. Fortunately for the deer he managed to get out on the opposite side some distance below, while the dogs crawled out on this side. But they showed spirit and pluck in staying with the chase so long. [Barnes]

Sunday, the twenty-third, was a pleasant day, and the men remained in camp, enjoying a well-earned rest, except for Christie and Hayes, who sojourned upriver "in hopes of gaining some information regarding the country beyond." Two hours of travel brought them "to the lower end of a deep, black canyon," whose walls, composed of black slate, were nearly vertical. Noting "several well defined veins of quartz formation" in the east wall, the men did some prospecting. While on their way back to camp in the evening they shot a deer and hung it up for future use.

Though the day had been pleasant, during the night six to eight inches of snow fell, covering their bedding. They did not mind the snow, but the temperature was so mild that it began to melt and at times became rain; the water soaked through their blankets and "made a rather uncomfortable camp." They spent half the next day digging the camp out and drying the blankets. In the afternoon they moved a load several miles up the river to The Forks. "This is the *ultima thule* of their [homesteaders along the Elwha] exploration. But if their exploration is no better than their reports it is well that it went no further. The only fork we could find was a little creek that a man could jump over."

The country traversed that day consisted of bottomland,[5] which alternated from one side of the river to the other. On the twenty-fifth of February, camp was shifted close to The Forks, to a point on a flat where a large creek entered the Elwha. They had now arrived at the eastern base of the mountain uplift thought to culminate in Mount Olympus. Immediately opposite was another creek, which flowed into the Elwha from the east.[6] The remainder of the outfit was temporarily cached at Backbone Camp, and to protect the cache from animals the men built an elevated structure, utilizing four small trees which grew close together. First they chopped the trees off about seven feet above the ground, then constructed a platform on the tall stumps. The provisions were piled upon the platform and covered with a tarpaulin.

On this day [7] the party first saw the mountain which they mistook for Olympus. Christie, however, had previously observed it from Macdonald's Butte on January 24, a month earlier (see pages 55–56). From this new viewpoint they "obtained a photograph of the mountain." It appeared to be "a huge, spreading mountain, bell shaped, covering a great area." In the center rose the peak, "snow crowned, regular in outline, clear cut against the dark blue sky beyond."

In the afternoon the sky became overcast, and a cold, raw wind began to blow from the southwest, chilling them when they stopped to rest. Before they reached The Forks on the second trip a furious snowstorm was in progress, the wind driving the flakes into their faces and clothes. "It was with hands chilled and blue that we made camp that evening," Barnes noted, "and the greatest fire we could make in that wind hardly took off the edge of discomfort. We pitched the tent and in the shortest possible time got into our blankets."

[5] These bottomlands now lie under the waters of Lake Mills, a reservoir impounded behind the Glines Canyon dam.

[6] It is not clear on which side of the river they were presently camped, although they had been coming along the east side. According to Christie's diary they must have been on the west side; the next day, however, a tree was felled for a bridge to enable them to cross to the west side. This would indicate that they were still on the east side.

[7] According to Barnes, February 25; according to Christie, February 24.

They also wanted to explore the country lying west of the river, and since at this point the Elwha was too deep for wading, they needed a bridge of some kind. On February 26 the men cut a two-hundred-foot tree which stood by the river. It crashed at right angles to the current, with the topmost branch coming to rest upon the snow-covered bank on the opposite side, the trunk spanning the river and forming an excellent bridge.

> The day was for the most part devoted to the homely and necessary task of repairing clothes. The rough travel of the river has already begun to tell upon the clothes of the party, and a patch of canvas here and a piece of blanket sewed on there already gives the clothing a picturesque effect. [Barnes]

On the morning of the twenty-eighth — while sitting about the fire after breakfast, smoking their pipes — the men caught sight of two large grey wolves walking quietly along the opposite bank of the river. The guns were close by, and as the larger of the two animals advanced to the water's edge to investigate the Press Party camp, he was greeted by a slug from Sims's Winchester, "which did not agree with his digestive organs." The animals broke for the brush, followed by Sims for a hundred yards, "where he found his wolfship and packed him to camp." Sims saved the pelt and later gave it to a Seattle friend for his den.[8] The other wolf "escaped with a piece of lead somewhere in his carcass, for several drops of blood indicated the point of his disappearance."

While the dead wolf was being skinned, Sims spied a good-sized wildcat, also on the opposite side of the river.

> It was a beautiful sight for a moment to see it stand as it did, surprised, wondering what kind of animal we were. Sims was the lucky man, and "got" it with the first shot. Tom made one jump of about five feet into the air and then doubled up in a heap. As Jack was fetching him across our tree bridge he seemed almost as large as Jack himself, but by actual measurement the cat was three feet nine inches in length from the front of the nose to the root of the tail. The tail measured eight inches. He was a

[8] Apparently the pelt was taken down to Macdonald's and sent to Seattle by way of Port Angeles. On June 6, 1890, Edmond Meany received a bill for twenty dollars from a Seattle furrier, for dressing and mounting the skins of a deer, an elk, and a timber wolf.

dim color on the back, with greyish spots in stripes on the sides. We saved and stretched the skin.[9] [Barnes]

The men named the creeks which entered the Elwha at their campsite in honor of the two kills. The creek coming from the east they called Wolf Creek; the stream from the west — draining the northern slopes of what they thought was Mount Olympus — they named Cat Creek; and these names still appear on today's maps. The site where the shootings occurred, however, now lies under the waters of Lake Mills.

> But this was not the end of the day's shooting. Wolves and cats are not grub, and the camp was almost out of meat. So in the afternoon Hayes was sent out to kill an elk, of which there were numbers on the hills around. He returned to camp after a couple of hours, having left a dead elk about a mile from camp, on the mountain side above. All hands were called, and with pack-straps and gunny-sacks we started off to fetch down the meat. We found a magnificent specimen of elk lying with his throat cut and a ball through his head, which accounted well enough for his death. We removed his hide for preservation, and his tusks for mementos, and brought away all we could carry of the meat — some 300 pounds. We got many a tumble and roll in the soft snow before we reached the bottom of the 1500-foot slope, and we were wet to the skin when we arrived in camp. But that is something we are accustomed to by this time. The weather is frosty and cold, but providing there is no wind blowing it is easy to be comfortable. [Barnes]

It was the end of February — winter was almost gone; spring but three weeks away. The Press Exploring Expedition, provisioned for six months, had been in the wilderness nearly three. In three months the men would be compelled to return to civilization. Still they had only begun to penetrate the mountainous interior of the Olympic Peninsula, had little more than breached the perimeter of the mountains. They had traveled less than one fifth of the distance across the Olympics. Their greatest adventures, hardships, and difficulties lay ahead, in the depths of the "terra incognita."

[9] At another point in his narrative, Barnes states that the wildcat was shot on March 1.

Chapter VI

MARCH, 1890: GOBLINLAND

AT THE beginning of March the snow was soft and deep, making travel almost impossible, especially when the men had to pack heavy loads. Nevertheless, on March 2 Captain Barnes left the camp at The Forks to search for a route through the country ahead. He proceeded up the west bank of the Elwha, returning by the east. During this trip, he stumbled upon the Goblin Gates, an unusual topographic feature which is practically unknown today.

Barnes departed after an early breakfast, carrying a gun, a camera, "and some provisions, consisting of tobacco, coffee, bread and a handful or two of beans." Fifty yards above the tree bridge spanning the Elwha he crossed Cat Creek, which entered the river opposite Wolf Creek. Immediately above the confluence of the three streams the river emerged from a deep canyon,[1] with precipitous sides composed of broken rock. Barnes climbed three hundred feet up a steep slope leading to the top of the canyon walls, and as he traveled southward he found that they gradually increased in height. From the lip of the canyon the mountainside sloped upward at a lesser angle and was "overgrown with small firs, sufficiently dense to make it quite gloomy beneath them." For half a mile the terrain permitted fairly rapid travel, then suddenly the mountainside was cut by a deep ravine, in the bottom of which flowed a stream, "milk white from the melting snow mass which crowns the summit of Olympus."

Because the ravine was "filled with soft melting snow and a

[1] Goblin Canyon, they later called it, but today it is known as Rica Canyon.

75

vast quantity of fallen timber," Barnes was some time making his way across. Upon reaching the opposite crest he caught a glimpse of a large animal running swiftly along the slope below. First he thought of Dike, his dog, who had followed him halfway across the tree bridge when he left camp.

> But the next instant it came into full view — a large gray wolf. He caught sight of me, stopped at the same time, double the size of Dike, although Dike was as large as a good-sized Newfoundland. I unslung my rifle and shot him through the lungs. As he jumped I gave him another one which laid him out. As he lay dead on the snow with his long tongue hanging out he was a horrible sight. I got a photograph of his carcass. [Barnes]

Perhaps a third of a mile beyond, Barnes came upon another milky stream — larger than the first — "plunging down into a deep cut or gorge in the solid rock." After many minor cascades and an imposing plunge of a hundred feet, finally "amid much spray and foam, the torrent sank into a quiet pool and thence flowed noiselessly into the river." From a small point of rock on the right bank, he obtained "a glimpse of the river below, . . . flowing in its canyon, deep, green and quiet."

The canyon appeared to continue southward for a considerable distance, and the farther Barnes went the deeper it became. Occasionally he could see across, through openings among the trees, to the eastern side. The canyon walls on both sides of the river were "almost perpendicular for from nine hundred to a thousand feet," and out of the depths rose "the sounds of mad and roaring water, sometimes deafening." From the top of the cliff or precipice, the mountainside sloped upward at approximately a forty-degree angle and was "broken by ravines and canyons and rough beyond description."

All day he clambered along the mountainside, "sometimes through deep snow, and sometimes over little patches of bare ground protected by the foliage overhead, but always over fallen timber." His progress was slow, and when, toward sundown, he at last found a suitable camping place, he was quite fatigued. Choosing a bare spot "at the foot of a great fir tree on the mountain side, whose spreading roots made a capital fireplace, and enclosed a little shelf about ten feet square," Barnes unslung his pack and placed it, together with his gun and photographic equipment, in a dry spot. "All around was snow for water," plus an abundance of dry wood. He cut enough wood to keep a fire going through the night.

> I made a fire, put on a pail of snow to melt, and in a very few moments the aroma of coffee filled my solitary camp. After a frugal supper — for I had been disappointed in killing game today — I gathered an abundance of spruce boughs [2] for my bed, and, having prepared my fire for the night and lighted my pipe, turned in just as it was beginning to grow dark.
>
> By the way, there is a science in laying spruce boughs, if comfort is desired. Throw them down carelessly and the sensation of lying on a grid-iron will be the result. They should be laid shingle fashion, the bushy foliage of one layer covering the sticks and stems of the lower. Given plenty of depth it rivals any bed that panders to the demands of luxurious civilization. The yielding springiness and aromatic odor of the spruce will transform a tired man into a fresh one in the shortest possible time. And how pleasant one's pipe tastes under such circumstances. Poets have sounded the glories of the chimney corner, the easy chair and the comfortable dressing gown, but they know nothing of the roaring camp fire and the bed of boughs spread within its circle of warmth. Around about the fire-lighted snow, and, beyond and encircling all the gloomy blackness of the woods, encloses one like a cosy room. Soon the wet clothing is dry, the hard day's work contrasts with the present comfort, the burned-out pipe is refilled and one can drop into the pleasantest of dreams. The fire, replenished once or twice during the night, lasts till morning, and at the first gray signs of dawn one can spring to his feet with the elasticity of boyhood. [Barnes]

Barnes continued his trek up the canyon the next day. The only animal he saw was a lone wolf, which treated him "with scant ceremony," disappearing before he could fire his rifle.

On leaving the camp at The Forks, Barnes had not carried any meat in his pack, as he expected to kill all that he required. But although he saw a number of deer and elk tracks, the game itself gave him not so much as a "whisk of its tail," and that, he declared, was rather short. For this reason he welcomed "a happy affair which occurred after breakfast." He had packed his kit and

[2] In their narratives, Barnes and Christie use the terms "spruce" and "pine" rather loosely. Spruce is not commonly found on the Elwha, and its sharp-pointed needles would hardly make a comfortable bed. Barnes was probably referring to Douglas fir, sometimes called Douglas spruce.

was on the verge of leaving his temporary camp when, startled by a light rustling in some nearby bushes, he reached for his gun and waited. Presently he heard another rustle, and from the thicket emerged

> as beautiful a doe as ever leaped a mountain stream. I raised my gun. I had her sure and was in no hurry to shoot. I caught her eye for the first time and she stopped, her front half concealed by the clump of laurel not 20 yards away, and stood gazing from curiosity. As she stood I could not help admiring her — the light-brown coat, the graceful neck, the gentle eye — it seemed like murder to kill her. It was too bad. I felt sorry for the beautiful animal, but I needed meat. After what seemed a long time, but which was actually about a minute, she turned half around and I shot her through the heart. One spring and she was dead. I was at her side in a moment and cut her throat. [Barnes]

He placed in his pack the liver and as much of the meat as he could comfortably carry, then hung up the remainder for future use by the expedition. It was still early when he left, blazing the trees as he went in order that he could again find the cache. Three quarters of a mile from his campsite he came to a large creek and, because his trail could be picked up easily at this point, discontinued blazing. He then followed the stream about two hundred yards and, "where it made a bold jump into the river . . . still a deep gorge below," found a good place to cross the ravine and climb up the other side.

Here he encountered little snow. The dense foliage of the trees had apparently protected the ground. For the next mile the forest floor — bare of snow and covered with Oregon grape — was "a veritable elk pasture." Hoof marks were everywhere, and a large elk herd was evidently in the vicinity, for some of the tracks appeared to be not more than two days old. He therefore proceeded cautiously, alert for "still fresher tracks."

Because of the unevenness of the terrain, his progress was slow. Gradually, however, the slope eased, and Barnes anticipated that he was nearing the end of the canyon. He expected to find bottomland again, where the traveling would not be so difficult. He had not reached the terminus of the canyon, however, when he was "surprised by the coming on of dusk." The dense forest had deceived him; all that day he had scarcely glimpsed the sun, so shaded had been the mountainside beneath the thick foliage of the trees. Now, as the darkness gathered, rain began to fall. During the less than thirty minutes of dusk that remained, he must locate and make a camp, as well as prepare for a rainy night. He was forced to utilize the spot where he presently stood, for there was no time to search for a suitable place.

> The available wood was rotten and wet, and it was not until I had fumbled about for some time in the dark that I was able to boast a camp — and a wet camp at that. I potted the nearest patch of snow for coffee and had venison for my supper. A hasty thatch of cedar boughs shed a part of the rain, which was now falling in torrents. A good fire dried one side of me and then the other alternately as I would wake up and turn over during the night. Nevertheless I was quite wet when morning came. [Barnes]

The sky was clear and bright, however, when the sun rose, and Barnes dried his clothes and gear. Then he broke camp, shouldered his pack, "and stole again to the southward." He had not gone far when he reached the end of the canyon and could see through the trees "a lovely valley" five or six hundred feet below. He descended to it by following "a charming little ravine" that was radiant with the glories of the spring-like day. At the bottom of the ravine he caught his first view of a scene that caused him to pause in wonderment — a spectacle which he later concluded "must become famous among the natural marvels, not alone of the Olympics, but of the whole continent."

> Along one side of a little valley the river thundered in great rapids, with a volume of sound, which, echoed by the bounding mountain walls, became almost stunning. The water of the river suddenly comes to a standstill in a deep, green pool, or basin. On the opposite side of the pool, the mountain is sheer perpendicular rock, smooth and bare. This rock is broken at right angles to the direction of the river, and down this cleft the water of the pool glides as noiselessly as a serpent. It is like the throat of a monster, silently sucking away the water. [Barnes]

Barnes had, indeed, encountered the most unusual sight in the mountains that any of the expedition members had thus far been privileged to see. He gazed at the pool and the cleft, where the

Goblin Gates (Courtesy National Park Service)

An Olympic creek in May, still bordered by deep snow. The Press Expedition spent much time traversing terrain of this nature (Photo by Robert L. Wood)

whole river entered the canyon through portals not more than twelve feet in width, and the longer he looked, the more impressed he became. As his enthusiasm grew, so also did his imagination.

> These portals are guarded by two gigantic heads of rock . . . which are 15 feet in height. About 30 feet inside of these heads is another pair of heads, making a kind of inner gateway, with a vestibule between the outer and inner. Upward and backward from the gateway, the canyon walls rise to a height of several hundred feet, making the bottom quite dark. For several hundred feet, as far as can be seen down the canyon, a multitude of faces appear in succession near the water's edge. One could conceive in them tortured expressions, which, with the gloomy and mysterious character of the whole, justified us in giving it afterwards the name of "The Goblin Gates."
>
> The geographical strata here is tilted on edge and consists of alternate layers of hard slate and soft sandstone. The sandstone has worn away, leaving alternating slate projecting into the canyon and forming in profile the heads as they appear from the entrance. The spectacle is one which alone would well repay a tourist for the trouble of a trip to see. [Barnes]

The miniature valley was thirty to forty acres in extent, "nearly encircled by the slopes of Olympus." Lying well to the sun, the place was bright and warm, with soil of rich sandy loam "covered partly by a growth of maple and alder, and partly by fir trees." The valley would be "a charming place for a tourists' hotel," the expedition later concluded, since it faced the Goblin Gates. No hotel was ever built, however, although some years later a settler named Anderson took a homestead on the little valley. No one lives there today, and small bands of elk often graze on its grassy expanses, now included in the national park.

The bottomland appeared to continue up the river and would likely afford good travel. The purpose of his solo trip — the finding of a route — thus accomplished, Barnes prepared to return along the other side of the Elwha to the camp at The Forks. He decided to ford at a point about two hundred yards above Goblin Gates, where the river was broad and shoal. Removing his clothing, he packed everything on his shoulders, and with a pole in each hand started wading carefully through the icy cold water. In the middle of the stream the water came above his waist, but he reached the other side without mishap and then commenced to ascend the mountainside. Here the "stone wall of the gateway" broke into a steep slope eight hundred feet high, "for the most part a sliding mass of thin, shaly stones." He managed to reach the top, however, "by dint of hard climbing"—occasionally swinging onto a bush, and pausing now and then to rest among some scrubby trees. "The view was excellent. It was now four o'clock, and as dry wood was plenty I camped there exactly on the summit. A good fire and some boughs made a very comfortable camp, and I boiled down some snow as usual and had venison stew for supper."

He rested well that night, and the next morning he had gone but a half mile when he shot a deer and hung the carcass up for use by the expedition, which would be along "in a few days at most." The distance to the camp on this side was shorter, "being the chord of the arc made by the river." The terrain was still rough, however, and he found the snow "trying in places, deep and soft." Often he slid into holes and had to struggle out. But traveling was much easier than on the west side of the river, for he did not have to clamber across ravines. Nevertheless, it took him about seven hours to reach The Forks.

While Barnes was on his upriver excursion, the other men explored various creeks which entered the Elwha from the west in the vicinity of The Forks. "The country lying between Olympus and Indian creek valley," Christie wrote in his diary, "is occupied by two magnificent ranges of heavily timbered mountains, intercepted by several small creeks and valleys." The land, he declared, held "great prizes in store for venturesome nimrods"—a region where the elk and deer roamed freely, "the seclusion of their retreat being seldom disturbed by the foot fall of man, although within easy reach of Port Crescent and Port Angeles."

Christie also had an appreciative eye for the natural wealth of the Olympics. He gazed at the "miles on miles of magnificent timber"—forests that stretched "from the river bank to the very summits of the mountains without a break in the dark confines"—and predicted that fortunes awaited the lumberman. But there was also room, he stated, "for many a happy homestead in the well sheltered valleys amidst the mountains." The day was not too distant, Christie concluded, when "rare benefits" would accrue to those who settled in the region.

The weather on March 6 was clear and warm until evening, with colder temperatures and rain during the night. The soft, slushy snow made any attempt to move camp impractical. Nevertheless, in order to make observations, Barnes returned to his "eagle's nest camp[3] above the Goblin canyon," where he had stayed on March 4. Upon arriving there in the afternoon, he shifted his camp a few yards in order to utilize a new backlog for his fire. The wind built to a steady gale that continued through the night, accompanied by incessant rain. Protecting himself as best he could, Barnes built a windbreak by stacking up a number of small firs and weighting them with stones and sticks.

By the next morning he realized that he would not be able to make the planned observations because of the weather, and he decided to return to the downriver camp. After caching his outfit under a log, Barnes descended to the river. Although he had intended to ford the Elwha and return by the west side, the river had risen a foot and crossing was impossible. He therefore climbed back up the mountainside and traveled down the east bank. Tramping through the slushy, thawing snow was laborious. When he finally arrived in camp, the place was deserted, the others having returned to Macdonald's for the mules. Barnes lighted a fire, cooked some venison for supper, then wrapped up in his blankets and wrote letters. The rain continued without a break all night. In the morning he rigged a tepee over a small fire and dried his wet clothes.

On March 6, while Barnes was at the "eagle's nest," Christie, Crumback, Hayes, and Sims descended to Macdonald's to bring up the mules, "as there was a prospect of being able to use them." They had to break trail almost the entire distance because of the deep snow, and they arrived at Macdonald's in the evening. The next morning the men awoke to find it "raining as if a second flood were threatened." The rain continued all day and detained them within the shelter of the Scotsman's cabin. On Saturday, the

[3] This was probably the present-day "elk overlook" just south of Whiskey Bend, near the Elwha trail.

eighth, they packed the mules at daybreak, bade farewell to Macdonald—who "seemed rather cut up at losing his pets, the mules"—and left for camp.[4] Progress upriver to The Forks was slow. "The pleasure of plowing through slush and snow to the waist was somewhat heightened by being under a down pour of rain all day," Christie noted, "compelling us to camp near a maple swamp all night."

The weather on March 9 was still foul, for snow and rain fell all day and night. It snowed very heavily at daybreak, the flakes "completely concealing objects at 15 paces distant." The men shook themselves clear of the snow, packed up again, and started, "wet, miserable and just a little inclined to use bad language." On the north side of the Devil's Backbone, they met Barnes, who was en route to Macdonald's to post the letters he had written.[5] Men and mules pressed on through the blinding snow, and upon reaching the Devil's Backbone "found the trail slippery with the mud and snow, which rendered extreme caution necessary in getting round some of the worst points."

About a half hour after meeting Barnes, the party reached the point where the trail became "a mere narrow ledge or shelf over a chasm 400 feet in depth." As they were traversing the mountainside, Christie was ahead, cutting away fallen trees and other obstructions, followed by Crumback leading Jennie. At a cry from Crumback, Christie "turned in time to see Jennie plunging down into the gulf below." The earth beneath the mule's feet had suddenly given way, and although the animal made a desperate effort to save herself she was dragged down by the two-hundred-pound load on her back. They heard a rattle of gravel, succeeded by a

[4] On April 21, William D. Macdonald wrote to Edmond S. Meany: "A balance of twenty Dollars being due me for feed and care of mules for the winter, belonging to the Press Exploring Party, when taking the mules away J. H. Christie stated that he had written to you, and that you would forward the amount to me by mail.

"As I have not received the remittance would you please to write me and state if Christie had any authority for making such a promise, and oblige."

[5] This was apparently the last time the expedition was in contact with settlers in the Elwha Valley. From this point on they were out of touch with civilization.

dull, sickening thud as the mule struck a cleft between the cliff and a large tree about one hundred feet below.

> Hastily undoing our life lines, and tying them to trees above, Sims and I lowered ourselves some hundred and 50 feet down the face of the cliff to find poor Jennie lying wedged between an enormous tree and the wall of rock. Her back broken and her poor body bruised, in the last agony. A cut from my hunting knife released her from the pack saddle and trappings, and poor Jennie went thundering down 300 feet, bounding from ledge to ledge, until she disappeared in the bush. [Christie]

A few seconds later, the heavy sounds of Jennie's body coming in contact with the rock told them "the fate of a faithful mule."

The animal's load had consisted of 150 pounds of flour and about 50 pounds of "colored fire." But signaling from a mountaintop held little interest for them at the moment. The flour was retrieved and hoisted to the trail, but the sounds of Jennie's plunge to the depths below had hardly died away when "with a kick the 'hell fire,' as it was familiarly known in camp," was sent after the mule, to find "a fitting resting place by her side." Christie and Sims then clambered up to the ledge above.

That evening the men arrived in camp at dark — cold, wet, and discouraged.

> The loss of poor Jennie to the expedition is greatly felt by us. She was the heaviest and strongest animal. Upon her we depended largely for the transport of our supplies. Without her we must do that work ourselves so that the accident will result in great loss of time and expenditure of labor, which might be devoted to the objects of the expedition. After struggling through this long hard winter surrounded by mountains of ice and snow and seeing at last the snow disappearing and before us a practicable route to the other side, — after all this, is it any wonder that we all feel blue. [Barnes]

The Devil's Backbone — where the incident occurred — was a buttress at the base of a snow-capped mountain which was connected by a ridge with Mount Angeles. They named the peak Mount Eldridge, "in honor of Mr. William Eldridge, of Washington, D. C.," but the mountain is known today as Hurricane Hill.

The expedition made one round trip each day from March 11 to 14, packing stores from the cache at Backbone Camp to The Forks.

On the fourteenth, Crumback and Hayes returned to the Devil's Backbone to bring up the last load of stores. While they were gone, Christie, Barnes, and Sims broke camp at The Forks and moved everything—"rather a tough pull up hill"—to a bench five hundred feet higher and about a half mile distant. The three then descended to The Forks and met Crumback and Hayes coming up from below. During the afternoon they packed another load of stores to the new location and established "Camp No. 16."

On the last trip the men were "treated to a circus by Capt. Barnes, as he plunged down the face of the butte to head off Dollie." The recalcitrant mule, apparently reluctant to go further into the inhospitable mountains, had broken away from the trail and was headed downhill toward Macdonald's. Barnes thwarted the attempted escape, but in the process "took some wonderful handsprings with a fifty-pound pack."

> With cries of "head her off" from those on the trail above, Jack and I, who were behind, rushed down packs and all, as Jack said, "to beat" his satanic majesty "on tan bark." We headed her off but in the tumble I tripped over a vine and went heels over head down the slope with my 50 pound pack on my back. I went over three times to the consternation of all hands before bringing up in a heap under a fortunate log. On extricating myself I found that my stock of worldly possessions had been increased to the extent of a severe sprain in the groin. [Barnes]

March 15 brought stormy weather, with heavy clouds hanging low in the gulches and canyons and occasional rain showers. The day proved to be "toilsome and laborious" for the expedition, each man packing two loads from The Forks up the steep hill to the new campsite. Together with an extra mule load, these comprised the entire remaining outfit.

The rigors of their journey were beginning to tell on the men. All were ill with dysentery—caused, they believed, by drinking from mountain streams swollen from the melting snow. In addition, Barnes was suffering from the sprain he had incurred; and because everyone was, as Sims expressed it, more or less "decomposed," the men were glad of the opportunity to rest on the following day, a Sunday.

While the others recuperated, Christie and Crumback left in the morning and reconnoitered upriver "to gain if possible some idea of the country ahead." Their camp was presently located on a bench that extended southward. Because the terrain looked promising, Christie and Crumback "struck out cheerfully enough," expecting to find a good trail. They had not gone far, however, before deep gulches and fallen trees compelled them to clamber up the mountainside. After struggling through the windfall, they found a better route five hundred feet higher, and for two miles traveled through an excellent tract of timber. Here Crumback shot a buck deer, bringing it down, according to Christie, "in a very sportsman-like manner." Upon examination the animal was found to be in a fair condition, considering the severity of the winter. The carcass was hung up for future use, and the men again headed southward. Before they left the hillside, however, Christie "succeeded in hanging two other deer on stumps along the trail."

About ten o'clock that morning the reconnaissance party reached a rocky point overlooking the river and valley. Immediately opposite them the Elwha was joined by a large tributary, which they later named Belle River; but today it is known as Long Creek. Below them a beautiful valley extended several miles upstream — "a magnificent stretch of low river flats, comparatively open." Apparently unclaimed, awaiting "some venturesome squatter," the unspoiled paradise impressed Christie.

> The course of the river could be traced far away to the southeast, whilst immediately opposite our lookout point, away to the south, arose a grand chain of peaks as far as the eye could reach, an exquisite panorama of mountain scenery to a lover of solitary natural grandeur. Enraptured with the scene before me I demanded of Crumback if he did not think it glorious, and was shocked to hear him give his opinion, low but impressive, that he considered it a "damned rough lay out." [Christie]

For several minutes they gazed upon the mountains, then sought a trail to the bottomlands and after some difficulty reached the bank of the river. Here, fortunate enough to find a place clear of snow, they made themselves comfortable and ate their lunch, having "no qualms of conscience" with respect to whether they had earned it. "A smoke was next in order."

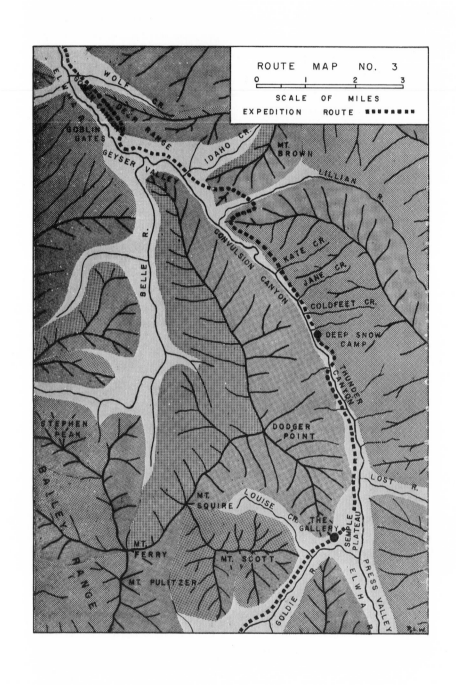

ROUTE MAP NO. 3

0   1   2   3

SCALE OF MILES

EXPEDITION ROUTE ▪▪▪▪▪▪▪▪

While they sat, quietly smoking, the snort of an elk caught their attention and acted upon their nerves "much like an electric shock." They jumped up, glanced in the direction of the Elwha, and "there in full view stood a magnificent specimen of the bull elk within a hundred and fifty yards . . . upon the bar on the opposite side of the river."

The men waited, hidden behind a stump that completely concealed them, and watched the elk's movements. Confident that it could not escape, Christie wished to afford the animal an opportunity to cross the river before he killed it.

> From his actions he had every intention of crossing as he advanced up the bar toward the head of a small ripple slowing step by step and sniffing the air as he came on; for fully 10 minutes he remained in front of us, giving us an excellent opportunity of studying his every movement. At times he seemed to make up his mind to step boldly across, whilst at others he would half turn toward the opposite bank and hesitate as if about to retrace his steps. His every motion was grace in itself. In spite of the wishes for stores of dried meat the thought would force itself upon me that it was barbarous to kill such a fine specimen of animal life. But by the time I had arrived at this conclusion a whiff of wind had carried to his sensitive nose a suspicion of danger, and one bound from two feet of water landed him on dry land, but ere he could gather himself for a second spring a 40.82 ball had pierced his lungs and furnished me with 400 pounds of good meat for pemmican. [Christie]

The report of Christie's rifle had scarcely died away when he and Crumback were "surprised to see elk after elk plunge into the river from a low point of the bank some 50 yards down stream." Christie ran down the bank a short distance, covered what he considered the fattest bull in the band of seventy-five head, and pulled the trigger. Nothing happened, and he was chagrined to find that his rifle had malfunctioned, leaving him "much in the position of a fool at a fair, gazing at the tail end of a procession of elk meat" walking away from him.

> On examining my gun I found that the point of the trigger had broken off, thus rendering the arm useless. Whispering sundry compliments to the man who forged that particular trigger, we prepared to cross the river and dress our elk and hang it up. The day by this time was well nigh spent and we made what haste we could to reach camp. [Christie]

During the return trip they killed another deer and hung it up by their trail, and on reaching camp at dark "horrified the boys when telling them of the amount of venison hung up; some 1500 pounds." They now had enough meat to make an ample supply of pemmican — about 250 pounds — which would "save the provisions of the pack."

The mountainsides east of Goblin Canyon were composed of slate and yellow and brown sandstone. A "succession of benches" on the long western slope of a high mountain led to the barren, snow-covered peak. Because the mountain slopes were "literally alive" with deer, they called the benches and mountainside Deer Range. The peak they named Mount Brown, "in honor of Mr. Amos Brown of Seattle." It is known today as Lost Cabin Mountain.

The expedition spent four days, March 17 to 20, on the lower slopes of Deer Range above Goblin Canyon and the stretch of river flats — later called Geyser Valley — which Christie and Crumback had observed on March 16. The weather remained warm, with occasional rain showers, and the melting snow was very soft. The men worked steadily, however, packing supplies up the mountainside as they moved their camp to the head of Deer Range, five miles up the Elwha. The trail followed old elk and deer paths over hills that were devoid of fallen timber, free of underbrush, and partially clear of snow.

From Deer Range they could see to the west, across the Elwha, "a magnificent range of snow-clad peaks" stretching generally from east to west and containing three notable summits. The easternmost peak, which rose abruptly from the river and lost its top "in the clouds," they named Mount Hunt, after L. S. J. Hunt, proprietor of the Seattle *Post-Intelligencer*, a competitor to the *Press*. West of Mount Hunt sprawled an "equally imposing" triple-peaked summit which they called Mount McClure, "in honor of Col. A. K. McClure of the Philadelphia Times." The striking series terminated in the west in a peak shaped like "a long thin white wedge, in a north and south direction," designated Mount Agnus, for General Felix Agnus of the Baltimore *American*.

When they had completed the packing across Deer Range, the

expedition established camp on the crest of a bluff overlooking the valley at the head of Goblin Canyon. According to the expedition's aneroid barometer, this bluff — "crowned by a kind of eagle's nest of jutting slate and shale" — towered more than eight hundred feet above the valley. Barnes had stayed alone at this site on March 4 and 6.

> On this eagle's nest we made the camp. The view was glorious. Mount Olympus, with many new crags and spurs unseen before, visible to the southward. Many new and unnamed peaks bounded the horizon all about. At our feet lay a large valley extending to the southward and eastward. [Barnes]

They had reached a significant vantage point. The men were exhausted after struggling with heavy packs over inhospitable terrain for many weeks, much of the time during adverse weather. The little valley below looked very inviting and held forth the promise that there they could rest and recuperate and also strengthen themselves for the ordeals which must still lie ahead in the depths of the mountains. They resolved to take advantage of that promise.

Chapter VII

MARCH, 1890: GEYSER VALLEY

ON THE twentieth of March the Press Exploring Expedition descended from the bluff into Geyser Valley, which Barnes estimated was "about four miles long and one mile wide in its broadest part." First, however, they slashed a trail down the steep mountainside, through logs and young fir trees, then packed the outfit over this primitive pathway to the bottomland along the Elwha. Here, in the midst of a dense growth of large trees, camp was established on the valley floor, about twenty yards from the confluence of the Elwha and Belle rivers. The latter — a large tributary — skirted the eastern base of "Olympus," which it drained, then flowed almost due north to join the Elwha. The Elwha itself extended "in a southeasterly direction, evidently draining the western watershed of the Sound range."

The expedition spent nearly two weeks in the valley. The men needed to rest, "and an opportunity to repair clothes as well as physical fiber." And they must take time "to explore the surrounding country and to discover the best route or pass through the mountains to the southward." Christie also desired to make some pemmican to add to their stock of provisions. The elk he had killed during the reconnaissance on March 16 would furnish an ample supply of meat for that purpose. The carcass still lay, undisturbed, on the other side of the river, not far from their present camp.

Dollie, the "survivor of the excellent pair of pack animals," was suffering from overwork. For a week they permitted her to rest, while "she chewed the succulent Oregon grape in peace, and her sides took on flesh."

> One virtue of the mule must be noted, they will live and grow fat upon anything that grows in these woods. Greenstuff — to wit, ferns and cedar boughs — are devoured by them with a great appetite. Grapevines, twigs, and, in short, everything that can be chewed, furnishes them with substenance [*sic*]. [Barnes]

Oregon grape and salal — which Barnes called ground laurel — covered the forest floor and provided nourishment for the herds of elk and deer that lived on the surrounding hills. For a "hard working mule," however, they were a poor substitute for oats. But since the expedition carried no oats, Dollie "had to live on faith in the 'bunch-grass country' ahead," of which the expedition "had heard so much and seen so little." When packing, they had worked the mule as lightly as they could, "never loading her with more than 150 pounds, but even this she sometimes found difficult to lift over logs."

> The little valley nestling in the mountains, an oasis in the desert of snow, won the affection of us all. So much so, in fact, that at least two of the party determined to return to it after the expedition had finished its labors, and to hold down a claim upon its fertile bottoms. Peaceful and happy, covered with mammoth trees, through whose interlacing boughs gleamed the golden sunshine lighting up the long trailing vines, the creepers and mosses of many hues, it seemed a little paradise in contrast with the snowy peaks around us. [Barnes]

The mountains, which rose steeply and enclosed the valley on every side, "were alive with game animals, tame in the happy ignorance of the gun." The river, broad and rippling as it flowed across the valley floor, "teemed with salmon, and its deeper pools were filled with trout."

Crumback decided to make the valley his home. As unsurveyed government land, it could be held only by "squatting" on the claim and waiting for a survey. Undaunted, however, he resolved to build the foundation of his cabin, and the others willingly assisted. On the afternoon of March 21 — "the opening day of

spring, 1890" — each man took his axe and proceeded to the spot
Crumback had chosen for the cabin, close by the river, in the
midst of a heavy growth of timber. Four trees, each a foot in diameter, were selected and soon lay upon the ground. Fifteen
minutes after the men commenced chopping, four logs had been
cut the proper length, "saddles" incised in their ends, and the
foundation of Crumback's log cabin — which measured twenty-five
by thirty feet — was in place.

> This was the first cabin in the Olympic mountains. A big blaze on a
> neighboring fir was made to bear the following notice to all comers: "John
> Crumback, his claim." An "expedition blaze" upon the opposite side of the
> tree was carved to give notice to all would-be claim jumpers and the world
> in general that behind "John Crumback, his claim" ready to make good the
> same, were five men, four dogs and a mule, armed with five guns, four rows
> of teeth and a pair of heels — let him on "jumping" bent beware! These
> formalities concluded, feeling that we had just had a hand in an event
> which might some day become historic in the annals of the Olympic moun-
> tains, we returned to camp to celebrate the occasion. Crumback was host,
> for we were now his guests, and on his claim. It was a royal banquet, and
> Crumback earned a lasting reputation for his hospitality.
>
> Elk tail broth, fresh trout and roast venison comprised the menu as
> served. But some of the boys, not satisfied with these delicacies, said
> that, although it was not Sunday, we ought to have an extra allowance of
> bread, because the occasion was important enough to justify the indul-
> gence and we needed something unusual to remember it by, and besides,
> they asked, what was a celebration without dessert, anyway? These reasons
> were deemed cogent, and we had bread with our coffee on this happy and
> memorable occasion. [Barnes]

Because they were now "living like princes and kings," they
could make the event a festive one indeed. This easy life was in
sharp contrast to their mode of existence during the preceding
winter months while they struggled over mountain spurs and
through canyons along the lower Elwha. Then the "formula for
meal calls" — as Barnes expressed it — did not include elk tail
broth or fresh trout: "Gentlemen, dinner is ready: pork and beans
are on the table, venison on the hills and quail on the fence." Now,
however, they enjoyed an abundance of game of all kinds — elk,
deer, grouse, quail, salmon, and trout.

No bears had been seen as yet, although on frequent occasions the explorers had noted evidence of their presence in Geyser Valley, where they apparently fed upon kinnikinnick berries. The men concluded that most of the bears were still in hibernation, "owing probably to the severity of the winter."

> The mountains were a game preserve. There was really no sport in shooting; the deer stood and gazed at the unaccustomed sight of man, until one could hit them with a stone. It was no unusual thing to see a band . . . comprising 30 or 40 deer grazing on the hillside within sight of camp. Hayes went out one day hunting and returned an hour afterwards having killed five. . . . They stood and gazed in wonder, and he could have killed half of the band but for the rules strictly enforced in camp of killing no more than we actually needed. Mr. Christie returned to camp one day during the absence of all hands and killed a doe as it stood with its head inside the opening of the tent, probably wondering what kind of a cave it had found. One started them up singly or in pairs, from behind every knoll, like jack rabbits on a desert. [Barnes]

Because game was plentiful, they now lived largely upon fresh meat, and they devoured large quantities. "It seems almost incredible and we could hardly believe it ourselves," Barnes states in his journal, "when we calculated up the amount of venison consumed for six days ending on Saturday night." In less than a week they had eaten four deer, one of them an unusually large buck! In addition, they had partaken of all the salmon they desired, plus "a certain quantity of the provisions of the pack." Their dogs —who had been on slender rations for months—quarreled over "the bones, fish heads and other refuse."

A "most delicious salmon trout" could now be taken in abundance from the Elwha. In less than thirty minutes one day, Christie caught fourteen in a pool adjacent to their camp. The catch weighed forty-two pounds, and the fish measured from twenty-two to twenty-six inches in length. These fish were apparently among the first of the season to ascend the Elwha, for the men had fished the river before but caught nothing.[1] During the stay in the valley, however, they had all the fish they wanted.

[1] The precise date when the first fish were caught cannot be determined. Obviously it was some time in the latter part of March, shortly after their arrival in Geyser Valley. According to Christie's diary, on March 26 he caught the fourteen "salmon trout," his first on the Elwha. Barnes also men-

In order to have some fish when we should next move camp, which would take us away from the river, we partially smoked a quantity, splitting them down the back, and stringing them on poles behind the fire where they would dry and get an occasional whiff of smoke. About two days of this treatment made them ready to stow away for future use, and lightened them of considerable weight for packing. Toothsome as the fresh fish were, we were unanimous in preferring these half smoked fish to the fresh, and after the first trial hung up all we caught, if there was time, for a little touch of smoke before cooking.

Venison is also improved by being hung where the smoke can get at it now and then. It becomes dryer and more tender and takes on a new flavor, and when put into a pan with a bit of good bacon over a hot camp fire, it becomes a tid bit for an epicure. [Barnes]

From the base camp located in Geyser Valley, the men explored the adjacent region with some interesting results. On Sunday, March 22, Captain Barnes crossed the river to make a preliminary reconnaissance of Belle River Canyon, while Christie and Sims went up the Elwha to find a trail through the burnt timber, or brûlée, that Christie had discerned in the distance the preceding day. Hayes and Crumback remained in camp to dry elk meat, preparatory to making pemmican.

Using butcher knives, they cut the flesh from the bone, then sliced the meat into long, thin strips and placed these on a rack suspended over a fire. In two to three days sun, air, and fire combined to dry the meat thoroughly. They then pounded the meat into a "kind of coarse meal," placed it in a sack, and poured liquid grease over the contents, "thus forming a compact mass." Bear grease was the proper fat to use, but since they had none, they obtained "a moderate amount" of fat from the elk, to which they added some bacon grease. The pemmican was then salted to taste and allowed to harden. The elk yielded about one hundred pounds — a generous quantity, since one pound of pemmican requires several pounds of fresh meat, most of the weight loss resulting from evaporation.

---

tions this particular catch as being the first fish taken by the party, but he also states that "fresh trout" were served at Crumback's dinner on March 21. Barnes further confuses things by twice mentioning the expedition being in Press Valley at this point in his narrative, when he must have meant Geyser Valley.

When one of the men left camp for a day or two, he would carry a chunk of the pemmican. It could be eaten raw in its smoked condition or cooked in various ways. According to Christie, "the Indians of the plains oft times introduce sundry condiments that are not always considered an improvement by the white man, but that is according to taste."

While the boys in camp prepared pemmican, Christie and Sims, trekking upriver, first crossed the Elwha and found themselves in a large river bottom. Christie noted that the timber in the valley was large, and he was particularly impressed when he saw that the upper end was "covered by a wonderful growth of bird's eye maple."[2] Upon reaching the head of the valley, they found the river "emerging from another great dark canyon."[3] Looking up the gorge they could see splendid cascades, "the river pouring over the ledges with a roar almost deafening." It began to rain heavily, and within a few minutes both men were "saturated to the skin." For two hours they cowered under a sheltering rock, then headed down the valley for camp, "a much more comfortable place."

Two days later, on the twenty-fourth of March, Christie, Barnes, and Hayes "left camp to explore a trail up the pass," carrying with them two days' provisions, a gun, two axes, blankets, and a camera. They followed the west bank of the river for a mile, then clambered above where the Elwha swept against the steep mountainside. Their course returned to the bottomlands, through "tangled thickets and fern" so dense that in places they had to cut a way. Here they came upon a large tract of old brûlée. The burn had occurred so long before that young trees had grown into an almost impenetrable thicket around the logs that lay strewn upon the ground in every direction. They could find no way to avoid the brûlée, so they crawled through — deciding, in the process, that "it would be necessary to cut a number of the logs to let the expedition mule through and to make a good trail." Beyond the

[2] This was undoubtedly big-leaf maple, a large deciduous tree that grows on river bottoms throughout the Olympics.

[3] Later called by them Convulsion Canyon, it is known today as the Grand Canyon of the Elwha. See photograph, p. 104.

burned area they came upon "a magnificent grove of curly maple,[4] each tree of which was worth hundreds of dollars."

Here, as elsewhere in the valley, the ground was "covered with a rich carpet of moss inches thick," reflecting bright shades of green in the sunshine. "The warmth of spring was calling out the buds, and tender leaves were bursting on every tree." They concluded that a lovelier valley could not possibly exist elsewhere in the mountains. Immediately beyond the maple grove, the valley was divided into two nearly equal parts by a bluff. As the men neared this bluff they struck a fresh elk trail leading steeply upward for three hundred feet to the crest of a ridge or spur stretching from the mountainside to the river. Beyond, they could see that their path was crossed by a succession of similar ridges extending from the mountain on their left to the river on their right. The river was lost in the depths of a deep gorge from which issued the "sounds of roaring waters."

As they continued to follow the elk trail, they found that the entire upland had been burned at some former time and was covered with a dense growth of young timber, like the patch of brûlée they had crossed earlier in the day. The trail passed over and under logs — "for the beggars have long legs and can jump the side of a house" —and held continuously through the dense growth of young fir. In many instances they made cuts to allow passage. By noon they had penetrated only a mile and a half of this, and the men stopped, made coffee, and filled their pipes before proceeding.

A few hundred yards further the reconnaissance party made the expedition's "first discovery of the former presence of man." The explorers came upon a tree which they concluded had been "double-blazed, after the Indian fashion." Declaring that Robinson Crusoe could not have been more surprised upon discovering footprints in the sand, they pronounced this "the first evidence of the old Indian tribes now gone to the happy hunting grounds, who once hunted and lived in the fastnesses of these mountains, and whose memory is now a legend." The tree was twenty inches in diameter and "bore two trail blazes, made when the tree was a

[4] This, too, was undoubtedly big-leaf maple.

sapling." The bark over the subsequent growth of the tree almost met across the blaze-faces.[5] Christie expressed the opinion that the purported blaze — considering its shape — "could have been done only with one of the old Hudson Bay hatchets, which were shaped after the fashion of the Indian tomahawke, such, for instance, as the general reader will remember in the pages of Feneimore [sic] Cooper."

> By cutting the tree down and examining the rings and the blazes in cross sections it would be easy to arrive at the exact age of the blaze, but we were reluctant to destroy this ancient relic of a pre-historic race and besides, since we had found one, it was probable that we would fall in with others in the future, upon which we could carry our researches. [Barnes]

They had gone but half a mile beyond the "blazed" tree when they came upon more evidence of "ancient Indian life."

> Upon a little knoll a few feet to our left, as we followed the old elk trail, overhung by firs of enormous growth and wide spreading foliage, stood a post about six feet in height and 12 inches in diameter at the base. The base was about two feet high and covered with the decayed remains of what was once bark. The upper part of the post had been hewed down to a diameter of seven inches. This was at once identified as an Indian wringing post for dressing skins. The post bore signs of great antiquity. Although standing in a dry and sheltered place it was extremely rotten — so rotten that a hard blow with the back of an axe would have shattered it, and a hunting knife could be driven into it to the hilt. [Barnes]

Further investigation of the "wringing post" was deferred until they should pass that way while moving camp, for now they had "work of another kind on hand and hoped to make a number of miles before nightfall." They decided, however, to photograph the post in place and then remove and cache it nearby, to be recovered later "for the benefit of antiquarians." The immediate surroundings, they believed, would repay careful investigation and probably yield interesting results. "Here the Indians, who are now gathered to their fathers, were accustomed to resort, for the pur-

[5] On the basis of annual rings counted in a chip chopped from a similar tree, they concluded that the blaze was more than two hundred years old.

pose of dressing the skins taken in the chase, and the little knoll and its surroundings had furnished them with a camping place."

In December, while visiting Indians living at the mouth of the Elwha, the party had been unable to gain any information regarding the interior of the mountains.

> Their fathers hunted the same foothills, and so far as we could learn, handed down no traditions, which would indicate more extended travel by their immediate ancestors; or any better knowledge of the country by them than is possessed by their living descendants. The only traditions, so far as our present information goes, relates to long ages ago, similar in character to those related by ex-Governor Semple. [Barnes]

The men concluded, therefore, that they were justified in believing they were now "threading passes and gorges long accustomed to the presence of man."

For two miles their route continued across rough country covered with dense stands of second-growth firs. These higher slopes, constituting the rim of Geyser Valley, were "literally alive with deer." Because the men made considerable noise with their axes in chopping out the trail, they did not see the animals, who remained hidden in the underbrush. However, their tracks — continuously visible in the snow and mud — were silent evidence of their presence. Apparently this end of the valley was a hunting ground comparable in quality to Deer Range.

About three o'clock in the afternoon the party reached "an elevated point overlooking the river." The Elwha, surging swiftly through a deep canyon, made a "slight bend to the southward" and received the waters of a large tributary flowing from the east through a similar canyon. To this stream they gave the name Lillian River.[6] The "triple canyon" at the confluence of the two streams was about five hundred feet deep, its sides almost perpendicular.

> We followed the friendly elk trail some distance up the Lillian river and then down, fording its cold waters to the knee, and then with much labor

[6] Neither of the diaries mentions relatives of expedition members (other than the one reference to the illness of Dr. Runnalls' wife). When they gave feminine names to natural features, they never indicated whether the name was given to honor a specific person or merely used in a general sense.

and shortness of breath, clambered up the opposite side to an altitude of eight hundred feet. "Poor Dollie" we thought "how she will suffer." It was evident that over this canyon we would have to pack everything on our backs. Dollie would get over, if at all, as the elk do, light. [Barnes]

Once across the Lillian, however, they found "an excellent trail skirting the mountain . . . three or four feet wide, cut deep into the steep slope of the mountain side." Apparently the elk had used this path for centuries. The trail was now free of snow, and fresh elk tracks indicated that a large band — perhaps fifty or sixty animals — had recently passed by. The mountainside the route now traversed was "timbered with a comparatively small growth of mountain fir," the first of this species they had seen. Beneath the trees the forest floor was thinly covered by undergrowth, primarily Oregon grape.

One little discovery we made here, which we knew would gladden the hearts of the boys in camp. We had brought with us 48 pounds of tobacco. The unexpected delays which we had met incident to the extraordinary winter, and the difficulties apparent ahead, were beginning to create an apprehension in camp that our tobacco would not hold out. This worried the boys not a little. On this sidehill we found, growing, beds of kinnikinnick, in some places covering the ground as a trailing vine for many square yards. The leaves of this plant, when dried, furnish an excellent substitute for tobacco. When smoked it has a peculiar flavor not at all unpleasant. [Barnes]

After two miles of good traveling along the old elk trail, the party halted at sunset and camped on a little bench two hundred feet down the mountainside, where dry wood was abundant. Making themselves comfortable, the men prepared their supper, then rolled up in their blankets and were soon asleep, "with the starry heavens for a tent." [7]

As dawn appeared we were stirring, and from our perch on the mountain side there spread out before us a view which would gladden the heart of the most hardened explorer. The shelf overhung the river, which roared

[7] They were camped on the slopes of Mount Fitten, which they named "in honor of Mr. DuBose Fitten of Seattle." The name does not appear on present-day maps, but the peak they intended to be so designated was probably the high point on the ridge northwest of Windfall Peak.

800 feet below, and which appeared foamy white and light green with here and there the deep green so characteristic of these mountain streams. The canyon ran for miles up the river. Above the canyon the gap appeared to broaden into a beautiful valley with sloaping [sic] sides clothed in the dark green of the conifer forests, terminating in the distance, perhaps 20 miles away, in a huge solitary mountain [afterwards named Mt. Dana] swathed in snow from base to summit, standing in the pale light of early morn like a great white spectre, with outspread arms guarding the hidden and unknown region beyond. As the light increased we could gradually distinguish vague and shadowy outlines of other peaks, a cloud of spectres, hovering a ghostly throng behind the mighty chief. Suddenly as we gazed a ray of the rising sun swept the summit. In a moment the spectres of the night vanished and in their stead stood mighty peaks, gilded with the rosy hues of morn seeming to welcome instead of repel. [Barnes]

Soon the aroma of coffee brewing and venison steaks broiling added their cheering influence to their now buoyant spirits, and the men were "as eager to be off as school boys for a vacation."

Again they followed the elk trail southward as it wound around the mountainside high above the rushing Elwha. For several miles the river flowed through a canyon from seven hundred to a thousand feet in depth, "with walls of solid rock inclined at an angle of eighty degrees." In about an hour the party arrived at a great landslide which extended from the trail where they stood to the river below, a vertical height of eight hundred feet. The slide was about four hundred feet wide and slanted at approximately a forty-five-degree angle. Little or no debris had accumulated at its base, "the slide having occurred gradually by the slipping down of material as it became loosened by natural causes." The river, where it passed the slide, made "a double bend, in form like a very flat letter 'U,' the bottom of the letter being towards the slide." On the opposite side of the canyon wall was "a great flat rock, 800 feet high and 500 or 600 feet wide, standing on and leaning against the mountain side." The top of the rock was detached from the mountain by a chasm fifty feet deep, so that the rock seemed to have "been lifted from the slide cavity and tilted bodily across the canyon against the mountain opposite, the stream then changing its course and running around the rock."

The wild and rugged appearance of the slide and the peculiar character of the wall of rock on the opposite side of the canyon brought to our mind at once the legend related by Governor Semple, of the convulsion of nature or catastrophe which had overwhelmed the Indians while attending the last powwow in the mountains, in which the "Spirit of the Mountains" shook the earth, opened great chasms and swallowed up the returning bands. [Barnes]

Barnes went on to explain that "to one unacquainted with the record of the rocks as they tell their own history regardless of legends or traditions," this formation did, indeed, seem to confirm the Indian story. A moment's examination, however, revealed "the groundlessness of the convulsion theory."

Aside from the fact that the rock would in that case have to be lifted upward to gain its present position, the stratification of the rock conforms to that of the mountain side behind it, while it does not conform with the side upon which the slide occurs. The same peculiar conformation of rock is repeated in two other places in this canyon without any corresponding cavity opposite it. Nevertheless out of respect to the old tradition we named this "Convulsion Canyon." [Barnes]

For half an hour they gazed into "the great gulf below," and amused themselves by rolling a few boulders down the face of the mountain. These would go bounding down, "detaching a hundred others on the way and rock and gravel would continue to clatter down for several minutes," the larger stones being shattered into fragments at the bottom. "It was great sport for the boys," Barnes commented, "but we could not remain for much of it."

They had by this time "recognized" their pathway as "an ancient Indian trail, which the elk continued to follow after it had been deserted by the Indians." At frequent intervals they saw old blazes, which they asserted were correctly made "and not to be confounded with the scars on the trees made by the horns of the elk as they brushed the bark." All the blazes appeared to be ancient. When the men stopped and made coffee, they cut into one of the blazed trees — a fir nearly three feet in diameter — and counted 210 rings of annual growth, "indicating a probable age of over 200 years for the blaze." Furthermore, Barnes declared,

Elwha River near the lower end of
Geyser Valley (Photo by
Robert L. Wood)

Elwha River emerging from Convulsion Canyon at the head of Geyser Valley
(Courtesy National Park Service)

"the blaze had grown with the tree, and was now about 10 feet long." [8]

A few hundred yards further, in a little glade by the side of a brook, they came upon another "wringing post." Like the first one discovered, it was very old and rotten, "and had similarly been a standing tree dubbed down to the proper size." Their trail was thus becoming more and more interesting.

> We had found a trail blazed by the old Indian and still kept fresh by his successor, the elk. Logs lay across it in every direction, but it was still well defined and could easily be made passable. Moreover, we were cheered by finding ourselves on a road. Roads lead somewhere, and this one possibly led into some beautiful valley with lakes, or perhaps a pass through the mountains. But our little party of three was now out of provisions and we had to turn back to camp. Eight hours at a rapid gait back over the trail which we had partially cleared, brought us in shortly after dark, and over our coffee and pipes we cheered the boys with the news of a good trail ahead. [Barnes]

The expedition's base camp was still located in Geyser Valley. On March 26, Hayes, Sims, and Crumback — working in the upper end of the valley — cut a trail across brûlée in order that the mule could get through when packing supplies upriver. Christie, resting from the long jaunt the preceding day, spent a half hour fishing in a pool above camp. He gently dropped a lure "beneath the

[8] This last statement raises considerable doubt as to whether the marks were, in fact, bona fide blazes, and arouses the suspicion that the men were drawing erroneous conclusions. A scar made on the trunk of a tree by an axe does not, of course, grow larger as the tree grows. The Press Party's "Indian blazes" may have been scars cut on tree trunks by neighboring trees falling during winter storms, a not unusual occurrence in the Olympics. One should note that Barnes states the "blazes" were not to be confused with marks made by elk antlers. Also, the explorers could have mistaken a rotting tree trunk — the remnant of a tree whose top had been broken off in some long past windstorm — for the Indians' "wringing post."

Perhaps in their enthusiasm to discover traces of ancient human activity in the mountains, the judgment of the expedition members was impaired and they mistook natural phenomena as evidence of the handiwork of man. One should be cautious, however, in assigning error to their conclusions. Some of the things they discovered may have been genuine artifacts. It is improbable that they could have mistaken natural phenomena for so many things which would have had to be formed by the hand of man — the trail, wringing post, blazes, and, later, the "village" on Semple Plateau.

shadow on the rock opposite," and within moments after his first cast had struck a fish, his first salmon trout on the Elwha.[9] He landed it "after five minutes of careful angling, the fish fighting to the end." "Then followed one-half hour of as fine fishing as any I ever enjoyed on the thousand streams I have had the pleasure of fishing in, carrying to camp fourteen splendid trout; weight about forty pounds; no mean basket from any water."

For a few days everyone kept busy, making general repairs, caching unnecessary articles, going on excursions to neighboring slopes to take bearings, and hunting for elk and deer. They often fished the Elwha in the evening hours, for the river was "fairly teeming with fish."

Geyser Valley lay but a few miles beyond the fringe of foothills explored by settlers along the lower Elwha; therefore, the Press Exploring Expedition had not yet penetrated the mountains to any great depth. Now, with the end of March approaching, the expedition had been under way nearly four months, and the men were obliged to move faster and to locate a route across the mountains. Therefore, Barnes intended to explore Belle River, the large stream that swept around the base of the peak thought to be Olympus and had its source "in a majestic range of mountains to the southward."

> Viewed from the mountain side north of our camp, the course of the stream presented the appearance of a deep canyon with steep sides, formed by the easterly spurs of Olympus on the one hand and by the slopes of a lower range on the other. In the distance could be seen through the gap two remarkable peaks, visible from base to summit, glittering white in the sun. Yet there was no certainty that the stream ended there. There was an appearance as of a pass making to the westward between Olympus and the range containing the peaks observed, through which we might reach the watershed of the Quiniault. To settle the doubt I determined on the trip. Besides this reason it was reported that Olympus cradled a glacier on its eastern sides. We had examined every stream draining its northern slopes without finding in their waters any evidence of its existence. By this stream, then if by any, the glacier must drain, and I wished to examine it. [Barnes]

On Saturday, March 29, Barnes crossed the Elwha to commence his Belle River exploration, carrying his blanket, an axe, and pro-

[9] See footnote 1 of this chapter.

visions for four days. An hour earlier the men had heard strange, elusive sounds, which they had taken to be landslides or avalanches on neighboring mountain slopes. As Barnes started up Belle River, he heard the whirring sounds far more distinctly. Puzzled and uncertain as to their origin, he returned immediately to camp and told the others; he again crossed the river, this time accompanied by Christie.

The two stood and listened intently to the "low, rumbling noises" for several minutes, then the suggestion was made that they "might be from a geyser." The men carefully clocked the intervals between the reports and found them to have a duration of about four minutes. At ten o'clock, when Barnes made his final departure for Belle River, the sounds persisted, and he continued to hear them until he entered the Belle River Canyon half an hour later.

The canyon was "wild and rocky" at its lower end; to his left, as he looked up from the entrance, Barnes could see a towering rock overhanging the stream, which looked as if it were "about to roll out of its place." The rock bore, he thought, "a remarkable resemblance to the head of an enormous buffalo," and the hillside behind it swept upward in a manner that resembled the animal's shoulders, thus strengthening the illusion. Belle River was fairly large and, at this point, "most romantic in its scenery." Delicate streams cascaded down into it from heights of one hundred to two hundred feet, "sparkling and bright, against the deep green of the mosses and ferns." He concluded that the entrance to the canyon — being close to the Elwha and easily reached — was "well worth the turning aside for half an hour to see."

Once within the canyon, he followed deer trails up its eastern side to heights of seven hundred or eight hundred feet. He marked his route by cutting the Press Party blaze on trees along the way, always careful to chop the lower of the three cuts on a level with the surface of the snow. "Future explorers will be able to note the depth of the snow and understand, as well," he explained, "how the blazes came to be so far up the trees when I had no ladder. In some places the lower one will be found ten or twelve feet high. I made a practice of thus blazing the trees on the entire trip."

All day he scrambled along the mountainside — "many times holding on for dear life to keep from slipping" — and late in the afternoon arrived at a large mountain creek "which came down between the two great eastern spurs of Olympus." The stream was crystal clear and, as far as Barnes's examination disclosed, showed no evidence of glacial origin. Apparently he did not know that glacial streams in the Olympic Mountains show few, if any, indications of their origin in the spring. At that time of the year the stream flow comes primarily from rainfall and snow melt, the ice itself being deeply buried beneath the winter's snow pack.

For about three hundred yards he ascended the stream bed, which was buried in logs and snow. He then crossed over and again climbed through snow until he reached a great landslide, down the face of which fragments of rock and gravel fell constantly, detached by frost. "I had to descend nearly to the bottom to cross," he wrote, "and when I did . . . it was quickly, and with my heart in my mouth, for the falling rock made it ticklish business across a space of about two hundred feet."

The sun had set by this time, and Barnes hastened up the mountainside again. He found a little space clear of snow, camped for the night, and dried his clothing "as well as circumstances permitted."

During the day he had seen two deer, plus a great many tracks, including those of a bear. He also noted that the formation of the canyon and mountainsides was chiefly slate and sandstone, "twisted and contorted to an astonishing degree, with here and there deposits of gravel and clay."

The next morning he was up and away before the sun rose. He traveled along the west side of the canyon, sometimes high above the stream, sometimes ascending to avoid heavy snow or jutting walls of rock. Because this side of the canyon was broken by gullies and small streams, he crossed Belle River, hopeful of finding easier terrain on the eastern side. However, the canyon became increasingly precipitous.

Toward evening I found myself painfully struggling around the face of the mountain side at the head of the canyon overlooking a little basin encircled by Olympus and the peaks of the Bailey range.[10] I was so fatigued with travel through the heavy snow that when at last I found a spot from which the wind had blown the snow I could scarcely stand. I sketched the main features of the scene before me, took several observations for my chart and then made camp for the night.

There was no pass here to the southward or westward. Across the little basin, which formed a head of the watershed of the stream up which I had been traveling, rose a solid wall of rock 5000 feet high,[11] with great precipices here and there of a thousand feet. The peaks formed at their base a little amphitheatre, crescent-shaped, with one end touching Olympus and the other sweeping around the mountain, from the side of which I viewed it. From its seemingly narrow wall towered the pinnacle, and more conspicuous still was a thin wall-like peak, shaped like a great eagle's beak, clear out [cut?] against the dark blue sky. [Barnes]

They had first seen this remarkable mountain from Deer Range and called it Mount Squire, "after Senator Watson C. Squire of the state of Washington." However, it is known today as Ludden Peak, perpetuating the name of a Geyser Valley pioneer.

On the third day of his exploration of the canyon, Barnes again rose very early, hoping to cross the snow-covered terrain before the crust was softened by the afternoon sun. By the time it became light enough to see, he had eaten his breakfast and was on the "downhill road homeward." He had gone but fifty yards, however, retracing his trail of the evening before, when he came upon the tracks of what was apparently a very large mountain lion. The footprints — which measured six inches across — indicated that the cougar had been following his trail, but had at the last moment circled around to avoid his campsite and then gone up the mountainside. The tracks had obviously been made

[10] This is the first mention in Barnes's narrative of the Bailey Range. Actually, the name was given to the range at a later date by the expedition.
[11] Barnes had entered a cul de sac on the eastern flanks of the Bailey Range, where its narrow spine widens perceptibly into a complex of cliffs and rugged mountain spurs. His statement about a "wall of rock 5000 feet high" is understandable, if somewhat exaggerated — assuming that this was his mistake and not a printer's error in the published account of the expedition.

shortly after Barnes passed that way, for they had been clearly imprinted before the frost of night had hardened the snow.

"Here was a surprise, and I challenge any man to find in the morning that a great cat probably five or six feet long had been prowling around him during the night, without twinges of conscience." His mind went back to his fire of the night before, surely his protection, but only by accident. When he carried blankets, Barnes usually neglected to build a fire, and he had not done so on his first night out on the Belle River exploration.[12]

> Rolled up snugly, and comparatively comfortable in them, I had permitted the fire to burn down and, finally, to go out, but last night I was too tired to make a respectable fire. I had simply pulled from the hill side, immediately above the bare spot selected, six or eight small cedar trunks, laid them parallel and made the fire at the lower end. Thus, quite by accident, the fire had an excellent opportunity to burn gradually up hill. This it did, and in the morning it was still smouldering. It was to this, I had no doubt, I owed my life. There is considerable question whether a cougar will attack a man unless driven to it by hunger, but fancy a great cat with such an opportunity as a sleeping man in the woods. As I studied that cougar track I had precious little doubt as to where I would have been that morning but for being close to a good fire. I was without my gun for I was traveling against time, as light as possible, but of course even a gun is no use with a cougar clutching one's throat.

While retracing his steps back toward the Elwha, Barnes discovered that the mountain lion had first struck his trail where he crossed Belle River the previous afternoon and had followed him from that point.

When he reached the place where the mysterious rumbles had been heard most distinctly on the preceding Saturday, Barnes again heard the sounds. He listened from eleven o'clock in the morning until noon, "noting the characteristics, apparent direction, etc., hoping thereby to obtain some clue to its whereabouts." Because they might possibly find another "geyser" later, he wanted to identify the particular one in question.

He therefore carefully observed that the wind was light and

[12] It is improbable that the cougar would have attacked Barnes. Mountain lions often follow the lone traveler without attacking, apparently motivated by curiosity.

variable, the clouds overhead drifting slowly west-southwest, the weather generally clear. He also painstakingly timed the interval between the reports, which varied from three and a half to slightly more than six minutes, but was most generally from four to four and a half minutes. "The sounds lasted exactly eight seconds, beginning slowly like the clicking of a ratchet on a cog-wheel, gradually increasing in rapidity, and at the end becoming too rapid for the ear to distinguish, and ceasing abruptly at the end of a few seconds."

The muffled rumbles seemed to be coming from the southeast — the direction of the head of the valley — but he thought the high surrounding mountains "rendered the real direction of the sound extremely uncertain." After listening to them fourteen times, he left at noon, intending to return later to "observe the phenomenon until it should cease." As he departed, the rumbles faded to a murmur, gradually becoming fainter until they ceased altogether. "It was evident," he concluded, "that the sounds were reflected to the spot where they were most distinctly heard from a considerable distance."

Barnes crossed the river and found that during his absence the camp had been moved to a new location further up the valley. He ate lunch at the old campsite, however, then returned to the "listening post" at 2:00 p.m., "but the sounds had ceased." Barnes again left, and arrived about three o'clock in the afternoon at the new campsite, "glad to be once more in more lively society."

Barnes noted that the "geyser" had been in action on March 29 from 8:00 to 10:30 a.m., and again on April 1 from 11:00 a.m. to 12:15 p.m., with an interval of about three days between. Whether it had been active within that three-day period he did not know, nor did he know how long it continued in action, if more than two and a half hours.

The "geyser" was not heard from the new camp, nor did they hear it while packing supplies from downriver, although they frequently passed the point where the phenomenon had been most clearly audible. On the third day, however, Crumback heard the sound again.

> The geyser has therefore an interval between its times of activity of about three days. Acting upon the knowledge thus gained, we were particularly on the alert thereafter on every third day. At length, on April 13, we again heard the geyser, between the hours of 4 and 5:30 in the morning. We were then in camp opposite a large island on the Elwha four miles below Lillian river. On April 4, 7 and 10, it is probable that we would have heard it if our position had been more favorable. [Barnes]

They did not hear the sounds again. Because of the necessity for traveling constantly, relaying supplies upstream from downriver points, they were unable "to make any explorations for the geyser and were compelled to leave it for future explorers." They suspected, however, that it was located "in the canyon below the mouth of the Lillian river." [13]

They did name the valley after the unseen geyser whose location they could never pinpoint. Unlike many of the names the expedition gave to natural features of the Olympic Mountains, this one endured, and the place is still known as Geyser Valley.[14] Since 1890 other "explorers" have wondered what the men actually heard, for no geyser, or anything else that would explain the phenomenon, has ever been discovered. The general belief now is that the men were deceived by the elusive drumming of the ruffed grouse.

The men gradually moved the expedition's camp from the lower end of the valley toward its head, then up a bluff to a new campsite on the rolling uplands.

> Here much cutting of logs and clearing of brush was necessary to make packing at all feasible. The growth of small fir which covered the ground held in its protecting shade a great quantity of snow. In some places the snow was three feet deep, and extremely soft. We had showers nearly every night, so that while working, and afterwards while packing, through this portion of our route we suffered great discomforts. These small trees held the water; upon every needle point trembled a tiny drop, and a touch would precipitate a quart of water upon us. Thus constantly drenched to the skin, and in snow which held water like a sponge, it was like a continual bath. [Barnes]

[13] Between the confluence of the north and east forks of the Quinault and the lake, near their journey's end, the men again heard the sounds of a "geyser."

[14] On some maps it appears as Geyser Basin.

Preparatory to moving their camp out of Geyser Valley, the men spent the last day of March cutting a trail through brûlée to the Lillian River. Still "suffering a good deal from dysentery," they were reluctant to leave the peaceful "oasis" encircled by the snowy peaks. But they could not linger. The *Press* had stated that the expedition was to explore the country thoroughly and not rush through the mountains; and rushing through they were not. The party had been provisioned for six months, and two thirds of that time was now gone, although they were just beginning to pierce the depths of the mountains. If they were to succeed in crossing the Olympics, they must still travel four times as far as they had come. Ahead were the highest, most rugged mountains, where further adventures and hardships awaited them; where they must find a route to the Quinault. The Olympic Mountains were only beginning to test their mettle, their "abundance of grit and manly vim."

Chapter VIII

APRIL, 1890: UPPER ELWHA

In a time period spanning almost four months, the Press Exploring Expedition had slowly progressed southward toward the interior of the Olympic Peninsula, carving in the process a crude trail through the mountains. During this four months — in which the men had done trail work, constructed the *Gertie*, pulled her up the Elwha, and finally resorted to backpacking — the expedition actually had not traveled very far. As a raven would have flown, the men were now approximately twelve miles south of Canyon Camp, where their journey up the river began. Because they had no trails and the terrain was inhospitable (especially so in the winter months), it must have seemed to them a much greater distance. For the mountain miles were long, backpacking was arduous, and carrying heavy packs from downriver to upriver points, repeating the process over and over until the entire outfit had been moved to a new location, must have been a seemingly endless struggle. Then, too, they faced the constant problem of route finding and collateral exploration of the surrounding terrain.

When he returned on April 1 from his trip up the canyon of Belle River, Captain Barnes reported that there was no way across the mountains in that direction, and that the expedition must seek elsewhere for a pass. However, Christie, Barnes, and Hayes, scouting on March 25, had observed above the confluence of the Lillian and the Elwha, apparently at a considerable distance, a valley far larger than Geyser Valley, "and from which four passes or gaps appeared to radiate like the spokes of a wagon wheel." This val-

114

ley — which they later named after their sponsoring newspaper — was most likely the key to the mountains. Because it would probably make an excellent base camp and center for exploration, the valley now became the expedition's immediate objective. Christie decided to cache their provisions temporarily at the Lillian, then proceed at once up the Elwha Canyon, "to reach the valley ahead and gain more knowledge of the country before moving up the supplies." They would travel light, for if elk and deer were as plentiful above the Lillian as they had been below, there should be no difficulty in living off the land.

Of the stores with which we started we now had remaining 250 pounds of flour, 60 pounds of beans, 30 pounds of bacon, 20 pounds of tea, 15 pounds of salt, 5 pounds of prunes, 7 pounds of tobacco, 20 pounds of sundries, with 50 pounds of pemmican, a total of provisions of over 400 pounds.

Besides the provisions we had remaining four Winchester rifles, 40–65, one shotgun, plenty of ammunition, fishing tackle and re-loading tools.

One tent, 12 x 14, two large canvas sheets.

Kitchen outfit, comprising a nest of sheet iron camp kettles, one large and two small frying pans, tin plates, etc.

Tools: Several light carpenter's tools, two 6-pound axes, five 3-pound axes, one shovel, one spade, one pickaxe, one goldpan and a rock hammer.

A 4 x 5 inch dry plate camera, with films for 250 exposures, instruments for topographical work, a field glass, an aneroid barometer, etc.

A few medicines.

Each individual was provided with a good, comfortable pair of blankets, cartridge belt, sheath knife, etc.

The weight of this outfit was about 800 pounds. [Barnes]

Although their provisions had been greatly reduced by the winter's consumption, if they were economical, the supplies would last for a considerable period of time.

Our supply of ammunition would provide us with meat as long as we chose to stay or the meat consented to be killed. The sugar had been gone some time. We used the last of the coffee in Geyser valley, but we still had tea. We started with 50 pounds of salt, now reduced to 15, more by shrinkage than by use. Lest any evil minded person should imagine that "sundries" in the above list means *wet goods* it may be just as well to state that it does not. We had some excellent whiskey in the medicine chest on starting, but during the first two or three weeks so much palative [*sic*] was required for cramps in the stomach, nausea, sore thumbs, etc., that it was all consumed. Fortunately all recovered from these diseases and the camp has since had no necessity for the remedy.

Baking powder was out, so that we relied upon raised bread, and carried with us from one camp to another a small lump of sour dough. We made bread whenever the opportunity presented, baking a large quantity at once. It was difficult at times to raise the bread as well as could be desired, out of doors, with cold weather and other unfavorable conditions, but once raised, our loaves, baked before the fire, made bread that was not to be despised. At other times, when unable to spend the time required for raising bread, we made thin cakes of flour and water, unleavened, and baked them in frying pans. These are familiarly known as "gillettes." [Barnes]

The men packed supplies to the cache site on the Lillian, then on April 3 they broke camp at daylight and carried the remaining outfit to the Lillian, where they built a staging for the cache.

For the reconnaissance trip the men took the necessary items for camping — a canvas shelter, cooking utensils, blankets, guns, and axes — plus provisions for a week, consisting of bacon and beans and twenty-five pounds each of pemmican and flour.

The cache was made snug to protect it from molestation by wild animals, and the expedition again headed up the Elwha, with one hundred pounds on the mule and the men packing the camp outfit. They had anticipated serious problems getting Dollie across the Lillian, but these failed to materialize, and she also climbed "Difficulty Hill" — as they referred to the steep mountainside above the Lillian — with less trouble than expected. Skirting the slope above the canyon, the party followed the elk trail that Christie, Barnes, and Hayes had blazed a few days before, passed above the great landslide in Convulsion Canyon, and late in the afternoon established camp at Kate Creek.[1]

The men were astir early the next morning and proceeded southward in the gray dawn, naming creeks as they crossed them. For two miles — during which they crossed Jane Creek — the traveling was good, they noted, if three feet of snow could be considered an improvement. Then came rougher country, and they traveled until noon "over rolling spurs, heavily timbered and deep in snow." By the time the expedition reached Coldfeet

[1] This was probably the stream known today as Bowman Creek.

Creek, Christie was "confronted with a conundrum hard to solve." Dollie was suffering from skinned legs, and to take her over more snow-covered terrain would mean "sawing her legs off from the knees," and a good mule without legs, he asserted, was not worth much.

Finally, blocked by deep snow beneath the trees, they could lead the mule no farther on the bench, and the party was compelled to climb the mountainside. A thousand feet above the river they found better going for a couple of miles, but well on toward evening they were stopped abruptly by "a deep gorge, at the bottom of which a mountain torrent was wearing still deeper its bed." The stream could not be crossed, so for three hours they attempted to follow this "creation of the devil" toward the river, only one mile distant. It was, Christie declared, "hard, tiresome work," with the last three hundred yards being the worst.

> Logs, snow and debris of the woods lay so heavy and deep toward the bottom that it was extraordinary how Dollie ever got through. A rough and headlong tumble and roll would carry her down 100 feet and land her over head and pack in a snow drift. We would dig her out — fortunately we had the shovel to do it with — and another tumble would put her down a little farther, until at last we reached bottom with a level space to camp. But such a camp for April! Snow waist deep and no feed for Dollie after her exhaustive struggle. [Barnes]

The poor mule was "rather the worse for wear and tear," and the men were no less exhausted, being "pretty well played out." Nevertheless, they set to work at once to make as comfortable a camp as the circumstances permitted, and "the shovel soon produced wonders." First they cleared the snow from a camping space, then spread their shelter, cut logs, and before darkness overtook them "succeeded in having a good fire going and things looking comfortable." They called the place Deep Snow Camp. "We managed to gather a handful of ferns for Dollie, and gave her a pound of our precious beans, but she got most of her provender that night by munching spruce boughs from our bed — filling, but indigestible."

That night the expedition was battered by torrential rains which continued during the forenoon of the next day, Saturday, the fifth of April. Because they were all, including Dollie, "badly knocked out by the preceding day," they called it Sunday and rested.

They had reason to be concerned. The mountains were not opening out into a great central valley covered by rolling prairies of lush grasses as the legends had related. Instead, the country was becoming increasingly wild and rugged, the snow deeper, the mountainsides steeper, and the canyons narrower. Supplies were beginning to run low, and for the first time it looked as if their provisions might not last long enough to enable the expedition to cross the mountains. Because the party was now past the general winter range of deer and elk, in the last several days they had seen only two deer which the dogs chased away before the men could fire their rifles.

> Below the Lillian we had plenty of game. Deer and trout were easily gotten, and we lived for the most part on fresh meat and fish. The greatest economy began to prevail at this time in camp with regard to reserve stores. When we left the Lillian we had expected to find game as easily as before, and had brought with us as meat only the pemmican already mentioned. But our experience at this stage of our exploration is illustrative of the vicissitudes of a hunter's life. With the exception of the two deer chased by the dogs we had not seen so much as a fresh track of any kind of animal since crossing the Lillian. Pemmican was made to last us two days, so that when we reached the present camp we had been two days without fresh meat, and the inroads into the more valued provisions of the pack had been unfortunately great. Our stores were valuable — valuable from the amount of toil and hardship borne in getting them in, and also because they were dwindling to small proportions. Flour and bacon were a luxury, not to be eaten as common food.
>
> Nero's dish of nightingales tongues seemed less extravagant to us than one of bacon and beans. As Jack said, as he dandled a couple of the succulent beans upon his fork preparing to masticate the same, "Many a millionaire has no beans for supper to-night." Until we reached the camp in the bottoms we had no time for hunting, unless the animals were considerate enough to come our way — which they had not been. It hurt our feelings, this extravagance, but there was no help for it, and we punished the stores with vigorous appetites. [Barnes]

There was nothing to do but go hunting the next day. They had to obtain a supply of fresh meat at once, "for even of the precious company stores there was but two days' supply left in the advanced camp." But that night it stormed, and five inches of snow fell upon the bottomlands where they were encamped, and more on the mountainsides above.

> The morning grew warm and by 8 o'clock water was dripping from the trees and little pats of wet snow fell from the branches as they became heavy in melting. It became impossible to distinguish or follow any tracks and the hunters returned empty-handed toward evening. Not a single animal had been seen during the entire day. This was a state of things we were not used to, and as we looked at each other and the small amount of flour in the bag and thought of the distance back to the cache, the conviction came home to every man that to-morrow it must be an "elk or bust." [Barnes]

The next morning they started early, "with injunctions to shoot everything in sight from a herd of elk to a jay-bird on the fence." Christie and Barnes went upstream along the river bottoms to hunt elk, Crumback and Hayes took to the mountainside back of the campsite in quest of deer, while Sims remained by the river to try his luck at fishing.

A mile from camp Christie and Barnes climbed the lower slopes of the mountain and came upon a "long and narrow glen" running up the mountainside. Scanning this with the field glass, they saw an elk in the lower part, about eight hundred yards distant.

> He was lying upon the ground apparently asleep in the sun. His wide branching antlers lay against his back, his feet drawn up. That we had surprised his majesty asleep seemed certain. It was long range, but the wind was right for a successful stalk. I dropped behind a log, covered him with my rifle, while in an instant Christie divested himself of unnecessary hamper and disappeared in the bushes on the right. I waited, and the elk seemed entirely unsuspicious of our presence. Presently I saw Christie emerge from a clump of undergrowth and glide as silently as an Indian to the shelter of a fallen log. Now and then I could see him slowly and cautiously getting nearer and nearer until he reached a big stump covered with mosses and vines within easy range of his prey. Ten minutes had passed and I began to feel the tension relaxing a bit as I saw him take careful aim through the vines. Already broiled steak and marrow bones seemed to greet my hungry palate. But there came no report. I wondered if his rifle had jammed. Presently his gun slowly dropped and his head cautiously appeared as he seemed to survey the animal in surprise. Then he came out

from his hiding place, walked up to the prostrate elk and beckoned to me. [Barnes]

Barnes hurriedly descended the slope, wondering if the animal was dead. As he approached, it became evident that the elk had been dead for at least a month.

"As he lay upon the ground we could not but admire his mammoth proportions. It was a bull, and his antlers, which we saved, measured 5 feet 6 inches across, and the animal when alive must have weighed 600." They concluded that the elk had died of starvation, unable to find forage because the mountainsides were "buried beneath the unusual snows." They were severely disappointed, and as they turned and climbed the hill once again, "visions of marrow bones were more shadowy." Half a mile further on, however, they struck fresh elk tracks less than an hour old, leading upriver. They resolved to stalk.

Realizing that the wary animal would be difficult to approach, Barnes and Christie hastily prepared themselves for "what might prove a long trail." If the animal became alarmed, pursuit would be impossible, for elk were "fleet and tireless of foot." Therefore, the stalk would have to proceed in careful Indian fashion, for the shy animals were always alert and watchful.

> Absolute silence was necessary for we might at any moment come upon his lordship. For two hours, over ridge and spur, climbing logs and through the dense shade of the woods, we patiently followed his tracks, sometimes easily seen in the snow, and at others with difficulty as we passed over grassy or stony places. Then we became aware that it was after noon and with sharp appetites we sat down beside a tiny rivulet to lunch sparingly upon what we hoped would be the last gillettes we would be compelled to eat for some time. [Barnes]

They had a drink from the rivulet, then resumed the chase. Upon climbing a ridge bordering the stream, the men realized that the spoor was suddenly becoming fresher.

> At the top of the ridge and down the other side the animal had traveled with great leaps, going down twenty feet at a jump. We must have surprised him upon that very ridge, and he had gone down the other side as we approached the rivulet. Blaming ourselves for stopping to lunch, we hastened on . . . but with little hope of seeing him again. At the foot of

the ridge water was still trickling into the foot track he had made in the soft mud. . . . Presently we saw where he had been joined by two other elk and they all traveled on together. . . . Now their tracks lay straight ahead. . . . Instead of now and again stopping to take a bite from a tempting sprig of laurel, they hurried on with great strides. All our exertion seemed to bring us no nearer our supper. We had little hope now of getting anything better than a snap shot . . . but even that was desirable in the reduced state of the camp larder.

At last the trail struck the river bottom, and passed over a wide space covered with cobble stones and boulders. We wore spikes in our boots, a necessary precaution in these log bestrewn forests, against slipping, for one is nearly half the time running along logs. In spite of the most careful stepping our spikes made a slight noise. We also found difficulty in tracing the trail here, which might lead across the river or up the mountain side at any point, and this necessary care delayed us.

Finally we reached a wooded tongue or low spur running quite to the water, and as we crossed this, bringing to our eyes a large valley beyond, we got just one glimpse of golden yellow disappearing in the brush, not 100 yards away. It was an elk and he had been on the alert. It was too bad. [Barnes]

They gave up all hope of shooting one of the elk. Alerted, the animals would probably travel for miles before stopping. Barnes and Christie sat down on a log, and several minutes passed while they gazed up the river in the direction the animal had disappeared.

Suddenly there emerged from the thicket and quietly stepped down to the river's brink four or five hundred yards away, a magnificent elk — a stag as artists attempt him. But no brush can picture the splendor of that animal, as with head erect and wide branching antlers he appeared to be searching for his enemies. [Barnes]

Unfortunately, Barnes had leaned his gun against a tree four or five yards away. Christie, however, hastily sighted his rifle for the distance and fired. Apparently the shot struck the animal, for the elk turned "and with one bound was in the thicket again." By this time Barnes had grabbed his own gun and fired, simultaneous with Christie's second shot. It was long range, however, and the animal did not fall. They hurriedly followed his tracks up the mountain — convinced by the way the elk had turned after the first shot that it had been hit. The trail, however, "showed no blood."

At one place the bull had laid down for a moment, and several times had apparently stopped and made tracks "as if trying to lick a wound." Thus they believed the shot had entered the animal's shoulder and passed inward — in which event it "might not drop blood for miles."

> As it was growing late and our devious track had led us seven or eight miles from home we were compelled to give up the hunt. So we comforted ourselves with the thought that the boys had had better luck and that liver and marrow bones were awaiting us in camp. But as we entered camp tired and hungry from our exertions of the day we saw no meat hanging from the tree. Not a living thing had they seen all day, not a bird, beast or fish excepting one poor solitary duck. The duck was in the pot. We had this poor duck, together with our last handful of beans, for supper. [Barnes]

Sims had had no luck either. Although he had patiently fished the river all day, while smoking "15 to 20 pipes," he had not had a single bite. Apparently the salmon — which were so plentiful in Geyser Valley — had not yet come this far upstream.

Now practically without supplies, the party was forced to return the next morning to the cache on the Lillian.

> We had on the morning of the return nothing for breakfast, but a little flour and some tea. The flour we mixed with water, for we had with us nothing to lighten it with, and baked it into gillettes before the fire. We made an insufficient meal of these, put by a remnant for lunch on the road, and started back. By good traveling, having no loads but a half blanket for each man and an ax and a rifle, and having now a knowledge of a better route to avoid the heavy snow, which we encountered on the second day coming up, we could make the cache in a day, for the real distance was not great. [Barnes]

The day was marked by "only two incidents of interest," the first being the rebellion of the mule.

> About two miles from camp, while floundering through some heavy snow drifts, she broke out of the path, which we were tramping for her, on to the river bank, and in spite of the honeyed and seductive promises swam across to the opposite side, and there stood regarding us with a "what-are-you-going-to-do-about-it" expression in her peaceful eyes. The promises and threats, which we sent across, were alike disregarded, so that

one of the boys had to ford the cold stream to his waist and catch her. Dollie has fewer tricks since the demise of her companion, but what they lack in number is usually made up in cussedness. [Barnes]

Barnes noted in his narrative that the second incident of the day was more worthy of comment.

> The little caravan had passed the snows and was winding quietly and with quickened footsteps around the sloping mountain side above Convulsion canyon. Mr. Christie, with the only gun in the party [2] was on some distance ahead. . . . Suddenly those of us behind became aware of a rustling in the bushes below the trail. . . . The dogs pricked up their ears. They were all fortunately at once held and prevented from giving chase. Almost at the same moment there came into sight not twenty-five yards away a great cow elk. Here was meat — but by all the angels where was Christie and the gun. The animal stood still, and silently sized us up. Imagine our feelings. No meat for almost a week and here was three or four hundred pounds of it waiting to be put out of its misery. We were afraid to stir — almost to breathe. If we had had a club or a rock we could have struck her with it. We had involuntarily sunk to the ground on seeing the animal and there we squatted.
>
> "For God's sake, where is Christie," were the muttered feelings of each of us.
>
> Great as my anxiety was I could scarcely refrain my laughter as I perceived our ridiculous situation. Here were hungry men and an elk quietly chewing her cud . . . waiting to be killed. After a couple of minutes, which seemed like hours, one of the boys could stand it no longer and uttered a half stifled cry.

Still the animal did not move, but remained standing where she was, apparently regarding them with curiosity. As they had not tried to molest her, she evidenced no alarm. Another man, "encouraged by the continued standing of the animal," called for Christie, and a moment later the call was repeated several times "by all hands . . . with full strength of lung." But Christie did not reply.

> I was in advance of the party and nearest Christie, and as the only chance of getting the four-legged meat was to get the gun at any hazard, I laid down the ax which I was carrying and slowly crept away a few feet, then a few yards, and finally gaining my feet whipped over a knoll out of

[2] The explorers had taken firearms on the reconnaissance trip, and it is not clear why, at this point, Christie alone carried a gun.

sight and ran, it need hardly to be said, break neck up the trail. I soon got within ear shot of Mr. Christie, called out to him and together we hurried back. The cow was still there. As the boys crouching upon the trail holding the struggling dogs caught sight of us we could see their excitement. With wild but half concealed gesticulations they indicated the direction of the elk, and with breathless lips formed the words "there — there — there." [Barnes]

As the elk stood gazing at the boys, less than fifty yards from where they were "sitting in a row struggling with the dogs to keep them quiet" and making signs to attract his attention to the animal, Christie got an excellent shot from a place within easy range, fired again when the cow turned, "and the dogs were loosed in chase." A hundred yards down the hill she fell to the ground, dead, "and all hands were made happy at the prospect of liver and bacon for supper."

While the men skinned and cut up the elk, Barnes took the gun and ascended to the trail, to the place where the mule had been left standing, "quietly munching her favorite Oregon grape." He arrived in time to see a small band of elk coming up the mountainside. He quickly dropped out of sight behind a fallen log and observed that the leader of the herd had caught his scent, "and the whole band crossed the trail and were traveling up the hillside as if forty devils were after them." The band was composed of an old bull, the leader, and eighteen cows. One after another the animals leaped uphill and crossed the trail within a hundred feet of where Barnes sprawled, concealed behind the log.

The leader, with wide-spreading horns, guided the advance, followed by the cows in single file. I had plenty of time to observe them closely as one by one they passed before me. They were of a dun color, graduating into a bright yellow on their flanks. Monstrously heavy they looked, but with what lightness and speed they sprang up the hillside! The old stag was plainly alive to surrounding danger, but he showed none of the fear so evident in his convoy. He led his charge up the hill. They had left behind a trail like a wagon road, so beaten with hoofs. [Barnes]

Barnes had plenty of time to pick out the "youngest and most tender looking of the does," and he brought the animal down with a single shot. He found it difficult to refrain from shooting the leader, so majestic did he look, but the expedition did not need him for meat, "and it seemed a shame to kill so noble a beast."

After a supper of fresh liver, the party continued their journey, crossed Coldfeet Creek, and followed the old elk trail northward, reaching the Lillian River toward evening. From their cache in the bottom of the canyon they packed one load to the top of the hill and made camp there.

The elk had been killed on the hillside above the lower end of the valley ahead, which broadened to a considerable width, "with gaps leading into the mountains." This valley, first viewed by the scouting party on March 25, appeared to be well suited for their cache and base of supplies.

For seven days — from Thursday, April 10, through Wednesday, April 16 — the expedition relayed supplies and provisions from the Lillian to the lower end of the large valley, making intermediate stops at Kate Creek and Big Island Camp. The weather was raw, cloudy, and chilly, with flurries of snow in the afternoons. On April 10, eight inches of snow fell during the night.

Their mule was now suffering terribly because of the deep snow. Her hind legs had been abraded into a mass of raw flesh, and every step she took dyed the snow with blood. On one occasion, while carrying a two-hundred-pound pack up the mountainside above the Lillian, the poor creature "took a most remarkable tumble. She slipped off the side, crashed down over the snow, striking two or three logs, turned several somersaults, and brought up all standing about 50 feet below without injury." When the men saw her begin to tumble, they were certain she had gone to join Jennie.

Beyond Big Island Camp the expedition continued packing up the Elwha. On April 13, while the others set up camp on the river bank, Christie — scouting ahead upstream — killed a bull elk, "and felt happy in the knowledge of having bacon and liver for supper once more." The next day the party crossed the Elwha, ascended the lower mountain slopes, and came upon "a good elk trail running up the mountain side," which enabled them to cross several deep ravines without too much difficulty, although at the expense of considerable labor. Their path then descended toward the river, to the brow of a deep canyon from the depths of which issued "a heavy booming sound, as of water pounding into a cave or hollow." Thunder Canyon they called it.[3]

The rock formations here were all slate. Near their camp the formation was peculiar, the strata being nearly vertical and "bent into waves for one half mile along the river. The river following these waves curves like a snake. At other places on the river this slate projects in massive headlands a hundred or two hundred feet in height."

On the river bottoms the snow was very heavy, but beyond Thunder Canyon they found good traveling for a couple of miles on a bench covered by giant firs. Several deep ravines barred the way, however, necessitating laborious crossings. Finally camp was established late in the afternoon at the lower end of the large valley they had observed while elk hunting. To it they gave the name Press Valley — "in honor of the newspaper whose enterprise fitted out the expedition." While camp was being made, Christie went on to reconnoiter and killed an elk a mile beyond, on the opposite side of the river.

On April 15 the expedition was established at its new campsite on the west side of the Elwha, at the lower end of Press Valley. Here the slightly rolling terrain was heavily timbered with fir and occasional large patches of alder and maple. The men left at daylight to go downstream to Big Island Camp for provisions, but encountered difficulty fording the river, which was five feet deep. Bad weather forced them to remain that night in Big Island Camp, although they were without blankets and had no meat, "some limb of Satan" having stolen their cache of deer hams.[4] Mountain lions were guilty of the larceny, Christie concluded, after examining the tracks.

During the next two days, supplies were relayed from Big Island Camp to Press Valley. They cached two hundred pounds, made the balance into seventy-five-pound loads — one for each man — and packed to Press Valley, arriving in the evening.

The new base camp, located on the floor of Press Valley, did not provide a point from which to observe the terrain ahead. There-

[3] This canyon is located about a mile below the present-day Elkhorn Ranger Station.
[4] Christie probably meant elk instead of deer.

fore, on the morning of April 18,[5] Captain Barnes reconnoitered to the northwest, ascending the mountainside until he obtained an excellent view to the eastward. Then, after dinner, accompanied by Christie, he climbed the hillside back of camp. The two had gone but three hundred yards when they came to "a level plateau about one and one-half miles long and three-quarters of a mile wide, rectangular in form." The little plateau or bench was covered with thin soil over white, gravelly sand, upon which grew stunted fir, spruce, and pine trees.

> Upon the plateau the trees are all small, there being hardly a tree over eight inches in diameter. The largest tree observed is not much over 200 years old. Fringing the edge and descending the bluff, which is everywhere very steep, the trees are very large. We were immediately struck with the number of trees upon the plateau which were blazed or otherwise injured. Examinations of these scars showed the hand of man. The scars were old. [Barnes]

In crossing the "plateau" they came upon a circular mound from which the snow had partially melted. The perfect regularity in the mound's form seemed to indicate that it had been artificially constructed, and the explorers "soon became convinced that this had been an old Indian village as well as a permanent one."

Barnes went on to explain that the location was ideal for such a village, for three sides of the plateau descended steeply, while the fourth was "an abrupt mountain side inaccessible except from the plateau itself." The place, therefore, could be easily defended, and it would be convenient in times of peace because of its central location in the valley.

Scarcely a tree more than seven or eight inches in diameter was not scarred or marked in some manner. They thought that most of the scars had been made with axes, and they also saw "where children had stripped off the bark of the pines for the purpose of getting the gum."[6] No fallen timber lay on the ground, which at this time was covered by about a foot of snow, and this, too, was

[5] An interesting item appears in Christie's diary under date of April 18: "The boys drying bears' meat." There is no explanation, no mention of their having shot a bear — or even having seen one thus far on the expedition.

[6] These scars may have been made by bears.

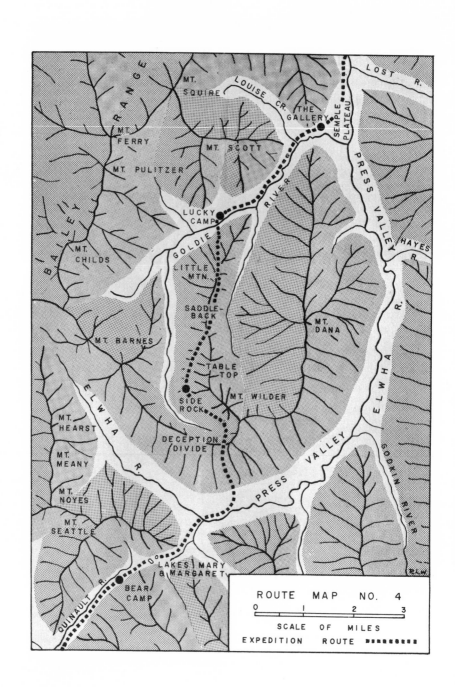

ROUTE MAP NO. 4

SCALE OF MILES
0 1 2 3

EXPEDITION ROUTE ▪▪▪▪▪▪▪▪

strikingly different from the "natural forest" surrounding the plateau.

> Every particle of wood had evidently been gathered for fuel. None of the younger growth of timber, under six or seven inches in diameter, indicating an age of 100 years or less, was scarred or blazed. The trees larger than this, having an age of say anywhere from 100 to 250 years or less, were, as already stated, all scarred. Nothing older than that, none of the patriarchs of the surrounding forest, existed on the plateau. [Barnes]

The men concluded from these facts that the forest had been destroyed, either for the purpose of admitting sunlight or for use as fuel. The scarred trees now found upon the plateau, they reasoned, were probably second-growth saplings during the existence of the village, and had been scarred either by accident or by children. They further concluded that the smaller, unscarred trees had grown on the plateau since the village had been deserted.

> The plateau was evidently the site of a large and permanent village. It is true that an occasional band of hunting Indians, camping at different times on different parts of the plateau, might in time scarify the trees over the whole surface, giving it the appearance of a large village. But a party of hunting Indians would never camp so far from water, as it must do if it camps near the mountains. With the choice of location the party would camp near the margin, where wood and water were convenient.
>
> An Indian in his village, however, surrounded by his squaw and family, does not care how far his habitation is from the necessaries of existence, for the labor of fetching devolves upon the squaw. There is no water upon the plateau, but springs are numerous on all sides, just below the margin.
>
> The snow prevented any extended investigation. We were accomplishing our purpose, however, if we discovered the ledge, and left to others the work of developing the mine. It is evident from the tokens observed that this plateau will repay careful investigation. In view of the fact that this ancient village may have furnished the basis for the legends of the Indian conventions and games so beautifully related by ex-Governor Semple, we named the place Semple plateau.[7] [Barnes]

[7] The benchland or "plateau" in question is located along the west side of the Elwha River, immediately below the confluence of a large tributary stream later named Goldie River by the expedition. For unknown reasons, the name Semple Plateau has been shifted in subsequent years to the southern part of the Bailey Range, just north of Bear Pass.

The validity of the Press Party's conclusions concerning this place being the site of an ancient Indian village is subject to serious doubt. The scars on the trees may have been made by elk or bear. Thin, poor soil on the bench-

Barnes and Christie crossed to the southwestern corner of the plateau where the mountainside came down to a point. Leading up this buttress was an old elk trail, which they followed until they reached the top of a crag-like rock that jutted from the side of the mountain, approximately three hundred feet above the plateau.

From this vantage point — which they called The Gallery because of the splendid view and the photographs obtained there — could be seen a magnificent line of peaks to the southeast. They mistook these peaks for what was then known as the Sound Range — the summits adjacent to and visible from Hood Canal and Puget Sound. In reality, however, the mountains they observed from the jutting rock stood farther to the west, deeper within the Olympics.

By mid-April the Press Exploring Expedition had penetrated rather deeply into the mountains, and the men had only to climb high enough to survey the surrounding country in order to see splendid snowy peaks wherever the view was unobstructed. But the irregular topography of the Olympics confused them, and they must have felt, at times, like blind men wandering through the tortuous passageways of an uninhabited castle.

They now faced the moment of decision. Should they continue up the Elwha, with the hope that it would lead them over the mountains? Or should they seek elsewhere for a way across the Olympic labyrinth?

---

land may explain why the trees were small, not large as on surrounding slopes. This would be a function of the "edaphic factor," where differences in the pattern of plant growth are a response to marked contrast in soil conditions. It may well be, however, that Semple Plateau constitutes a fruitful ground for competent archaeologists to explore. It is certainly not unknown terrain today, however, as an old trail crosses it, leading from the Elwha up to the Dodger Point fire lookout.

Press Valley from The Gallery, looking toward Mount Anderson, left, and Mount Norton, right. The Press Party mistook Mount Anderson for The Brothers
(Courtesy Arney A. Rodal)

Chapter IX

APRIL, 1890: THE GOLDIE

ON SATURDAY, April 19, Christie, Barnes, and Crumback left camp in the morning to investigate the country ahead for a trail through what they believed to be "a good pass to the southwest." If such a pass existed and they chose to use it, their route would be changed, and the expedition would move away from the Elwha. Ever since the party had left Canyon Camp in mid-January, the men had fought their way up the Elwha, through its bottomlands and canyons and along its steep mountainsides. But the question now presented itself: Would the Elwha lead them to the headwaters of the Quinault?

The reconnaissance party crossed Semple Plateau, ascended to The Gallery, then climbed upward. At first the slope was easy, but it steepened consistently. After a tiring climb they arrived, about one o'clock in the afternoon, at a benchland on the precipitous slope where they built a fire and ate lunch. Then, removing their boots and slipping into moccasins and snowshoes, they started westward along the bench, which contoured the mountainside for a half mile. Proceeding upward from this point in moccasins alone, the men arrived at the top of the mountain about four o'clock in the afternoon. They were now twenty-three hundred feet above their camp, and the view was even better than from The Gallery. "Press valley seemed to continue to the southward many miles. To the westward extended a gap for eight or ten miles, and then appeared to sweep to the southward and to form a pass in that direction."

Because the expedition was scheduled to emerge from the mountains by way of the Quinault, if possible, the men were "desirous of getting westward." If the maps then in existence were correct, the southward trend of Press Valley indicated that it would lead toward the Skokomish River. The decision was therefore made on April 19, 1890, that the Press Exploring Expedition would "take this westward gap," which seemed to be a practicable, logical route. It was a momentous decision, one they were to reflect about later. Through this gap they could see "a great white range extending from the direction of Olympus, southward, seemingly the backbone of the mountains." Bailey Range they called it provisionally, "in honor of Mr. William E. Bailey, the proprietor of the SEATTLE PRESS."

The weather was clear and warm on April 21. Crumback, Sims, and Hayes were detailed to move the expedition's camp from Press Valley up the zigzag, hazardous trail to The Gallery. They would not have used this lofty perch, "a dangerous place," had it not been convenient for their purposes. While the camp was being moved, Christie and Barnes took their guns and two days' provisions and explored Press Valley southward. First they crossed Semple Plateau to its southwestern corner, and there paused a moment "to survey the glorious view."

> The valley stretched to the southward. Seemingly in its center Mt. Egan reared its snow white crest. The main valley, however, or the one containing the river, seemed to sweep a little to the westward, between Egan and a great mountain on the right [Mt. Dana]. Up this valley, far in the distance, could be faintly discerned a snow white peak. To this we gave the name of "Old Snowback." To the left, eastward of Mt. Egan, could be seen the distant peaks of the Sound range, most conspicuous of which towered "The Brothers." [1]

[1] The Press Expedition's Mount Egan is today known as Mount Norton; their "Old Snowback" is Chimney Peak; and the men mistook Mount Anderson — a peak lying far inland from the peaks facing Hood Canal — for The Brothers, one of the prominent peaks of the so-called Sound Range.
Had the men retained the colored fire which was discarded when the mule Jennie was lost, and released it from a high peak where they now were, the display of fireworks would not have been seen from Puget Sound, for they were too far inland.

Descending from the plateau, they came to a large tributary (later named Goldie River) about a mile above its confluence with the Elwha. Unslinging their axes, they felled a large tree across for a footbridge. On the south side were some "lovely alder bottoms partially bare of snow." The two men traveled about three miles up the valley, which was "covered with incomparable timber," more or less free of underbrush. Here and there groves of maple stood on the river flats.

About noontime they came again to the Elwha, at this point bordered by a hundred acres or more of bottomland, the alluvial soil covered by stands of alder. Here the men ate lunch, then retraced their steps back toward The Gallery. While still a mile from camp, however, they were startled to hear two shots fired in rapid succession.

> As we had noticed fresh elk trails in the morning on the plateau, we thought the boys had killed an elk, and we hastened our steps a little. A few minutes later from the top of a spur, or little ridge, which crossed the valley, we thought we could distinguish shouts. Then came another shot and unmistakable shouts. Surely they were not hunting elk in that unseemly fashion. Something had happened and they were trying to recall us, we thought. Acting on this hypothesis we gave them an answering shot. After listening for perhaps a minute, another shot came from the hill. Surely something had happened. [Barnes]

The sound came from the direction of the day's rendezvous point, The Gallery, seven hundred feet above. Fearing that one of the men had fallen from the jutting rock and been killed or injured, they quickened their pace. Then a new fear crept into their minds. Perhaps some well-meaning but undesired relief party had followed their blazed trail and overtaken the expedition.

> This last fear mingled with the other as a misfortune second only to it. The progress of the expedition had been necessarily so slow, that we always had the fear of visitors in our minds. It was part of our mission to cut a trail into this region in order that the country might be opened to settlers. So thoroughly had we done it that a party leaving Port Angeles, could lope after us on horseback, and easily travel in a few days over a road which it had taken us months to come. So jealous were we of sharing our hard earned honors with exploiting and notoriety seeking strangers, that we

would have regarded it as a catastrophe ranking next to the loss of one of ourselves. [Barnes]

Almost certain that one or the other misfortune had occurred, and "unable to conceive a lesser reason for so much commotion," they hurried down the hill, crossed the log spanning the Goldie, then scrambled up the opposite mountainside. Halfway up, however, their anxiety was relieved, for they came upon a minutes-old "deeply plowed trail of a descending band of elk." The tracks indicated that the elk — apparently frightened and pursued — had gone leaping down the hill, traveling fifteen or twenty feet at a jump. Christie and Barnes, "now satisfied that the boys had been hunting elk, although in a most extraordinary manner," slowed their pace and climbed up the zigzag trail to The Gallery. Several minutes later "the boys came up with Dollie and the last of the camp outfit."

> They had indeed, while packing, run upon the band of elk, whose trail we had seen upon the hill side, and had killed one. But in the scrimmage, "Dike," one of the dogs, a large black retriever, had been killed also. It seems that the dog rashly attempted to head off one of the bulls. The bull striking "Dike" with his forefeet nearly cut the dog in two, killing him instantly. This explained the shouts that had so alarmed us. The boys perceiving the dog's danger had shouted at him in an endeavor to save him. We went down and visited poor "Dike's" remains. He was horribly mangled, and gave a most instructive object lesson upon the savage nature of the elk when brought to bay. [Barnes]

Taking the liver and tenderloin of the slain elk for their supper, they gave the dogs a feed from the flanks and hung up the remainder, for the pack contained sixty pounds of dried meat. Then, because water was not available at The Gallery, they took advantage of the remaining hours of daylight to proceed to a suitable camping place. The mule was loaded, "all hands shouldered their packs, and the expedition once more set forward." Immediately confronting them, however, was a great landslide; to pass it they must climb above and then descend. After a strenuous ascent they reached the top of the slide, then gradually worked their way down again "through vast quantities of snow, carefully edging along the steep, sliding mountain side."

This was the last day the mule Dollie traveled in their company. About a half mile beyond the starting place, she suddenly gave out and laid down. She had done her duty faithfully and well to that point, but where it became impossible to take her a mile further she gave up. "Played out," as Christie said. "All our endeavors could not induce her to rise. Persuasion, couched in the most honied [*sic*] phrases and emphasized by means of the large end of a fair-sized club, was unavailing. Poor Dollie was exhausted" [Barnes].

They unloaded the mule, cached the pack she had been carrying, and left her on the path. No doubt, they hastened to assure themselves, she would be "with fair luck . . . fat and fresh at the end of the month."

With the articles necessary for making a camp, men and dogs went on to the foot of the mountainside. There, where a snow-covered creek entered the Goldie several miles above its juncture with the Elwha, they stopped for the night and made camp in the dark beside the stream, which they called Louise Creek. "It had been a hard day's work. We had hoped for a better camp, but the best we could do this night was to camp in our wet clothes on a wet snow bank."

Their situation was critical. Even traveling as lightly and rapidly as possible, they could not hope to reach Lake Quinault in less than a month, and it could take twice that long. The expedition's original supply of provisions had shrunk to one hundred and fifty pounds of flour, twenty-five pounds of beans, ten pounds of bacon, five pounds of tea, five pounds of salt, and less than two pounds of tobacco. They supplemented this with a meager sixty pounds of partially smoked meat, expecting to kill game whenever they needed it. This stock of provisions would last only ten days on a full-rations basis, but "could be made to last indefinitely" if they put themselves on a strict allowance. With these supplies, then, they "commenced the search for the head of the Quinaiult."

> The meat we now had was most villainously tough and dry, absolutely devoid of fat. It was only possible to eat it in the form of soup. We would fill a four-gallon kettle with meat, boil it all night, and in the morning not

so much as a single globule of grease would be floating on the surface. Owing, as we supposed, to the want of grease, we were all suffering from dysentery, and sometimes we would be so weak from this cause that we could hardly stagger. We had no remedy available. We used browned flour, mixed with a little of our precious bacon grease, which was better than nothing. [Barnes]

After spending an uncomfortable night at Louise Creek, they started toward The Gallery the next morning, in order to bring up their remaining stores.

Dollie we hardly expected to get, but the snow was becoming so heavy that it would be impossible to use her even if she were in good condition. We found her standing where we left her. Although hungry and without water the poor mule had been too exhausted to wander in search of food. We removed her halter, patted her on the back and turned her adrift to get her living as the elk do. Dollie had done us good service, her small feet made it possible for her to climb steep mountain sides where a horse would have failed. [Barnes]

By ten o'clock they were back at Louise Creek, having packed their remaining provisions in two loads. They did not delay, but set out at once, following the deep, gloomy canyon west until darkness prevented further travel. Because the stream flowing through this gorge was "a large branch of the Elwha and worthy of a good name," they called it "Goldie river, in honor of Mr. R. H. Goldie of Seattle."

The expedition had now left the Elwha. The five men, accompanied by their three remaining dogs, had irrevocably set their course to the southwest, hopeful of reaching a pass that would lead them to the Quinault. Unwittingly, they had decided to cross one of the roughest parts of the Olympic Mountains — a labyrinth of steep-walled canyons and precipitous mountain spurs, without trails to this day. For a week the men fought their way up the Goldie Canyon, sleeping on the snow for lack of bare ground. Their progress was very slow. As they continued, the size of the river diminished, but the canyon through which it flowed gradually deepened and became increasingly difficult to negotiate.

The snow also became deeper as we advanced, and our daily progress slower. Beautiful scenery opened before us at every turn. At places the river was bridged with snow, so that we could cross with ease and safety. From the mountain sides magnificent cascades played hundreds of feet into the river below. Avalanches had at places stripped the mountain of its timber, and at these points the canyon was blocked up with a huge mass of mingled snow, rock and forest trees torn out by the roots. [Barnes]

They could no longer afford the time to rest in camp or spend an afternoon leisurely hunting for elk or deer. They put in "a succession of hard working days," during which the travel was generally "hard and disagreeable." In addition, the men continued to suffer from the dysentery that had plagued them. The many occasions when they were compelled to ford the Goldie, its icy water reaching to their armpits, recalled to their minds the early days of the expedition, when they had towed the *Gertie* up the Elwha in below freezing temperatures. Although winter was technically over, the weather was uncertain, for they were now high in the mountains. Along the river they sometimes came upon little patches of bottomland buried in snow, and they plowed a route through these on snowshoes. Most of the time, however, they were forced to keep to mountainsides "that seemed to be set on edge."

Our trail lay along the river bank, which at best was hard work getting through. The snow was very deep, and overhanging drifts in many places made our journey rather precarious and kept us always on the alert for chances of a slide. Crawling up one spur to clamber down the other side kept us engaged all day. [Christie]

The arduous work of backpacking under such adverse circumstances — particularly considering the length of time the men had been in the wilderness — was telling upon them, and Christie promised every fourth day as Sunday. While the others relaxed, however, Christie followed his usual practice of leaving camp "to get a look at the country ahead, if possible." He found it "rough traveling all through," and returned to camp "having gained no definite knowledge of the route."

On the morning of April 26, the expedition had, in Christie's words, "another dress parade of stores and camp outfit"; or, as Barnes preferred to say, their equipment "underwent another weeding." They cached a number of dispensable articles. As the

canyon became rougher and the snow deeper, they were daily
made more aware of the necessity for reducing their packs to the
lightest possible weight.

A lot of bullets, a frying pan, two axes, a pick-axe, the large kettle and
several other articles went over the fence. Some old clothes were discarded and we retained only those we wore. They were our best, but even
they were ragged and torn. Tougher looking tramps never bummed along
the roadside than the once well-dressed "PRESS Exploring Expedition."
We had each started with good, strong suits of serviceable Scotch wool, a
suit of overalls, a change of underclothing, stout flannel outside shirts,
good leather boots and waterproof garments throughout. These were now
reduced to the actual clothes we wore, all in rags. Our hats we threw
away long ago as unnecessary and we were tiding over the winter bare-
headed. A piece of blanket served for a stocking; of our boots there is
little left but the soles. All other apparel has been left by the roadside, a
prey to bears, cougars and other varmints. So much the less to pack over
the mountains. At this rate, if we reach Grays harbor with our ammunition belts we will be doing well. We can hide in the woods while we negotiate a trade with some clothing merchant. [Barnes]

After caching the discarded items, they left camp at 9:00 A.M.,
crossed a snow bridge a hundred yards above camp, and continued their trek up the Goldie Canyon. As they trudged slowly
through the deep snow, many beautiful waterfalls captured their
admiration. One of the largest — which they named Adeline Cascade — fell about a hundred feet from the northern wall of the
canyon into the snow-covered river.

All day long we traveled without seeing a bare spot large enough to
camp on, and we expected to have to make our beds in the snow bank
again. But just as we were about to camp we discovered a little bench
above the trail, 15 by 20 feet in dimensions, enclosed by the hillside behind and two jutting rocks. Sunny and warm and bare of snow it was the
cosiest little camping place imaginable. A low spreading spruce tree overhung it, which when cut down fell into camp and furnished us with a
splendid bed. Two dead trees a little above also fell into camp and gave
us an abundance of firewood. Twenty yards away ran the creek. It was the
best camp that we had had. The boys wished that they could pack it along
with us.
We were now at the base of the range which seemed to divide the watershed. From this camp we would begin the next day to climb the mountain side opposite, and camp for a week or two would be likely to be cold

and disagreeable. If we could only have packed this camp along. We named this Lucky camp. [Barnes]

Two miles north of their route stood a high, pyramid-like peak, somewhat isolated from other summits. The men named it Mount Scott, "after Mr. James W. Scott of the Chicago Herald." An outlier or spur of the Bailey Range, the peak remains almost inaccessible to this day and is seldom climbed.

April 27 was Sunday, but the men gave no thought to "going to church" — which meant, in this wilderness, a day spent resting in camp or hunting in the nearby woods. Their supplies were now dwindling at an alarming rate and travel was a necessity. Crumback and Hayes were sent back to retrieve two packs left at the last campsite, while the others

> shouldered 60 pounds each, crossed the raging Goldie, and struck up the mountain side, headed for the water shed of the Quinaiult. The lower slopes of the mountain incline at 55 to 60 degrees and we had to go at it side hill fashion, slowly and painfully, kicking a foothold in the snow, sometimes finding footholds five or six feet deep. We plowed through this deep snow on the mountain side for three hours and our packs made it laborious work. At an altitude of 4500 feet by aneroid we made cache of our pack. The snow was here 10 feet deep. In some places on the trail upward we had found it to be over 15. Around every tree a little well was melted, enabling us to see downward to the roots. The timber on this mountain side is heavy, and although the day was clear and warm, so impenetrable was the foliage overhead that a deep gloom pervaded the woods. [Barnes]

They had only one view of the sun that morning, from a point halfway up the mountainside where a small landslide had occurred, creating a break in the timber. While seated upon a root projecting from the top of the slide, the men caught "a glimpse of the canyon below" and, opposite them, "a glorious range of mountains."

> Snow covered from base to summit, the range seemed to rise in a perpendicular wall. From its central position and lofty height it was evidently the backbone of the Olympic mountains. We called it Bailey range,[2] after Mr. William E. Bailey, proprietor of the PRESS. Two splendid

[2] On April 19, Christie, Barnes, and Crumback — scouting ahead for a pass to the southwest — had provisionally called this chain of peaks the Bailey Range. See page 133.

The "terra incognita": Bailey Range, foreground and left background; Mount Olympus Range, right and center background (Courtesy Pacific Aerial Surveys, Inc.)

peaks in the range rose immediately opposite us. The peak to the northward we gave the name of Mount Ferry, after Governor E. P. Ferry of the
state of Washington. The one to the southward we called Mt. Pulitzer,
after Mr. Joseph Pulitzer of the New York World.[3]

Bailey range from where we sat seemed like a long thin wedge. Its edge,
sharply defined against the sky, was covered with snow, through which
sharp jagged rocks protruded like the teeth of a saw. The west wind
which here prevails throughout the year, had drifted the snow along the
summit in places into a huge overhang on our, or eastern side. It was like a
great wave curling over. It seemed in some places to project thirty or forty
feet. [Barnes]

Throughout the day the rumbling of avalanches broke the mountain stillness. From a little opening in the trees where they had
stopped to rest, Christie, Barnes, and Sims were privileged to
view a massive slide. A low rumbling noise attracted their attention to the Bailey Range. On the face of Mount Pulitzer, directly
opposite them — at a distance they estimated at not over a mile
but which must have been double that distance — a great mass of
snow was slipping and sliding down the mountainside. The rumbling noise was soon amplified "into a perfect hurricane of sound
as the mass gained in volume and speed," and the whole face of
the mountain seemed to be in motion.

A glance revealed the origin of the movement. A piece of the overhanging snow had broken from the crest. The snow below it lay upon the
mountain side a hundred feet in depth. Dislodging a great quantity of this
the combined mass began to descend the almost perpendicular descent,
gathering momentum and fresh accumulation every moment. To us as we
watched it from a distance it seemed to move slowly, but in fact it was
plowing and plunging down the shining white plane at a great velocity.
Before it bounded great balls of snow, like sputtering drops of oil on a
heated surface. As it neared the timber line we watched it with increased
interest. From the base of the mountain the timber belt extended up its

[3] It cannot be determined with certainty which peaks the expedition designated as Mount Ferry, Mount Pulitzer, and Mount Childs. Immediately
south of the peak known today as Mount Ferry (which is probably properly labeled) stands a higher one known locally as Snagtooth by reason of its
appearance from the Dodger Point lookout. This peak may have been Pulitzer. However, if the Press Expedition considered Mount Ferry and Snagtooth as one — which they very well might have done — then Pulitzer was
probably the peak standing a mile NNE. of Bear Pass. But this peak could
have been the one designated as Mount Childs by the expedition.

sides some three thousand feet and lay directly across the path of the descending monster. We had not long to wait.

Before the head of the avalanche struck the timber the trees began to go down. It seemed as if a rushing column, or cushion, of air pressed forward, and sustained by the mighty downrush of the avalanche, struck the timber. It snapped them off like matches and hurled them before it hundreds of feet. Great forest trees gnarled with the hardy mountain growth of hundreds of years were torn up by the roots by the breath of the monster. [Barnes]

They had had an unobstructed grandstand seat from which to view nature in one of her most violent moods. As they watched — their attention focused on the avalanche to the exclusion of everything else — the plunging masses of snow left behind a dirty yellow track extending up the mountainside.

The crash of timber and roar of the avalanche came to our ears like thunder — like the continued roar of artillery. It cut a swath through the timber hundreds of yards in width, and poured — a dirty mass of snow, broken timber, rocks and earth — into the canyon below. It was all over in about the space of a minute, but to us who watched it seemed an hour. The movement of a mountain side, the tearing up of rocks and crashing of trees made it a most thrilling spectacle. After it was over, we had time to observe the awful effects which ensued from that little break at the top. Broken and splintered stumps marked all that was left of the great trees in its path. The smaller trees had bent forward with the weight of the snow and had remained comparatively uninjured. Great patches of bare earth and naked rock showed here and there where there had been pure, white snow a few minutes before. [Barnes]

Although Barnes succeeded in describing the avalanche in vivid terms, Christie found himself at a loss for words to describe "the scene of awful destruction" that lay outspread at their feet.

This immense body of matter lay spread out in the valley of the Goldie river completely concealing it from view for the length of half a mile. Snow, ice, rocks and trees broken and twisted in every conceivable manner, piled high in one conglomerate mass. On the conclusion of the infernal din we found our tongues to exclaim "Thank God that we were not on that side of the river!" [Christie]

The Bailey Range was "peculiarly liable to avalanches," Barnes concluded, because of its precipitous terrain which, at the higher

Mount Ellinor as it appears in M
Although not on the expedition ro
this scene illustrates the nature of
terrain crossed by the party w
climbing above the Goldie. Note
snow cornice in lower center (Pl
by Robert L. Wood)

Scene in the Olympic Mountains in
May, showing development of snow
cornices on leeward side of ridge
(Photo by Robert L. Wood)

altitudes, nearly approached the perpendicular. Heavy winter snows apparently piled up to immense depths on the range — the spine of the Olympics — and, swept by the prevailing westerly winds, formed great cornices that overhung the leeward side. The men could see this side of the range from their present position. Thus, whenever the burden of snow became too heavy or warm temperatures created instability in the snow masses, slippage resulted and tons of snow cascaded down the sheer cliffs.

> Avalanches are not common in these mountains, as a whole. The timber extends everywhere in an unbroken belt along the lower slopes, unbroken, save by the present winter. Mountain slopes nearly approaching the perpendicular are everywhere heavily timbered, which would not be if such heavy snow were a common occurrence, or even happened once in a hundred years.[4] [Barnes]

[4] Weather Bureau records for four stations — Port Angeles, Tatoosh Island, Olympia, and Vancouver — reveal that the winter of 1889–90 was severe in western Washington. Although temperatures during October and November, 1889, averaged near normal, the period from December 1, 1889, to March 1, 1890, averaged 5.24 degrees colder than normal at these four points. Significantly, at the two northern stations, Port Angeles and Tatoosh Island — which were nearest the expedition's location at that time — the mean temperature for this three-month period averaged 5.61 degrees colder than normal. The trend continued through March and April, 1890, which averaged 2.6 degrees colder than normal at the four stations.

On the other hand, precipitation at the four stations from November 1, 1889, through April 30, 1890, averaged only 0.19 inch per month greater than normal.

Port Angeles was the nearest weather station to the expedition's location. From November 1, 1889, through April 30, 1890, the temperature at Port Angeles averaged 4.4 degrees below normal, the precipitation 1.0 inch per month above normal. February was the coldest month, averaging 7.8 degrees colder than normal, with 1.70 inches more precipitation than usual.

Although the precipitation was not greatly excessive, the low temperatures caused most of it to fall in the form of snow. This meant heavy snow in the valleys — such as the expedition experienced in December, January, and February — when normally the snow line would have been up two or three thousand feet. However, the amount of snow at the higher elevations probably did not greatly exceed the normal. Barnes was no doubt incorrect in his conclusion that "such heavy snow" would not occur more than once in a hundred years.

On August 14, 1890, John P. McGlinn, United States Indian Agent at Neah Bay, reported: ". . . the past winter was the most trying and discouraging that I ever experienced. The rainy season (it is no Oregon mist) set in the 1st of November, and it either snowed or rained incessantly till

After watching the remarkable spectacle — and the avalanche was the most awe inspiring phenomenon they had thus far observed in the Olympics — the men "again entered the gloom of the woods" and retraced their trail to Lucky Camp much more quickly than they had made the ascent.

The next morning, April 28, the weather continued clear and warm. At daylight, the men began arranging their packs for "another trip up hill."

> Last night the dogs got away with the bacon, leaving us only two or three pounds. In the remaining piece was very little fat, the only grease in camp. We have of late been very saving of bacon, and the loss amounts almost to a disaster. With the exception of a minute allowance of bacon we have been for nearly two months past without grease, which is beginning to tell on the health of the expedition. As for the dogs they have had scarcely anything to eat since we left the dead elk at the Gallery, for we cannot pack for dogs. They are hardly to be blamed for last night's theft. We would probably steal ourselves if we were hungry. [Barnes]

As the sun rose over the mountains to the east, the expedition was afoot once again with the second and final pack. The men crossed the Goldie, bade it an affectionate adieu, and commenced to climb with the hope in their hearts that they would be across the central divide of the mountains three days later. The snow provided better footing that morning — in itself a good omen — and they were able to follow their tracks that had been tramped hard the day before. "Still, it was long and hard work, and many a drop of perspiration fell and many a breath came short before the day was over. 'I am leg weary of this job,' quoth good Jack Crumback, before the top was reached."

After climbing steadily for four hours, they attained their altitude of the previous day. They stopped, built a fire on the snow, prepared some lunch, and rested awhile. Beyond this point a bench sloped upward at an easier angle, and they were able to use snowshoes, only occasionally having to remove them in steep places "and go at it in bare moccasins."

---

the middle of April. At times storms from the ocean were dreadful, and would shake the buildings to their foundation." (*Reports of the Interior Department* [Washington: Government Printing Office, 1890], pp. 222–25.)

They had now left the valley-and-canyon country and had climbed into the high land near timberline. Deep snow covered everything except the trees, and it was pointless to look for a bare campsite. At three o'clock in the afternoon they selected a place on the sidehill where the snow was only six or seven feet deep. The men cut out a bench ten feet square, then chopped a tree into logs, which they rolled to the lower end of the bench and placed parallel. Upon this platform they built a fire and before it, on the bench in the snow, spread a layer of boughs a foot thick for their bed. "We were," Barnes noted when this work was finished, "as comfortable as we had any right to be."

While the boys completed preparations for the night, Christie and Barnes left to reconnoiter ahead on snowshoes. For a couple of miles they followed the mountainside on a gradual ascent. The forest remained so dense, however, that in the brief time available for scouting they were "unable to find an opening in the trees from which a satisfactory outlook could be obtained." Christie and Barnes therefore resolved to spend the next day climbing "above the timber belt," to a point where they could "see over the divide ahead." There appeared to be an excellent pass, but whether or not it existed was debatable. They had so long anticipated finding such a pass, however, that the idea had almost become fact in their minds.

The weather remained clear and warm. On the twenty-ninth, while Hayes, Crumback, and Sims went back to the cache made two days earlier, Barnes and Christie scouted ahead to search for a trail "and to endeavor to reach some high point." Snowshoeing straight up the mountainside, they soon reached "the summit of the low mountain," only to discover that a saddleback connected it to "a sharp snowclad peak directly south." [5] Here they paused a few moments.

[5] This was Mount Wilder. Christie heads his diary entry for April 30 "Mt. Barnes," and it is possible the peak now known as Wilder was the mountain which the expedition meant to bear the name Mount Barnes, after their historian and topographer. Present-day maps, however, indicate Mount Barnes as the northwestern of two peaks lying between the head of the Goldie and Dodwell-Rixon Pass, which peak does closely resemble the sketch of Mount Barnes in the *Press*'s story of the expedition. The men also gave the

The excellent view from here eastward induced us to rest and have a smoke while I made some negatives of a glorious mountain to the eastward. This mountain we recognized as being the great white peak previously observed from above Convulsion Canyon, but how different in appearance observed from here. Then we saw its northern side, pure white, glittering with snow, now its western and southern slope came under our view, heavily timbered almost to the summit. Great masses of snow however appeared near the summit, wind blown and curling over the summit to the northward and eastward, like a great wave breaking upon the beach. This mountain, though a part of Bailey range, is connected with that range by a low ridge only. It stands forth so independently and prominently that it reminded me of my favorite newspaper the New York Sun. So we called it Mount "Dana." [Barnes]

They rested awhile, admiring "the broad and generous proportions" of the peak. A short, easy grade led down to the saddleback. There the snow was "as much as fifteen feet in depth covering the smaller trees whose heads peeped out through the covering." They had now reached an altitude where the trees — mostly sub-alpine firs, with an occasional Alaska cedar — were stunted. Following the saddleback southward for about a mile, Christie and Barnes came at last to the base of "the steep ascent of the great peak" whose sides they wished to scale (known today as Mount Wilder). The summit stood two and a half miles south of the "low mountain." An hour of strenuous climbing brought them

to a small ledge and the knowledge that we were both mighty hungry. Rustling a fire of small twigs we soon had our kettles on, and but few minutes elapsed ere we were enjoying a cup of our fast going tea. Our lunch of dried elk meat and gillettes was soon a thing of the past. [Christie]

Once again they adjusted their snowshoes and continued to ascend the gradually steepening mountainside.

Thus lightened and fortified, we began the ascent of 1100 feet at an angle of seventy-five degrees. The mountain side was partially bare of timber. A few tree tops only protruded through the deep snow. We made the ascent

name Mount Childs to a peak in the Bailey Range. This could have been one of the two peaks adjacent to Dodwell-Rixon Pass; or it may possibly have been the higher summit about one mile NNE. of Bear Pass. See footnote 3 of this chapter, and footnote 1 of chapter X.

at considerable risk, for the snow, whose great depth we could only guess at, lay so soft and yielding on the mountain side that we constantly feared a slip of the entire mass. We made our way slowly up zigzag fashion. Mr. Christie went in advance, thrusting one snowshoe into the snow, edgewise, carefully bringing his weight upon it, then thrusting in the other foot a little above and ahead of the other, sometimes making a short tack then a long one. Mr. Christie, followed closely by myself, gradually approached the top. [Barnes]

As they neared the top, the face of the mountain became steeper with every step, and Christie was even more impressed than Barnes, declaring that he was "perfectly satisfied that the last 500 feet was done at an angle of fully 85 degrees — just about as steep climbing as there is any use for." [6]

After two hours of steep climbing that expended considerable physical and nervous energy, the men reached "a flat-topped table" eleven hundred feet above the saddleback. Their new vantage point commanded a view of the entire horizon except for a forty-degree segment blocked by the mountain. The main peak, which was separated from the "table-top" by a deep ravine, appeared to tower another thousand feet above them. As they stood upon the level bench, regaining their equilibrium, they decided — because it was midafternoon — to go no further, but to make their observations from that point. Around them the stunted tops of a few trees thrust upward through the snow — which they estimated to be at least twenty-five feet deep. [7]

It was an important viewpoint. They had climbed to a height that would permit them to see, for the first time, the Quinault watershed.

[6] Here, as elsewhere on the expedition, the explorers were guilty of pardonable hyperbole. Except for cornices and similar structures, snow slopes seldom exceed an inclination of 50 degrees. Barnes's and Christie's exaggeration is understandable, however. Even experienced snow and ice climbers sometimes have the feeling that a 45-degree slope approaches the vertical, particularly if the slope is exposed. And a snow slope greater than 50 degrees almost brushes the climber's chin. See expedition photograph, "Side of Mountain, May 1st," p. 158. The snow slope in the upper part of the picture has 40-degree inclination.

[7] This was not exaggerated. Snow in this part of the Olympics often reaches this depth in March and April.

Mount Christie as photographed by Asahel Curtis *ca.* 1924
(Courtesy Washington State Historical Society)

Mount Christie as photographed by Asahel Curtis Aug. 1, 1907
(Courtesy Washington State Historical Society)

Mounting a small pinnacle of naked rock, we obtained a glorious view. The whole mountain system south of us came for the first time under our view, and for the first time under the view of any white man. Before us what a jumble of mountains. Range after range of peaks, snow-clad from base to summit, extended as far as the eye could reach, in splendid confusion. [Barnes]

Surrounded by an "unequaled spectacle of mountain scenery," Christie and Barnes nevertheless withheld their admiration for the moment.

One thought was uppermost in both our minds. For a moment we were almost stunned by the sea of mountains across the pathway to our journey's end — and we had but twelve days' grub in camp by the utmost economy. For a moment only we gazed — then in one breath we cried, "The Quinaiult!" Yes, there was the watershed of the Quinaiult, the aim of all our travel, separated from us at a distance of not over six or seven miles by a "height of land" somewhat less than the height at which we stood. But what a watershed! What a route to travel! A deep gorge it seemed, its precipitous sides all rock and snow rising gradually to the snow-capped, vapor-wreathed heights that formed its bounds. For some miles the pass appeared to run due south and then trended to the southwest, far away.

"One pack a man," said Mr. Christie, after several minutes of silence, during which we looked and pondered upon the situation — pondering in which pounds of flour and ounces of bacon largely figured.

"One pack," I assented.

This decision arrived at, the difficulties in the situation seemed to disappear, and we both felt relieved. By leaving behind all useless articles, by taking with us only what we could pack in a single load, and traveling right ahead, we might expect to reach Lake Quinaiult and a game country in ten or twelve days — sooner, if the road turned out better than it appeared; worse than it appeared, it could not be. All our slender stock of provision, our guns and ammunition, half a blanket each man, the camera and a few instruments — that was all we could take. Once near the lake, we had no doubt but that we could get plenty of game and fish. Our experience during the last 25 miles forbade us to expect any game before that. [Barnes]

Immediately to the left of the Quinault Canyon rose a cluster of giant pinnacles which the expedition named Mount Christie, in honor of their leader. These pinnacles formed in their midst "a great amphitheater in the clouds." To the right of the canyon stood the first and apparently highest peak of a range that "swept in a semicircle around to the westward."

The peaks of this range differed so much in height from the mountains of the other ranges which we had yet seen, and possessed such strong individuality, varying each from the other, that they formed the most striking and interesting sight we had seen in the Olympics.

The first peak on the right of the canyon of the Quinaiult we named provisionally "Mount Seattle" — provisionally, because we might yet find a greater one. From where we stood there did not appear to be a vestige of timber upon it. Pure white snow spread like a mantle from the double peak to the base. Its eastern and western sides seemed to slope gradually, but its northern was nearly up and down.[8]

Down the gap of the Quinaiult a second range appeared, and beyond it another range, crossing our proposed pathway like lions in the path. Beyond them, sky — thank heaven, there was an end to them. [Barnes]

But they could not indulge themselves to stand and gaze at the tangle of peaks and gorges that lay about them in all directions, for they had work to do. Already the sun was dipping low, and as the afternoon advanced the snow softened under the glare. How long the descent might take they did not know, but they were far from camp. They allowed themselves one hour to work, and "an hour never passed so quickly," Barnes declared. They could, he added, have "spent twelve with profit."

First they photographed the entire horizon, which here encompassed "a splendid panorama . . . mountains on every side." They needed data for Barnes's map of the mountains, and therefore took the bearings and altitudes of peaks and "the positions and courses of the canyons, valleys and streams." Quickly they made sketches and outlines which could be developed in detail later, and hastily examined the rock where they stood, "a needle-like mass of slate," the strata being inclined at an almost vertical angle.

Before descending, they named, in addition to Mount Christie and Mount Seattle, some of the surrounding peaks. Immediately to the westward, the Bailey Range blocked from their view what lay beyond, toward the Pacific.

In this range, due west of where we stood, rises to a considerable altitude above ourselves a grand old mountain clothed with snow, magnificent

[8] They were looking directly at the north face of Mount Seattle. Thus foreshortened, it appeared to be vertical.

in its proportions. It seemed one solid mass of rock and snow. It deserved a good name and we called it Mount Childs after George Washington Childs, the eminent philanthropist and proprietor of the Philadelphia Ledger.[9] [Barnes]

To the north stood the beautiful, pyramid-shaped peak they had previously named Mount Scott. Beyond it, still farther north, was Mount Squire — a spur of the Bailey Range known today as Ludden Peak — which they had observed from Deer Range and which Barnes had seen more clearly on his solo trip up Belle River in March.

As we were reaching for our snow shoes, Mr. Christie exclaimed: "See, a pansy!" Sure enough, upon the very summit, growing in a cleft of the rock six thousand feet above [sea] level, surrounded by oceans of snow, backed [basked] in the warm sunlight a little yellow flower. It was the first we had seen. We pulled it tenderly and took it with us, a souvenir of our visit. [Barnes]

When they started back toward camp, descending the steep slopes proved to be more perilous than climbing them.

The soft afternoon snow made dangerous work of that descent, where a little slip meant a plunge to the very bottom, unless the snow swallowed one up completely. But step by step, down the already nearly obliterated ladder of our former footsteps, we descended in safety to the saddle back. The sun was then setting, skirting the mountain side by a shorter route we arrived in camp soon after dark, hungry and tired. Pulling off our wet clothes and swaddling up in blankets, Indian fashion, we lighted our pipes, climbed down into the fire hole, in the snow and rested after the fatigues of the day. [Barnes]

As a result of the observations made the preceding day, the men spent April 30 preparing for the work ahead. Their situation was not exactly desperate, but the Olympic Mountains had obviously not finished testing their "grit and manly vim." The explorers could, of course, retrace their steps to Port Angeles — admitting failure — but they were in no mood to quit. They had come far, at immense labor, and had endured much hardship — too much to turn around and go back. The elusive goal now seemed almost

[9] See footnotes 3 and 5 of this chapter and footnote 1 of chapter X.

within their grasp. Therefore, like the Indians in the legends related by Eugene Semple, they held their own powwow high in the central Olympics and made their decision.

Christie determined that the packing should be as light as possible from their present position. Overhauling the provisions, he found only a few days' supplies left in camp. He therefore ordered that all blankets — with the exception of a single one for each man — be cached, together with all surplus clothing (very little), and otherwise reduced the packs as much as possible, "making a single pack for each member from this point." They simply could not carry one superfluous ounce. The gear to be taken was divided into five packs, and the remainder was cached in a tree.[10] Caching the discarded articles was apparently a precaution against the possibility that they might be forced to return via the route they had been traveling.

All that day, while they worked, they listened, at intervals, to the roaring of avalanches. With the advent of warm spring weather, the heavy snows burdening the mountains had become unstable. The slides were most common in the afternoons and evenings, when the snow was softest. Sometimes they averaged five or six in an hour, and they ended "only with the frost of night."

On their first night near the summit of this peak, deep in the central wilds of the Olympics — a peak that is still wilderness today, one of the mountains in the heart of Olympic National Park — their fire had burned through the base logs and reached the ground. The fire had gradually extended the hole until, on their last night at the camp, they were all able to sleep on bare ground.

The Press Exploring Expedition had been in the Olympic Mountains almost five months. Although the men did not know it, they were now approximately midway between the lower Elwha Canyon west of Port Angeles, where they had begun their wilderness journey, and Lake Quinault, where they hoped to emerge from the mountains. Nor could they possibly know how

[10] Vestiges of this cache might still be found by a lucky "explorer" today. This is a remote, seldom-visited area. The exact spot of the cache may not have known the tread of a man's foot since 1890.

long it might take them to travel the remaining distance to the lake — a distance as great as they had covered from early December to the end of April. They had taken five months to breach the mountains and reach the central divide. Once over that divide, however, their path would surely lead downhill and back to civilization. But it was an unknown path — a way that still held surprises.

Chapter X

MAY, 1890: HIGH COUNTRY

HOMEWARD *bound!*

With those two words foremost in their thoughts, the men of the Press Exploring Expedition broke camp at daylight on May 1, 1890, high on the mountainside above the headwaters of the Goldie. Their mood was one of unrestrained optimism, for, despite the hardships they had endured for months, their morale was good.

They divided the remaining supplies and equipment into five packs — weighing about seventy-five pounds each. These carried all their provisions — one hundred and twenty pounds of flour, three pounds of tea, and a half pound each of bacon and dried venison — plus their snowshoes, a single blanket for each man, three axes, three guns, ammunition, fishing tackle, some rope, and the scientific instruments of the expedition.

> Seventy-five pounds was a rather heavy pack for the work before us, but we had the satisfaction of knowing that its weight would diminish every day as we consumed the provisions, and of believing that, as we descended the Quinaiult, the traveling would improve with every mile. The first day or two would be the worst. With the heavy packs we must climb the side of the mountain ahead to reach the division between the water sheds. But the magic phrase "homeward bound" made a trifle of the burden and a molehill of the mountain. [Barnes]

They left camp at 9:00 A.M., their feet clad in moccasins and snowshoes, and began a gradual ascent of the mountainside. It was destined to be one of their most strenuous days, with "some of the toughest kind of mountain climbing." After two hours' travel, interrupted frequently for short rest periods, they reached the saddleback connecting with the high peak to the south. Thirty minutes later they had reached the place where Christie and Barnes ascended on April 29 to make observations. This time, however, the party carefully traversed around the west face of the mountain, avoiding the steeper slope. Still the going was difficult, for their packs forced them deep into the soft snow. Part of the time, however, they were able to use snowshoes, which permitted faster travel; but on steep terrain they had to struggle along in moccasins. Finally, on a little bench, they stopped, made tea, and divided their "last remaining half pound of venison."

> All day long we passed steep inclines, bare of timber and heavy with snow. In two places avalanches had taken place, and we were in constant fear lest the jar of our weight would start others. For this reason we kept, as a rule, far apart, in order to bring as little weight as possible on any one point. The snow was soft and melting; little pieces started by our feet would go rolling or sliding sometimes thousands of feet, becoming great masses before reaching the bottom. We had to check the dogs from running above us on the slope, for even the small pieces of snow detached by them would often become dangerous by accretion by the time they reached us a little way below. [Barnes]

Late in the afternoon they arrived at a point midway along the western slope of the peak. A rock, bare on its outward face, projected through deep snow on the mountainside below. As the men looked over the edge, they saw several small shelves or benches. Weary of the snow, they elected to utilize these warm, dry shelves for their camp. They were now at timberline, and the few treetops that poked through the snow were stunted and gnarled. The men had seen no moss since leaving Goldie River, but here lichens covered the trees and rocks.

> Upon one shelf we made the fire. Upon the ends of the shelf, and upon the shelves above and below, each man selected his berth, and made himself as comfortable as he could.
>
> The view from this rock was magnificent. Mount Seattle and Mount Childs were both in view. As the sun went down it flooded the mountains with a rosy glow, transforming this cold white drapery into soft garments of a warmer hue. This was again succeeded by white, then gray, until at length night obscured the view. [Barnes]

An original Press Exploring Expedition photograph, captioned "Side of Mountain, May 1st" (1890). Slope at upper left has angle of 40°; eases to about 35° at lower right. Last man is carrying a bucket; man ahead appears to be using his gun for an alpenstock (Courtesy Robert Hitchman)

They named their lodging spot Side Rock Camp. Neither comfortable nor safe, it offered the only possible relief from the steep, snow-covered slope. No one slept much, for all were made restless by the apprehension of falling off the mountain.

> My berth was not so very bad. I laid several good sized sticks from one jutting piece of rock to another, including one to keep me from rolling over. I could look down through the "slats" of my bed hundreds of feet below. Sims and Hayes sat up all night, not trusting themselves to sleep in their hazardous resting places. After the exhausting work of yesterday, the loss of sleep was unfortunate, but there was no help for it. [Barnes]

Strenuous as the day had been, the men were destined to be fatigued still more the following day. After a scanty breakfast of beans, they strapped on snowshoes and were on their way at dawn, scarcely pausing long enough to admire the alpenglow on the peaks. Because the snow was in "first-class condition," they moved rapidly across the shoulder of the mountain. At first their route led up the mountainside, which had a gradual slope in some places, but in others was very steep. On rounding a low spur, they found the divide only two miles distant, "but ravines necessitated a good six miles of tough travel to reach." Several hours later, suffering from near exhaustion, the men reached the apparent divide or watershed. "It was an interesting moment to us," Barnes declared. "We had no doubt that we would now have a down-hill pull for home."

They were standing upon the crest of a long, narrow ridge connecting the peak they had just skirted with Mount Childs.[1] Al-

[1] It is impossible to determine exactly which peaks the Press Exploring Expedition meant to bear the names Mount Childs and Mount Barnes. There are four high peaks in the immediate area, any two of which could have been these.

For the purpose of clarification in this footnote, these four summits will be referred to as peaks A, B, C, and D. Peak A, known today as Mount Wilder, is the easternmost of the four; Peak B, presently unnamed, is located about one mile southeast of Peak C, known today as Mount Barnes; Peak D, unnamed, is located in the Bailey Range about one mile NNE. of Bear Pass.

If the men were accurate in stating that Mount Childs was "due west" of the "table-top" from which they made observations on April 29, this would indicate that they were referring either to peak B or C; if so, then the expe-

though it was obviously a watershed, something was wrong, and the men were puzzled. Far below them lay a serene and peaceful valley, clad with luxuriant evergreen forests, stretching at right angles across their line of travel. Since it could not be the Quinault, the men wondered what river flowed there. As they stood, the fear crept into their minds that they might be looking at the Elwha.

Throwing their packs to the ground, they scattered in search of high points from where they could, Christie said, "gain a glimpse

---

dition gave the name Mount Barnes to Peak A (the mountain they were climbing on) or to Peak B. This conclusion is bolstered by Christie's diary entries for April 30, May 2, and May 3, all of which are headed "Mt. Barnes." Also Barnes's statement that they had reached "a long, narrow ridge connecting the mountain . . . just skirted [i.e., Peak A or Mount Wilder] with Mt. Childs" indicates, again, that Mount Childs was Peak B.

It must be admitted, however, that the etching of Mount Barnes appearing in the official story of the expedition, which was made from an expedition photograph, greatly resembles Peak C. The evidence is not conclusive, however, that Peak C was, in fact, the one photographed, because Peak A has a similar configuration.

The statement about Mount Childs being due west of the table-top is not necessarily accurate, for the men had made errors previously in regard to directions; i.e., they indicated Belle River as entering the Elwha from the southwest when, in fact, it flows directly from the south. Nor is Barnes's map conclusive, for it lacks the accuracy needed to determine this close question.

If Peak C was the mountain they intended to bear the name Mount Barnes, then Mount Childs undoubtedly must have been Peak D. However, this summit is considerably off the expedition's route. It is also possible that Peak C was their Mount Childs and Peak B was their Mount Barnes. Still further confusing the matter is the possibility that they considered peaks B and C as one mountain and gave to them one name.

Unfortunately, Barnes's map cannot be used for confirmation, for he was not consistent in placing the names of peaks either to the right or left of the cartographic indication of a summit. The name Mount Barnes lies between two peak designations, and thus it is impossible to determine which summit he was labeling. If he meant the one to the right – directly opposite Buckinghorse Creek – then the Press Party's Mount Barnes was undoubtedly Peak A. On the other hand, if he meant the peak shown to the left of the name, it was a minor spur of Peak A, or merely Deception Divide, the point at which the expedition had now arrived.

The preponderance of the evidence indicates, however, that the Press Party's Mount Barnes was Peak A and that Peak B (or B and C considered as one) was their Mount Childs.

of the water flowing two thousand feet below." The field glasses were brought to their aid, and they were "rather surprised to find the river running north instead of to the south, a disagreeable discovery which gave rise to sundry hard expressions not usually found in Webster, but quite excusable under the circumstances." Christie and Barnes climbed a knoll two hundred yards up the ridge in order to get a better view.

> On our arrival there we saw at once what we had done. At our feet lay the beautiful Press valley, broader and larger than where we left it at the mouth of the Goldie. This old friend and the still older friend, the Elwha river, we still had with us. But we felt toward them more like an enemy than a friend at this moment. Nevertheless it presented a pleasant contrast to the canyons we have of late been traveling through. It swept around the base of Mount Dana and ended at our feet, having an apparent width of two or three miles. In shape the valley is a crescent. We had left it at one horn, traveled over 20 miles of the roughest country and through the most rugged canyon in the mountains, and have experienced 12 days of the hardest work of the trip, only to find ourselves at the other horn of this crescent-shaped valley. We might have made the journey on snowshoes in a couple of days' easy traveling. [Barnes]

The men took this bitter, frustrating revelation well, considering the circumstances, just as they had accepted other disappointments on the journey.

> Such is the fate of explorers. We are here to find these things out. Still we felt a little mad and may have on this occasion expressed it. The gap we have been taking for the Quinaiult is on the opposite side of the valley near the head. It still looked like the Quinaiult, that was one consolation. [Barnes]

They could do nothing but return to the depths of Press Valley, then climb up the other side. But first they ate a frugal lunch, rested for a few minutes, and checked their aneroid, which indicated that they were at an altitude of sixty-two hundred feet. The instrument was in error, however, for they were actually nearer five thousand. They called the ridge Deception Divide, then started down into the valley at precisely noon.

> The descent was very steep. We plunged down in our "moccasined" feet through the soft deep snow and while the slope remained nearly up and

down we made rapid progress. . . . Then as the mountain gradually became less precipitous it became heavier work in the snow where gravity had less to do with pulling us out. We shaped our course down a ravine. . . . Then the snow in the ravine began to get hollow underneath and the water running below us became unpleasantly evident. So we climbed out of the ravine and found a mountain side bare of snow, most delightful after a couple of weeks in the deep snow, but much harder to descend upon. [Barnes]

They spent four hours descending the steep, pathless mountainside. When they reached the bottomlands along the river, they again checked the aneroid, which indicated their elevation as twenty-four hundred feet.[2] On the valley floor the snow was five feet deep beneath the trees. The men selected a favorable place beside the Elwha, shoveled a space clear, and made their camp on bare ground. The following day they rested.

We are all completely tuckered out by the experience of late, and particularly of the last few days. We are much in need of meat. Our sole food for the last few days has been flour soup. To make flour soup for five men one pound and a half of flour is added to three gallons of boiling water and well stirred. This is flour soup. It is not much of a dish for an epicure, nor is it found on the bill of fare at Delmonico, but it is very

[2] Apparently the aneroid was now functioning better. Actual elevation at this point was about twenty-two hundred feet. Thus, in descending they had lost elevation at the rate of about seven hundred feet an hour.

Even today aneroid barometers are unreliable as a means of measuring land elevation, unless the observations of a single point can be made over a long period. Not only does the air pressure measured by the aneroid decrease with increasing elevation, but the rate of decrease is also variable and depends upon the density of the air, which changes daily in response to pressure and temperature. On any given day, the density may differ as much as 20 per cent. This is unusual, but a 5 per cent differential is frequently encountered, and 2 per cent is quite normal.

In addition, the pressure at the base of a mountain or some fixed point also varies daily; therefore, a "fixed" base does not exist as a starting point. This, however, can be compensated for by adjusting the aneroid before moving to a new location. If some time elapses in moving, however, the base pressure may have changed, therefore the need for continuous observation over a period of time in order to insure reasonable accuracy.

The possibility that the aneroid may be defective — especially if it has been carried over rugged terrain for a long period of time — also militates against its use. If the instrument has been dropped, or goes a long period without standardization, it will probably register erroneous figures.

filling, and in the absence of anything else and with a good appetite is positively good. [Barnes]

They were indeed in a precarious position now, deep within the Olympics and completely isolated from contact with the outside world. In the afternoon, while Christie searched upstream for a "practicable trail" toward the summit of the divide, five miles distant, Hayes went hunting, hopeful of shooting something for dinner.

> He returned empty-handed, but said he saw rabbit tracks in the snow, and that he was going to polish up a club and try to get some of the tracks for supper if he couldn't get anything else.
>
> Hayes is a good hunter, but sometimes he makes a mistake. He came in breathless a few days ago, and said he had seen bear tracks just outside of camp. It was a little rough on Mr. Christie's feet, but investigation showed that they were made by his new moccasins. [Barnes]

The skies were clear on the fourth of May, and the day was warm. Following their established custom, the men broke camp early and headed up the valley on snowshoes. Their destination was the canyon bounded by Mount Seattle on the west and Mount Christie — "the amphitheatre shaped mountains" — on the east. This canyon ran to the southward and would, they believed, lead them to Lake Quinault. But they faced a steep climb en route to the divide.

The men "headed directly for the foot of the declivity," first crossing a branch of the Elwha that came in from the northwest.[3] This branch — which is considered today as being the main stem of the river — contained about one third of the water. Now the river became small — little more than a creek — and was mostly covered or bridged by deep snow. At the foot of the cliffs barring their way, the stream again divided,[4] "the main part pouring over rocks from above and forming beautiful falls about 50 feet high." These they called Elizabeth Falls. Here, at the base of Mount Christie, the men replaced their moccasins and snowshoes with

[3] Elwha Basin.

[4] The east branch is known today as Delabarre Creek and the west is an unnamed creek descending from Martin's Park on the northern slopes of Mount Christie.

boots because they would be forced to kick steps in the snow as they began once again to climb toward the elusive, long-sought divide.

For some distance their route followed the pathway of a recent avalanche. Though the slope was steep, the climbing was easy, for the snow was smooth and firm, and by noon they had ascended eleven hundred feet; "but from this point upwards the ascent was broken and consisted of bare ledges of rock for 600 feet."

Above the Goldie, the expedition had been forced to climb steep snow; now it was rock. The men paused briefly for lunch, then attacked the ledges, which were "very hard climbing," and arrived "at the foot of what appeared an impassable ledge of rock." After a little exploration, however, Christie discovered a route that looked climbable. He gradually worked his way upward fifty feet, then lowered a hand line to raise the packs and assist the others.

> At extreme hazard one of us, generally Mr. Christie, would climb slowly up to some jutting splinter of rock or stunted tree whose roots had a firm hold in the crevices, and then throw down a line. One by one and from one niche or shelf to another we gradually scaled the face of the rocks, some time hand over hand, and at others by means of a loop around the body, each man worked up after the leader. Our baggage we hauled up in the same manner. As for the dogs we would tie the rope around their necks and pull them up. Fortunately the rock work was free of snow. It was not pleasant to trust one's entire weight to a cod line, and when we reached the top we were all quite exhausted, more from the expenditure of nervous force than by physical. [Barnes]

According to their aneroid they had climbed seventeen hundred feet above the valley floor when they reached the top of the cliff at five o'clock. During the ascent the operation of using the hand line in scaling the rock ledges "was repeated some five times in all, as . . . the summit was only to be reached by rope in this manner." By sundown, however, they were safely above the rock face, and Christie felt relieved. Settling down for the night right there — for they felt disinclined to go further at the moment — they called the spot Bluff Top Camp.

All hands present for supper (flour soup), after a rather dangerous afternoon's work. Whilst the party prepared camp on a small ledge, I went ahead to assure myself that we are at last upon the Quinaiult. This I found as I had fondly hoped, returned and made the boys happy by the news, "Homeward bound again." [Christie]

Fortunately, the weather remained clear and warm. The next morning — the fifth of May — the men left before sunrise, once again wearing their snowshoes. "The water still flowed toward the Elwha, but it was a little brook plunging over the precipice. The canyon between the two mountains was buried in snow, even trees, if there be any at all, were covered."

For a half mile they walked on hard-packed snow, which provided "the first really good travel of the trip," then came upon a little lake about four hundred yards in diameter. Its waters were frozen and snow-covered, but at the lake's outlet the ice and snow had melted, affording them a glimpse of the waters as they passed by. They called it Lake Mary, and crossed the ice to the southern shore, from where "rose a little swell of ground, not 50 feet in height." From the top of this knoll, they looked down the other side, "and there lay another little lake." The swell, which formed a complete barrier between the two lakes, was "evidently the divide, or height of land."[5]

The Press Exploring Expedition had finally, after many long months, reached the central divide of the Olympic Mountains, the watershed — now known as Low Divide — that separates the headwaters of northward and southward flowing streams. The men paused but momentarily, however, with the somewhat anticlimactic feeling that they had "attained the object of the expedition," and could now say "homeward bound" in earnest. They had long since given up hope of finding the "great discoveries in store for some of Washington's explorers."

They crossed the ice of the second lake, which they christened Lake Margaret, and continued down the canyon. Below the lake

[5] Both lakes drain to the Elwha and the high point of the divide is just west of the second lake, the larger of the two. Evidently the deep snow covering the terrain deceived the explorers.

An original expedition photograph, caption "On the divide" — apparently Low Divide
(Courtesy Robert Hitchman)

the defile widened to about three hundred feet, its sides sloping gradually, "with a broad sweeping curve up the mountains."

There was no obstacle to their progress, for the deep snow covered everything. About six o'clock in the morning, after traveling for an hour, they came to a great rock "shaped like a vast cathedral, with spires and entrances." It stood on the right-hand side of the canyon, and through a hole in the snow at this point they caught their first sight of water running south. "As we stood looking at it, after having tasted its virtues — and it seemed to taste better than the Elwha — one of the dogs began to give tongue in a clump of trees about 300 yards down the canyon. The other two dogs were away like a shot."

"A bear!" one of the men cried, and at that moment a black bear, harassed by the three dogs, emerged from the clump of trees. The men seized their guns and started in chase. Barnes dropped his gun, and took instead the camera, but by the time he had removed the instrument from its case the others had covered half the intervening distance, and he was forced to "travel pretty hard" to get there before the finish.

> The bear was fighting the dogs, sometimes sitting back on his haunches and snapping at them and trying to reach them with his paws. Then one of the dogs would nip him behind and he would be off again. No sooner would he be off a few steps than one of the dogs would nip his heels, and that would bring him up all-standing once more, and the fighting and snapping would recommence. Meanwhile, the bear and dogs were nearing a little clump of trees, and to this we all hurried. I got three exposures while hastening toward them. [Barnes]

Barnes was afraid that they would shoot the bear before he got there. The men were fearful of hitting the dogs, however, and he arrived in time to obtain "several good negatives." Cornered as he was, the bear "made several rushes before concluding to give up the argument," and one of these was in Barnes's direction. The captain chose to "retire very quickly behind a tree," for he was not armed, he protested, "in precisely the right manner to cope with his bearship." Finally, however, Christie delivered the *coup de grâce* with a shot through the kidneys, and the bear "laid down and gave it up." Another bullet through the head ended his suffering.

> After it was all over we could hardly believe our luck. Here was fat! It is impossible to convey an idea of the craving we had for fat at this time. After having lived on plain flour for a week and little besides flour for several weeks, and before that, plenty of meat, but not an atom of fat, except a little dole from our precious bacon, for months, the prospects of grease seemed a delirious dream. It was not 15 minutes before we had that bear skinned and dressed and his liver and slabs of fat frying over a fire. No food ever tasted so good to starving men as that fat tasted to us, for we were indeed starving for fat. So we sat around the fire and kept the frying pans going and drank the grease as fast as we could fry it out. [Barnes]

Christie decided to adopt the Indian custom of camping by the kill, and they were soon established by the little southward flowing stream which had brought good fortune. The killing of the bear made a drastic change in their plans. Now that they had meat, the compelling urgency to hurry out of the mountains was alleviated, and they could take time to explore the surrounding country. As soon as they decided to remain several days at Bear Camp, Barnes began at once to make preparations to ascend Mount Seattle.[6] He took "the camera, instruments for topographical purposes, a blanket and meat enough for two days."

Snow-covered from base to summit, Mount Seattle towered immediately northwest of the lakes Mary and Margaret. Early in the morning on May 5, Barnes skirted northward along the eastern base of the peak for a half mile, until he came to a "practicable canyon." Then, removing his snowshoes, he commenced to climb in bare moccasins.

> The ascent was easy for about four hundred feet. After that I had to zig-zag up the steep slope, which generally had an angle of 55 or 60 degrees. The snow was extremely soft and yielding so I sank to my knees at every step, and sometimes sank bodily to my waist, and then had to struggle to extricate myself. As I got higher and could look down the long slope of a thousand feet or more at such an angle it was calculated to make a man proceed slowly and with caution — slowly, however, he had to. [Barnes]

[6] Christie's journal states that the captain ascended Mount Barnes, but this is obviously an error.

By late afternoon he had climbed two thousand feet above the mountain's base — or to a point sixty-three hundred feet above sea level, according to his aneroid — and he was greatly fatigued. He decided to camp for the evening and continue early the next morning to the summit "a thousand or more feet above." He had reached the back side of a ridge, and upon looking over the southern face was "gratified to find it an almost perpendicular rock wall with little shelves upon which grew stunted mountain pine, entirely free of snow and exposed to the warm sunshine." He chose a suitable camping place — a bench three or four feet wide, about four feet below the ridge crest. Upon its margin grew several of the little pines, which branched inward, to form "as cosy and snug a nook as can be imagined."

> My feet were wet and cold with the snow and the hot afternoon sun pouring upon my head for hours made me welcome the good fortune. Dropping into it and breaking from the pines a few dead branches I had a fire going in a very few minutes. I put dry duffles on my feet and soon had meat frying and tea brewing, and was as comfortable as in a drawing room. I spent the remainder of the afternoon and evening frying meat. [Barnes]

Barnes was up with the first streak of light the next morning, quickly made a fire, prepared and ate his breakfast, and was on his way toward the summit.

> The snow was a little harder by the frost of the night than it had been in the afternoon before, and although the upper ascent was the most abrupt I had less difficulty in getting along. It was a ticklish thing though to plow along the face of a soft and yielding snow bank, which has its base half a mile below. I was glad when I approached the summit — or rather a kind of thin ridge or saddle, which connected two sharp unscalable spires of rock, which constituted the actual double summit of the mountain. As I approached this saddle the question of what was on the other side became of absorbing interest. This range, together with the Bailey range, divided the Olympic mountain region into two parts. Their height had shut off from us the view of anything beyond, so that the western portion was a *terra incognito* [sic]. Therefore at this height I anticipated a glorious view unless a range provokingly near shut me off beyond. A final step brought my head above the sharp wedge like saddle and the curtain rose from before the unknown region.
> The rising sun at my back swept over mountain ranges as far as the eye

could reach and the view was all that I could have hoped for. At a distance of about two miles extending north and south was a range of mountains lower than the one upon which I stood. It was a range of solid rock nearly naked of soil and vegetation. The sides were so steep and precipitous that even snow could scarcely lodge, and it lay piled in sweeping curves from the base far up toward the summit. [Barnes]

Nor was this all. Over the top of this range he could see to the northwest a higher chain of ice-clad peaks — known today as the Mount Olympus Range — dominated by "a notable mountain of a peculiar gothic-like appearance." He was actually observing Mount Olympus, but Barnes failed to recognize this because the expedition had previously mistaken another mountain for Olympus. Therefore he named the gothic-like summit Mount Bennett, after James Gordon Bennett of the New York *Herald*.

> Over the first range due west could be seen a large and beautiful valley,[7] sweeping the base of a superb range of mountains beyond. . . . Toward the southwest were low hills, evidently the lake country. These wooded hills of low, rounded form were in sharp contrast with the lofty snow-clad ranges of broken rock, which came down from the north. [Barnes]

But the vista to the north most held his attention. There he could see the western side of the Bailey Range, which swept northward and westward until it culminated in the great peak believed to be Olympus.[8] Beyond this mountain, the range continued to the westward as far as Barnes had an unobstructed view. He also saw the valley of what he thought was the Quillayute paralleling the southern base of the range, with the head of the watershed lying almost at his feet. This was actually the upper Hoh Canyon. In 1890, however, the Hoh River was virtually unknown, and Barnes understandably confused it with the Quillayute.[9] The three ranges of mountains lying west of his vantage point each extended from

[7] Queets Valley.

[8] See footnote 4 of chapter IV.

[9] Two early maps of the western portion of Washington Territory, however, show the Hoh as being distinct from the Quillayute. On James G. Swan's map, illustrating his book, *The Northwest Coast* (1857), the river is labeled the Hooch; on an 1874 map, the Ohalaats.

Mount Seattle as photographed by Asahel Curtis, Aug. 1, 1907
(Courtesy Washington State Historical Society)

Mount Seattle from the
north (Courtesy Wash-
ington State Historical
Society)

the "Quillayute" [i.e., Hoh] on his right to the "large and beautiful valley" [Queets] on his left.

When he turned to the east, Barnes found the view more familiar. "Comparing the mountains on the east and west sides," he wrote, "those on the west are arranged with more order, less confusion, and possess more greatness and sublimity than those on the east."

> The sight of Olympus [Carrie] was particularly interesting, inasmuch as it was the first time that it had been seen since we left Deer range north of Geyser valley, so completely is it hidden by other peaks. Constance and The Brothers were also in plain view to the eastward.[10] [Barnes]

After admiring the spectacular vista, Barnes made a number of exposures with the camera. Then he spread out his chart, using his blanket upon the snow for a plane table, and worked for several hours. As the day progressed, the heat from the sun became very intense, and finally unendurable. In order to escape the pronounced glare on the summit, he descended from the mountaintop at about one o'clock and returned to his "little camp under the scrub pines."

The next morning Barnes was again up at daybreak. He returned to the summit and finished his work in a couple of hours. While he remained there he was "nearly frozen," for the weather had changed considerably from the preceding day. The wind was

---

[10] Here again Barnes was in error. What he took to be The Brothers — the most conspicuous peak of the Olympic Mountains when viewed from Puget Sound — was actually another mountain further inland. A few months later Lieutenant O'Neil named it Mount Anderson, after Colonel T. M. Anderson of the Fourteenth Infantry. Barnes's error stemmed from the Press Party's belief that they were crossing the Olympics closer to Hood Canal than they actually were.

Barnes obviously mistook Mount Anderson for The Brothers, but it is not clear which peak he believed to be Mount Constance. He may have been looking at Deception, Mystery, or Wellesley. Lieutenant O'Neil later concluded he confused Mount Claywood for Constance. Detailed analysis of Barnes's map, however, leads one to conclude that he probably did, in fact, observe Mount Constance. The map was primarily based on observations taken from Mount Seattle. A line drawn on this map from the summit of Mount Seattle and passing through Mount Egan (known as Mount Norton today) points directly to Barnes's "Constance"; a line similarly drawn on today's highly accurate United States Geological Survey maps does the same.

blowing strong from the southwest, and he found it necessary to ballast everything with rocks. A forerunner of worsening weather, this change indicated that clouds and rain would replace the sunny skies that had prevailed while the expedition climbed over the roughest part of the mountains.

On the western side of Mount Seattle's summit, the wind had blown away the snow, revealing the rock formation. The slate was tilted straight up and down, a pattern of vertical stratification that had characterized almost all the slate the expedition had observed. At the top, the slate "terminated in a sharp, jagged edge." Between this edge and the deep snow covering the remainder of the summit grew a few stunted pines, about two feet tall, "leaning toward the eastward as blown by the wind."

While Barnes was on the summit, the average reading of his aneroid indicated an altitude of seventy-six hundred feet at the saddle between the two spires, the southern of which he estimated to be one hundred feet higher, "making the height of Mount Seattle 7700 feet." Apparently the aneroid was again not functioning properly, for the actual elevation of the peak is 6,246 feet. The aneroid also indicated Bear Camp, on Low Divide, to be at forty-three hundred feet, or about one thousand feet too high.

When he had completed his work, Barnes began to descend the mountain and reached Bear Camp "after about three hours of heavy travel, tumble and slide." During his absence the men had killed another black bear,[11] and both skins were stretched upon frames, drying, in readiness for the projected start down the Quinault the next morning.

The men had eaten all of the first bear, killed three days before, except for part of a ham. Barnes felt that he could not say much, for he had taken fifteen pounds on his trip up Mount Seattle, and had eaten it all. Nothing, in fact, tasted so good to the men as bear's meat fried in fat, and they needed no encouragement to sit around the fire all day, frying pans in hand.

[11] Christie's journal entry for that day, May 7, states: "Capt. Barnes returned to camp this evening with the scalp of a fine full-grown bear, killed on his trip to the summit." Barnes says nothing in his narrative about this, another example of the discrepancy between the stories of the two men.

We don't often change our bill of fare, but when we do it is radical. Flour last week, meat this. We have old bruin in every style, roast, boiled and fried. His sides thick with fat we rolled up and boiled and ate cold. One of his hams roasted would tempt the most pampered appetite. In vain we courted indigestion with the frying pan. Soup consumed a great amount. The choice tid bits are the tail and the feet, which as Jack Crumback said beat "three of a kind." But the fat is the most highly prized in camp. It is the bears grease of commerce, pure white, the consistency of butter. Add a little salt and it has the taste of the purest dairy article, together with an indescribable flavor peculiarly its own.

The first bear was consumed in three days, and a pretty good sized bear he was. Then all hands began to look fat and sleek, and before the second bear was all gone it would never be suspected that only a few days ago the party was on a diet of flour and salt, and a precious small allowance of flour at that. [Barnes]

Bear Camp was apparently well named. Barnes had scarcely had time to relax after his return from Mount Seattle when Hayes came running into camp, breathless, crying "A bear! A bear!" The men grabbed their guns, gathered the dogs together, and soon were hurrying across the snow. They could see the bear up the canyon on the snow. Concealed by a little clump of timber, men and dogs hurried toward the animal, passed through the trees, and were several yards beyond before the bear caught sight of them.

We then instantly loosed the dogs and the race that ensued between the bear and the dogs was prettier than any steeplechase or handicap in the world. The bear had about 100 yards the start. He headed up the canyon toward a part of the hillside which was heavily timbered, the dogs hot after him. The bear was a large one and heavy and made poor work floundering through the soft snow, so that when he disappeared in the timber the dogs were close upon him. [Barnes]

Within moments the barking of the dogs indicated that they had cornered their prey. In the race among themselves to overtake the bear, Barnes and Crumback — being lighter than the other men and therefore sinking less in the snow — won in a tie.

There was bruin up a tree and the dogs barking at the foot. Crumback and I fired simultaneously. The bear instantly dropped into the hole in the snow at the foot of the tree. The dogs tumbled in after him pell mell. We had to pull the dogs out first before we found out that old bruin was stone dead. [Barnes]

The black bear was larger than the first one killed, its fur slightly tinged with gray. Examination of the carcass revealed that Barnes's shot had entered the brain below the ear, while Crumback's had passed through the heart and ranged upward until it lodged in the spine. Thus three vital points had been hit, which explained why the animal had dropped from the tree the moment the rifles were fired.

The men dragged the bear into camp, where they skinned and dressed it; and Christie deferred for another day moving to a new campsite.

The brief interval between Barnes's return from the summit of the mountain and Hayes's cry of "bear" had allowed little time for conversation, but after the camp quieted down one of the men asked Barnes if he had any tobacco. "Yes, a little," the Captain replied, incautiously, and produced a piece about the size of his thumb. "It proved to be the last small smoke. For the time being all other business was postponed that there might be no interruption to the last indulgence."

Clouds from the sea rolled over the mountaintops during the night, a development of the changing weather pattern which Barnes had noted while on the summit ridge of Mount Seattle. The sunny skies that had prevailed for some time disappeared, and the next day was rainy and foggy. The men spent the morning hours tanning the bear skins. The mountain pass where they were encamped afforded scant shelter from the elements, and that night the men were rather uncomfortable because of rain. At noon the next day, May 9, "the bear skin was pronounced dry, and a move was ordered." Because their facilities for packing were limited, they took only the best of the three skins. Their pack also included ten pounds of grease and as much meat as they could conveniently carry.

The Press Exploring Expedition had been on the Olympic Peninsula five months, and while the men had endured considerable hardship, they retained the optimism that had characterized their journey. Fortunately, the weather had been good for several weeks, clear skies and warm temperatures prevailing when the explorers climbed above the Goldie and over Low Divide. Thus, they were able to view the terrain that lay across their path and determine the most feasible route to the watershed of the Quinault. Had the steep-walled gorges been filled with fog — as they often are — or the mountainsides swept by rain clouds during this part of the trip, determination of the route would have been more difficult. And when they reached the divide and stood at last upon soil drained by the Quinault, the bears were dehibernating. The meat and fat obtained from the three animals they killed at Low Divide saved the undernourished men from starvation following weeks of inadequate diet.

Winter was past. Now, in the late spring, they were about to embark on the final stages of the exploration. If their luck held a few more days, they should presently emerge from the mountains and return to civilization. Tired of the struggle, they were eager for that moment.

Chapter XI

MAY, 1890: THE QUINAULT

EXACTLY five months from the day the men first set foot on the Olympic Peninsula, the Press Exploring Expedition left Bear Camp and headed down the Quinault Canyon. The men started out on snowshoes, and for a mile the travel continued to be easy, "the gulch being under snow from side to side, and the stream completely bridged." Then the Quinault emerged from its covering of snow, and they were forced to keep to the benches, climbing occasionally, "but for the most part sliding down hill," an agreeable change in their mode of travel. The mountainside, however, was steep and rough, broken by landslides and obstructed by timber and dense undergrowth. For the better part of the day the men traversed sidehills, "shinning old logs or scrambling across rocks, which was hard on both back and knees." It was difficult going, but they saw "some wonderful canyons and hard looking water." The Quinault River, Christie noted tersely, seemed to be but "one continuous long water fall."

After traveling steadily for four hours, the men completed the traverse of the mountainside and came to the confluence of the Quinault and a large tributary flowing from the west. They called this branch the Sims River, in honor of John Sims, but its present-day name is Promise Creek.

They made camp late, after descending eleven hundred feet in three miles. In a little bottom, opposite where Sims River joined the Quinault, they built a fire and spread their blankets. Here the

177

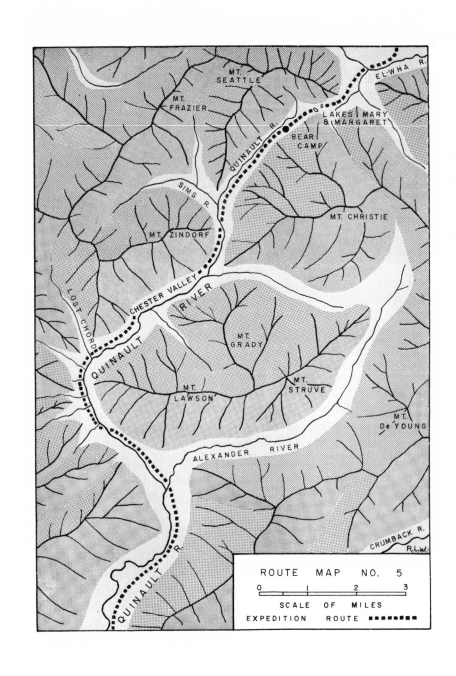

ROUTE MAP NO. 5

0   1   2   3
SCALE OF MILES
EXPEDITION ROUTE ▪▪▪▪▪▪▪

snow was eight feet deep, but they hoped that by traveling steadily all the next day they would "reach a country with at least occasional spots of bare ground."

The next day was cloudy and cool, and "packs were slung bright and early," as the expedition headed once again down the Quinault. The men followed the left bank of the river and frequently had to climb over rocky spurs in order to pass from one little patch of bottomland into another.

The addition of Sims River had practically doubled the Quinault, which now attained the proportions of a respectable river. In addition, nearly every hundred yards or so a tributary — swollen by the melting snows above — added its contribution to the river, further increasing the volume. A mile below the previous night's campsite, the left bank of the river became impassable, and the men were faced with the problem of crossing the forty-yard expanse of water. They felled a large maple thirty inches in diameter for a bridge, but it failed to reach the opposite bank. From the farther end of this "tree bridge," Christie forded the remaining distance, then chopped down a tree on the far bank. It completed the bridge, and the other members of the expedition crossed the river without getting wet.

The expedition had lost considerable elevation since leaving Bear Camp and was now less than two thousand feet above sea level. Consequently, a few spots were bare of snow, and the men "ran upon an old friend once more, an elk trail," which they followed along the mountainside — sometimes ascending, sometimes descending — over country as rough as they had yet experienced.

Presently we found that the trail was blazed like that upon the other side, but the blazes were very old, like those upon the Elwha. We were immediately pleased by this discovery, for it is the broad road to civilization again. Following this old trail we found that it differed in several respects from that on the Elwha. While the blazes themselves do not appear to be older they are invariably on older trees. We saw no blaze on any tree of less diameter than three feet. Fully half of the blazed trees are dead and broken off, say from 10 to 15 feet from the ground. These old yellow stumps, decayed and devoid of bark, are so numerous that they make a long line through the woods, which can be seen for some distance, marking the trail of the old Indian. [Barnes]

On the Elwha the marks that the men had taken to be Indian blazes had apparently been made on the trees when they were saplings. Here they were on mature trees. Barnes theorized that the "difference in the manner of blazing" might indicate that the marks were made by different tribes, and although the blazes in the two valleys converged near the "height of land" from opposite sides of the mountains, they perhaps did not constitute a thoroughfare. More likely, he thought, they were the respective hunting trails of the tribes living along the lower reaches of the Elwha and Quinault rivers.

Barnes speculated further that if one accepted ex-Governor Semple's story of an annual powwow, the two trails — which differed greatly in their characteristics — would lend credibility to the theory that two or more tribes with unlike customs did meet in the central part of the mountains. On the divide itself — and for some distance on each side — the expedition had failed to observe any trail. Barnes explained this lack by pointing out that the ground at this time was covered with from six to fifty feet of snow. He felt that, given time to search, the explorers would have found an easier way than scaling the rock to ascend from Press Valley to the watershed of the Quinault — and that if this better route had been free of snow, they would have found the Indian blazes.

That day the expedition covered a distance "of five or six miles as the trail went, but not more than two miles of air line travel." Most of the day they traveled opposite a great slide which extended for a mile along the other side of the river. The peak whose sides were scarred by the slide was "shaped like an old feudal castle, with battlements and towers crowned with snow." They called it Mount Grady,[1] after the late Henry W. Grady of the Atlanta *Constitution.*

The trail at last brought them back to the Quinault. There, in the midst of a pile of driftwood on the river bank, they found an excellent camping place, bare of snow.

[1] The Press Expedition's Mount Grady is now called Mount Lawson. The party gave the name Mount Lawson to another peak about two miles to the southwest. In later years the terminology apparently became confused, like many of the names, with the application of the name to a different peak than the expedition intended.

In leaving the Elwha and crossing over Low Divide to the Quinault watershed, the expedition had passed from the leeward to the windward side of the Olympic Mountains, and the difference in the appearance of the country was not lost on the men. "There seems to be much greater moisture here than on the other side of the range," Barnes noted; "the vegetation is ranker and the undergrowth denser."

On Sunday, May 11, they continued down the valley, starting "with the liveliest anticipations of getting out of the worst of the mountains and into better country for traveling." But it turned out to be one of their most dangerous days, involving long hours of arduous, difficult scrambling over wet, sodden canyon sides.

> Below camp the river entered a deep and gloomy gorge. Scrambling up the steep side of Mount Zindorf, as we named this mountain, we followed the mountain side to the southward. The underbrush became gradually more rank. The mountainside also became more moist and wet. The ground was sodden, water oozed up by the pressure of every footstep. In addition to this discomfort, which had to be borne in shoes of which by far the greater part, by weight, are worn away, it began to rain. We followed the side of the mountain until it curved to the westward, and then descended and found ourselves in a large valley. . . . There is so much moisture that a stick begins to rot as soon as it falls, and any kind of scar or blaze seems to kill the tree. The ground is cumbered with rotting logs, for the most part so decayed that they crumble beneath a man's weight. Everything is rotten. [Barnes]

The river ran close to the southern side of the valley they were now traversing. Named by the expedition Chester Valley,[2] it consisted chiefly of level benches of considerable width. The soil appeared to be excellent when they glimpsed it now and then where the deep snow permitted — although, Barnes noted, "it must be confessed that this permission was rarely given."

Because the snow in the valley was deep and soft, they had difficulty finding a suitable place to spend the night. In the afternoon, while hunting for a campsite with enough wood to build a fire, they came to a large torrent which they called the Lost Chord.

[2] The records do not state for whom Chester Valley and Mount Zindorf were named. Of the many masculine names given, these were the only ones not identified.

It flowed from the north, pouring over a deep, rocky bed; somehow they managed to bridge it with a log. For two miles they looked for a campsite, "without finding the right combination of dry wood and a dry hole in the snow," until finally, just beside the river and a half mile beyond the Lost Chord, they "stumbled suddenly from winter and dampness into summer and dryness, sunshine, moss and dry wood."

Showers fell occasionally throughout the day on May 12. A half mile below their camp of the previous evening the men came to a second "Lost Chord" plunging through the depths of a deep gorge, and a mile further brought them to a third. They had lunch nearby "in a most charming alder bottom."

> About here we began to be greatly puzzled by the outlook ahead. There is something much like exploring a dark rat hole in this following a stream in these woods, and enclosed by such hills as these. One can only see a few yards in any direction near the ground, and overhead the foliage shuts out even the sky. One cannot get a sight of the mountains or hills. At long intervals on approaching the river the most that can be seen is just sufficient to enable one by tracing the specks of light through the branches of the trees, to expect that the gap continues a little further in the given direction. [Barnes]

At the lower end of Chester Valley, their course led up a steep and difficult mountainside. In this region many tributaries entered the Quinault through cleft canyons and gorges, and the expedition had to cross all of them. This necessarily slowed the party's progress. At one point they spent an hour crossing a stream that tumbled down the mountainside through a deep gorge; they had to use ropes down one side and up the other. That evening the party descended to the river and made camp for the night on a small patch of bottomland.

Below Chester Valley the river swung in an easterly direction, a development that caused them no little concern. They were determined to emerge from the mountains by way of the Quinault, but the river's new course made them fearful that they had missed the Quinault when crossing the divide. If so, they were following some other river — one that would perhaps lead them to Hood Canal, definitely not their destination.

The river is now flowing due east, and we are very uncertain as to the identity of the river. It is away off the course laid down for the Quinaiult on the maps. The maps in our possession indicate the west fork of the Skokomish as draining this section, and, as the river we are now on flows in the direction by them given to the Skokomish, we have much trouble on our minds to-night. [Barnes]

The next morning, while preparing his pack for another day's hard travel, Christie was "surprised to hear the snort of an elk." Quickly scanning the surrounding forest, he spied a large bull elk as it stepped into view among the alders on the river bank immediately opposite their camp.

We ate the last of our bear meat yesterday, and had just risen from a repast of flour soup, and the appearance of the elk at once put life into every man in camp. All dropped flat on their faces and each man grabbed the dog nearest him. Mr. Christie crept to the bank, took deliberate aim, and, putting his whole soul into the gun along with the cartridge, fired. The elk started, moved two or three yards and laid down, just as Mr. Christie put another shot into him; but the first shot killed. Then there was joy in camp, as well as meat. [Barnes]

Within an hour and a half, they had felled a tree bridge across the river, retrieved and dressed their elk — "a magnificent buck, his new horns just sprouting" — and had his liver in the frying pan. The men then moved their camp across the river, cut up the elk carcass, and hung the meat up to smoke. Christie thereupon declared a rest day, for everyone was suffering greatly from fatigue, "all hands being worn out by the hard travel of the preceding four days."

We cannot help remarking on the fortunate way in which we have obtained meat on three occasions when we badly needed it. First, the elk at the lower end of Press valley; second, the bears; third, this elk. This morning we had only about 25 pounds of flour in camp. That was our whole provision. [Barnes]

The change in fortune made them very optimistic. "If this river should prove to be the Skokomish," Barnes declared, exuberant over the killing of the elk, "we can now with our present supply of meat gain the Quinaiult, if there should be a dozen ranges to cross." He added, however, that they were "anxious to explore the Quinaiult, if possible."

On the fifteenth of May — their packs once more replenished with meat — they started at daylight, their course following an old elk trail up the mountainside. Ahead they could occasionally glimpse "what seemed to be a little valley." In the afternoon they descended into the valley, found that "it was large and heavily timbered, with but little underbrush, and afforded good travel." They soon reached the Quinault at a point where it received a tributary from the eastward.

This stream — named by the expedition Alexander River but known today as Rustler Creek [3] — was large, but very shoal and rapid. Where it discharged into the Quinault it divided into three streams, "forming a kind of delta, obstructed, however, with timber." They crossed without difficulty and found themselves in a large, open bottom from where they could see up and down the valley. To their satisfaction and great relief, "the river and valley turned to the westward and was undoubtedly the Quinaiult at last."

There was no snow in the valley, and the afternoon was warm and sunny. The party's troubles and hardships seemed at last to be over.

> For the first time in months, and finally, we hoped, we stood upon bare ground. We seemed to be near home now and the satisfaction of all hands was complete. After resting up a little while and enjoying the novelty of the change in our circumstances we again shouldered our packs and followed the left bank of the stream. [Barnes]

The expedition had finally reached the unbroken bottomlands of the Quinault — covered with dense stands of spruce, cedar, fir, and hemlock — though at times the men were compelled to take to the sidehill.

It rained all the next day. After an early breakfast the party was afoot, and everyone was now quite anxious to reach the lake. But progress was slow as they fought their way through underbrush beneath towering trees, forded sloughs, crossed river bars, and

[3] It is also called The Rustler or The Rusher.

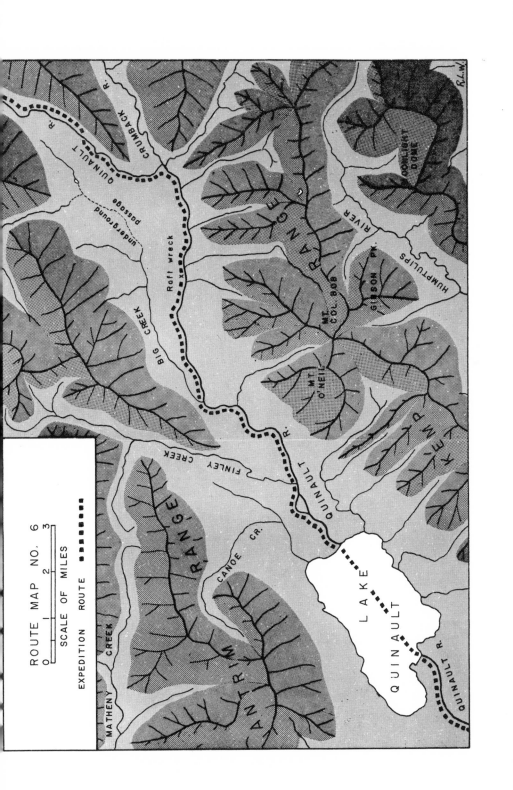

ROUTE MAP NO. 6

SCALE OF MILES

0   1   2   3

EXPEDITION ROUTE ▪▪▪▪▪▪▪▪

MATHENY CREEK

ANTLER RANGE

CANOE CR.

FINLEY CREEK

QUINAULT LAKE

QUINAULT R.

QUINAULT R.

MT. O'NEIL

MT. COL. BOB

GIBSON PK.

HUMPTULIPS RIVER

ELWHA RANGE

BIG CREEK

Raft wreck

underground passage

QUINAULT R.

CRUMBACK R.

DOSEWALLIPS DOME

R.L.W.

Douglas fir above Lake Quinault (Courtesy Washington State Historical Society)

occasionally climbed up and down steep hillsides. Noting that the land on the opposite side of the river was flat, they expressed a desire to cross and thus avoid the continuous scrambling over the rough mountain spurs.

> The river was unfavorable, however, for fording, and the driftwood was too rotten and heavy for a raft, so that we had to give up the idea and take again to the sidehill. Toward evening, descending again to the river, we made two more attempts to cross. The first attempt was made with a rope lashed from man to man, but our united strength could not resist the strength of the current. At a short distance above we made another attempt, in water to our armpits, and succeeded in reaching an island in the middle of the river. We arrived there wet and tired, and made camp on the sand of the island. This has been one of the hard days of the trip. We are all sick again with dysentery. [Barnes]

To multiply their troubles, it rained all that night — for they were on the wet, windward side of the Olympics — and on the morning of May 17 the men were almost as miserable as they had been the evening before. However, the sun came out shortly after breakfast and "made things cheerful again." They felled another "tree bridge," crossed over, and again headed downstream.

> We continued all day down the river, through dense underbrush consisting of a tangled thicket of salmon berry bushes, vine maple and all other usual small growth that can be imagined. About noon we came to a big bend of the river with a fork from the eastward. This fork at the point of junction is about equal in size and in its possibilities for navigation with the main river. This is the East fork which is laid down on some of the maps. But it deserves a name, and we gave it that of Crumback river, after John H. Crumback, a member of the party. [Barnes]

Below the juncture of the two forks of the Quinault (they had been following the north fork), the party suddenly emerged from the forest into a little clearing, in the midst of which stood a log cabin, the "first sign of civilized man for many months." The cabin was empty, but they did not linger. Apparently it belonged to a trapper, for "carcasses of beaver, fisher and otter were scattered about, creating an awful stench."

The Quinault was now large and broad, and as the men proceeded they encountered frequent signs of the presence of man, including a fisher trap "probably made by Indians." Next they came upon "the cold embers of an Indian fire surrounded by a frame work of drying fish." During the day's trek Christie shot an eagle, and the men observed many tracks of bear, elk, and fisher. They also noted numerous beaver signs, observing both their habitations and small trees that the animals had destroyed.

The underbrush on the banks of the river now became so dense as to be almost impenetrable. The men therefore moved away from the stream and followed dry sloughs; however, these led again to the river, where the men camped on a sandbar. For supper that night they consumed the last of their flour in making soup, but they had remaining "sufficient meat for two days."

Sunday, May 18, was clear and warm. "This has been the day," Barnes wrote, "long looked forward to, of meeting white men and getting a taste of civilization, but coupled also with our greatest misfortune." They broke camp at daylight and set out immediately. In order to reach the sandbars again, the men were obliged to climb and follow a long spur so "matted and jungled" that they could move through the dense growth only with difficulty. Therefore they descended to the water's edge and "scrambled along the rock, clinging to the overhanging foliage." Then they struck inland and followed a dry slough, which brought them out on the bank again after a mile.

For several miles the river had been smooth and quiet, its banks and channel free of drift timber. The men were tired and footsore, their packs were heavy, and the lake seemed to be as far away as ever. Looking down at the smoothly gliding stream — and realizing that it would carry them in an hour a distance that would take two or three days of bushwhacking along the brush-choked bank — the men persuaded Christie that they should build a raft.

Christie was "fain to give way" to their request for several reasons:

> We were getting rather short of grub; we were now almost naked. The continued hard work and travel which the party had undergone, backed by the fact that we were traveling or rather forcing our way along the bank of a magnificent stream, tended towards the making up of my mind to build a raft with which to reach the lake. On reaching a gravel beach

some six miles below the east fork, dry wood being handy, I determined to collect timber and launch a raft at the point. [Christie]

While chopping and rolling logs down the river bank to the gravel bar, they were suddenly surprised to see a man emerge from the brush on the opposite bank, several hundred yards downstream.

He caught sight of us at the same moment and stepped back again out of sight. After another moment he came out and we mutually signaled by waving our hands. "A settler!" cried one of the boys. "God help his plug of tobacco!"

Our pleasure on seeing him can be imagined. We stopped working on the raft and centered our attention on the stranger, who came down to the waters' edge for hailing, as Mr. Christie reached a point opposite. The distance made communication difficult, but fortunately there came in sight around the bend from below his canoe paddled by his two Indian guides. The white man stepped into it, and in a few moments was along-side of us. He was evidently a little doubtful of us, for which we could hardly blame him, for we did look tough, but after a few moment's conversation he became convinced of our honesty and became most kind and cordial. His name was F. S. Antrim of Aberdeen. He apologized for jumping behind the brush when he first saw us, because, as he explained, he was looking for elk or bear, and, not expecting to meet any man up here, his momentary impression was that we were game. [Barnes]

Since he had discovered his mistake in time and had not shot them, they laughed a little over this, then began plying Mr. Antrim "with questions varying from the grave to the gay." He gave them information about the river below and also offered to assist them in any way that he could.

He said the lake was eight miles down. We asked him if a raft would go down. He said he was ignorant of rafting, and turning to one of his Indian guides, asked him what he thought of it. The Indian nodded toward the hills on the north of the valley and said:

"Good trail over there."

"Yes, but can these gentlemen go down on a raft?"

The Indian looked thoughtful for a moment and then said:

"Yes, raft go down." But still he looked at the hills as he repeated:

"Trail over there." But if a raft would go down we wanted no trail. We were weary and footsore and half sick. Now that we were so near our journey's end we wanted to finish it, and so it was little attention we paid to the hints of a trail "over there."

We then came to the main point and broached the tobacco question. To our chagrin and disappointment Mr. Antrim informed us that he did not smoke. But learning our wants he secured for us a piece of tobacco from the Indians and presented us with a good brew of coffee and tea. [Barnes]

Antrim told them that he had a quantity of stores in a cabin where the river flowed into the lake, and they were welcome to help themselves. Antrim was going up the river, but would return in a few days; if they were still about, he would share his canoe with them. He then departed, leaving them to their raft building as he again headed upstream.

The tobacco afforded a morsel for each man. How can it be expressed the satisfaction afforded by that morsel of tobacco? A fire was built and water put on for the coffee of which we partook as soon as the raft was ready. We set to work and finished the raft in short order. Seven good sized stocks rolled into the water and lashed to good solid cross pieces with rope lashing, made a comfortable raft of about eight by fifteen feet. Upon this we spread a few boughs to raise the cargo out of possible wash, provided her with a steering oar, and our vessel was complete. [Barnes]

They did not give the raft a name, but it could have been christened the *Gertie II*. Like the ill-fated flatboat on the Elwha, which had proved impracticable as a means of ingress into the mountains, the raft on the Quinault would prove to be an equally unsatisfactory way of leaving.

Pushing out into the stream we were soon gliding quietly and swiftly down. The steering oar in Mr. Christie's experienced hands, assisted by an occasional check with the poles, served to keep us in mid channel. The river for over a mile continued as gentle as could be desired, and we congratulated ourselves on an early termination of our journey. It terminated earlier than we expected. [Barnes]

As the raft rounded a sharp bend in the Quinault, they were horrified to see the whole river gather into a narrow, rapid channel, sweep in toward the right bank and rush under a great pile of drift timber that lay on the bank and projected halfway across the stream.

The men made an effort to save the raft and their packs, but had little chance to do so, for the raft was traveling ten to twelve miles an hour, and the poles were useless. With his oar, Christie was able to swing the raft, however, causing it to strike the drift pile broadside and thereby preventing its instantaneous destruction. At the moment of impact, Crumback and Sims sprang from the raft to the driftpile and were safe. At the same time a huge volume of water poured over the raft, sweeping off Barnes, Hayes, the dogs, and all the baggage.

Hayes was thrown into the water and in danger of "being sucked under the drift and jammed by the raft." Christie grabbed him by the arm just in time to prevent his being borne directly under the drift timber, and helped him regain his footing on the logs. "It was a narrow shave for Hayes, for even if he had not met with an obstruction beneath, which would have terminated his career like a cat in a bag, the chances are a hundred to one that he would have bumped his head in the passage" [Barnes].

When Barnes came to the surface a few seconds after being swept from the raft, he had "passed under the outer corner of the driftpile and was grasping the pack which contained the records." He then managed to catch hold of a spar that projected out from the lower end of the drift pile. Barnes seemed to have clung unconsciously to the pack whose loss they would have felt most severely – the one containing the records.

After Christie had assisted Hayes to a point of safety and seen that Crumback and Sims were secure, he turned his attention to Barnes, "who was in a rather dangerous position." He had grasped a piece of timber about fifty yards below where the raft had struck and nearly midstream, with the drift pile still menacing him.

With a strong effort, Christie succeeded in turning the raft until it cleared the drift pile entirely and then steered toward Barnes, who "rather preferred to strike out and swim than run the risk of being struck by the raft." Barnes released his hold on the snag and was carried down the stream three hundred yards, but "succeeded in getting out of the boiling waters which formed the current." As Barnes felt under his feet "the gravel of terra firma on the opposite or left bank," Christie swept past on the raft, "happy to see that he was safe, but evidently exhausted from his terrible fight with the river." Christie then turned the raft to the river's edge and returned to assist Barnes "in spreading out his records and charts, saved by his exertion and at a very imminent risk of his life. We are indebted to his grit and pluck for preserving the records of our winter's work within the charmed circle of Olympus."

Barnes was philosophical about the wreck of the raft and their loss of gear, feeling that the expedition was fortunate that no one had been killed or injured.

> So ended the episode of the day. We lost everything except the contents of one pack and the clothes we were wearing. Guns, ammunition, bear skins, fishing tackle, and most of the mineral and other specimens which we had collected.
>
> All went.
>
> The loss to Mr. Christie of his box of flies and other fishing gear, the collections of a lifetime, can be appreciated only by a devotee of the gentle art of angling. It contained several hundred flies, many of them imported and very rare. On account of the difficulty of packing we had brought down the river but few specimens of the flora and the fauna of the country, but the few which we had were lost. The same of minerals, although of them a part were preserved by being in the pack saved. The fact of their being there, however, nearly lost the remainder of the pack in the shipwreck, for partly owing to them the bundle was heavy, and had to be supported in the water. We lost also many little curios, such as bears' teeth, elk tushes, etc.
>
> The pack saved contained most of the records of the trip – journals, the negative films, some 250 in number – and above all the map of the mountains which we had made.
>
> However, it was all over now, and the party was safe: that was one consolation. [Barnes]

Crumback, Sims, and Hayes were on the opposite side of the river. Inquiries and answers were shouted back and forth across the Quinault "to the effect that, barring a few bruises, all were well." Apparently they had dry matches, for Christie and Barnes set fire to a large pile of brush, then slipped off their few garments and spread them out to dry, "together with the contents of the pack saved." Everything had been soaked except the films, each roll of which had been separately packed in its case. At the same time

Crumback, Sims, and Hayes also dried their effects, and eventually the divided expedition again started downstream, Christie and Barnes on one side of the river, the boys on the other.

That afternoon they passed two log cabins, both untenanted.

> The claims on which they are located are valuable ones. The mountains are more than half a mile from the river there. The houses are mere travesties on houses, are absolutely uninhabitable, being put together merely to enable the claimant to hold the land. It is an outrage that the law should make such a thing possible. The same thing is practiced on the lower Elwha, where valuable land is being acquired by men who are in business at some distant place, whose only improvements are similar to those we saw to-day, and who do not even make a pretense of visiting them. [Barnes]

Slowly they made their way down the valley, walking close along the river's banks. Because of the dense growths of salmonberry and brambles, they did not progress more than a mile in three hours of hard work. Their only food was the tender green shoots of the raspberry bushes, and they nibbled on these as they went along.

Barnes and Christie finally reached a sandbar and camped there, protecting themselves as much as possible with half a blanket. Crumback, Sims, and Hayes, who camped opposite them across the river, were less fortunate, having no shelter at all. But they built fires on both sides of the river.

Making themselves as comfortable as possible, Barnes and Christie pulled their half blanket over themselves and were soon asleep. About midnight, however, it began to rain. Their fire had gone out, but they lay beneath the blanket until morning, wet to the skin. It was still raining the next morning when they got up and looked around. "The boys, on seeing us, came down the river bank, and we were able to communicate by shouting. They had sat around the fire all night, feeling, like us, too mean to look for cover."

From the information Antrim had given them, they estimated their present position to be about five miles from a settler's cabin at the head of Lake Quinault, and they were hopeful of reaching this cabin during the day and procuring food.

The boys having permission to go on started at once, and it was as good as a joke to see the speed with which they disappeared into the woods. Mr. Christie and I made a fire to dry ourselves by, and while I was drying the blanket he went into the woods back of camp to see if he could not find an appetizing-looking spruce tree for breakfast. The inner bark is sweet, and makes excellent food in the absence of better. He had not been gone five minutes when who should come around the bend from above but our benefactor of yesterday, Mr. Antrim, in his canoe, as handsome as ever, — indeed more handsome he appeared this morning to our famished eyes. [Barnes]

In response to a call from Barnes, Christie emerged from the thicket. Antrim had camped with his Indian companions at the confluence of the forks of the Quinault the previous evening and had started back down the river at four that morning.

It was a happy meeting. His offer of assistance was gratefully accepted, and we prepared to accompany him in the downward trip. He was, however, as wet as ourselves, and so we finished the drying out process and had the pleasure of adding to Mr. Antrim's wardrobe a pair of blanket "duffles" for his feet, an acquisition which, however comfortable, may create some amusement in the family circle at Aberdeen. Duffles are a style of hosiery not as yet prescribed by the tyrant, Fashion. Mr. Antrim killed a bear this morning, which was in the boat, and while we were drying out the Indians skinned it. [Barnes]

Once in the canoe, they thoroughly enjoyed the day. The rain ceased, the clouds rolled back against the mountaintops, and the sun shone. The Quinault, with its numerous piles of driftwood, was a surprise. It soon became evident that descending the river on a raft would have been impossible.

As we neared the lake drift piles became still more numerous, and it required most skillful handling to clear them with the canoe. But in the hands of the Indians, who had been brought up from boyhood on the river, and had frequently traveled as high as the forks, the voyage was made in perfect safety. Their knowledge of the current is wonderful. They know every submerged sandbar, rock, and snag on the river, and just the right stroke of the paddle at the right time sends the canoe past dangers which to us were invisible until we were by them.

About a mile down the river we picked up the boys who were stoutly trudging down the bank. Their surprise at seeing us may well be imagined. Eight men and three dogs made a large passenger list for the little canoe, but it arrived safely at last at the mouth of the river. [Barnes]

At the head of Lake Quinault they "found a house, and an actual, bona fide, settler." Antrim's stores were cached there, too.

> It was to them our first attention was directed. It was but a few moments before we had potatoes in the pot — real potatoes, and plenty of them. Baking powder biscuit on one side of the fire vied with more baking powder biscuit, light and flakey, on the other. Broiling ham and baking salmon mingled their savory odors with the aroma of coffee. But Mr. Antrim's treasures did not end here. He had butter, sugar, golden syrup, condensed milk, mustard, pickles — any single article of which we would . . . gladly and willingly have committed a homicide to attain. [Barnes]

Murder, however, was unnecessary, for Antrim

> spared not his grub. If we paused a moment he felt our pulses and prescribed another biscuit or cup of coffee with plenty of milk. The feast was of long continuance, though hastened somewhat toward the end by the desire of the boys to get the tobacco to burning, for of that precious weed we obtained another small supply from the Indians. [Barnes]

The repast was finally concluded at two o'clock in the afternoon. Because the days were long at that time of year, they could still cover a considerable distance before darkness. Now that they were at last in touch with civilization, the men were in a desperate hurry to return home, for they had been nearly six months in the wilderness, moving across primitive, unknown terrain. Once more they took their places in the small canoe and within a few minutes emerged upon the tranquil waters of Lake Quinault. The shores and surrounding mountains were clad in luxuriant forests, and the men were duly impressed by the scene.

> The dense verdure which covers the mountain side and descends upon the valley, extends quite to the border of the lake, where the overhanging foliage conceals and hides the shore. . . . There is not a clearing upon the lake, but it is all, we are told, taken up as squatters' claims, excepting that portion which is in the Indian reserve. . . . This broad lake, its wooded shores and high bounding mountains, its surface unruffled by storms, makes a peaceful picture of wild and entrancing beauty. [Barnes]

As the canoe moved across the lake, the Press Exploring Expedition emerged from the Olympic Mountains, for this lake lies on their margin or perimeter and is embraced by foothills to the north and south. But the party was not, as yet, out of the wilderness — for in 1890 the lowlands surrounding the mountains were still covered by uninhabited forests, and man had scarcely made an imprint on the natural scene.

> After our experience in the mountains it was to us a new and delightful sensation, the crossing of the lake with the easy motion of the canoe, propelled by hands other than our own. The surface of the lake was dotted here and there with ducks and the shores are alive with game. [Barnes]

Soon they were across the lake, gliding down its outlet onto the broad lower Quinault River. For a mile the stream was smooth, then for several miles the surface was broken by ripples or swift flowing water, and rocks appeared intermittently. The water was deep, however, and the channel free of obstruction. Seven miles below the lake a log jam made it necessary to portage the canoe about two hundred yards. Then followed two miles of good water, interrupted by another but much smaller jam. By this time it was nearly dark, and they landed, made camp on the river bank, and prepared "another wonderful feast" from the stores Antrim had furnished them.

The next morning — the twentieth of May — the men were astir before daylight, hastily prepared breakfast, and were on their way at four o'clock. As the canoe floated down the river, the men observed the fish weirs of the Indians, and they also met several canoes paddled by Indians headed upstream. Then, six miles from the river's mouth at the Pacific Ocean, the party stopped for awhile at the home of the tribe's medicine man.

> The house, which is well built, is about 30 feet long by 25 in width. The interior consists of one room and is open in the center of the roof to let out the smoke. Ten or a dozen bunks lined the side walls. From the ceiling was suspended dried fish and jerked elk meat. The ground was bare excepting at the further end, where a raised platform marked the space devoted to the incantations and mysteries of the aboriginal medical profession. This platform and the wall behind it were covered with the apparatus of the profession, and are calculated to terrify unwelcome and undesired spirits. [Barnes]

The party reached the Quinault Indian Reservation agency at the mouth of the river at ten o'clock, procured lunch, hired a team, "and were soon bowling down the beach." They arrived at Owyhut shortly after dark, where they boarded a sloop for Grays Harbor, arriving in Aberdeen at 2:00 A.M. May 21, "having by 22 hours of continuous travel made a distance of 60 miles."

Because of the late hour, they had difficulty in obtaining accommodations, but when they at last touched real beds — for the first time in almost half a year — "it was a luxury to be appreciated."

> When we arose late the next morning we found that the news of our return to civilization had been sent abroad, and we found telegrams of congratulation from the Seattle PRESS and from many friends, and many kind inquiries after the health and welfare of the party. As soon as we were awake we had at our rooms interviews with various merchants of the town, and with the barbers, so that when at last we were able to resume a civilized appearance, we hardly recognized ourselves. Bronzed faces alone remained to remind us of what we had been through. [Barnes]

On May 21, Christie wired Edmond Meany from Aberdeen, his message stating that the party's expenses to Seattle would approximate 125 dollars, and requesting that the *Press* remit the money that morning by telegraph. A group photograph of the five men and their three dogs was also taken that morning in the studio of C. K. Pratsch, an Aberdeen photographer, who sent the *Press* the negatives, together with a bill for five dollars.[4]

> The people of the town were very kind and showed us every consideration. Unterrified by our tremendous appetites, they took us to their homes and gave us white folk's food.
>
> After two days of rest, which we needed so badly, we at length parted from our kind friends at Aberdeen and took the steamer for Montesano, and thence to Seattle,[5] where our arrival at the steamer's wharf ended our journey after an absence of six months. Our exploration of the Olympics was completed. [Barnes]

[4] See photograph, p. 29.
[5] Christie sent another telegram to Meany on May 23: "Party left Aberdeen this morning & will arrive in Seattle this evening by Boat from Kamilchie."

Chapter XII

THE UNVEILED OLYMPICS

WITH PARDONABLE pride the PRESS speaks of its presentation of this account. It is believed no handsomer paper was ever published on the Pacific coast. Certainly the illustrations have not been excelled by any newspaper."[1] Thus did the Seattle *Press* describe its issue for Wednesday, July 16, 1890.

Eight weeks earlier, when the Press Exploring Expedition returned to Seattle in late May, the party had simply disbanded, each man going his own way, quietly returning to the monotonous routine of ordinary living.[2] Christie and Barnes did remain in the

[1] Seattle *Press* (July 16, 1890), p. 20.

[2] Copies of the Seattle *Press* for late May, 1890, apparently do not exist today, and what comment the sponsoring newspaper made immediately upon the expedition's return to civilization is not known. However, the Seattle *Post-Intelligencer* — which was, of course, a rival — ignored the event. An article did appear in the *Post-Intelligencer* on May 22 — while the expedition was in Aberdeen — under the heading, "The Promised Land." It related that a Mr. Pier [Pierre] Barnes, "brother of Capt. C. A. Barnes of the Christy exploring party" had returned a few days previously from a trip into the Olympic Mountains. He had gone into the Lake Crescent–Lake Sutherland area, and stated that this "would have been the best place for the Christy party of explorers to have entered the mountains. There is an almost level divide right back of the lake which cuts through the mountains and which could have been easily traversed. The Elwha river was the very worst route they could have chosen, for it runs in two forks through deep canyons from the very base of Mount Olympus, while the intervening country is a rich, level plateau. They could have reached the interior of the country much sooner than they did and with much less labor, if they had gone by the Crescent divide. The last I heard of them they were at the foot of

198

city, however, for some time, completing their narratives of the trip for the *Press*, and the results now appeared in this lavish edition, devoted almost exclusively to a "complete account of the exploration." Captain Barnes (who replaced Dr. Runnalls as historian) had carefully narrated many details of the more interesting incidents of the trip, and Christie's diary gave "a daily record of how the party moved and accomplished its work." The story began with the inception of the idea in the interview with Governor Ferry and ended with the return of the party "after six months of hard climbing over snow covered mountains and through dangerous canyons." In addition, it was liberally illustrated with zincograph etchings made from photographs taken on the expedition. A reproduction of Barnes's topographical map covered one entire page. The map had been drawn from his personal observations and information gained from triangulations and field notes "which were carefully preserved, even through the shipwreck on the upper Quinaiult river."

> There is no doubt whatever that this is the first time the country illustrated has ever been traversed by white men. Indeed, the reader will unhesitatingly believe that no party of men, less experienced in work of this kind and less elaborately equipped, could have conducted an expedition involving so great hardships and productive of so comprehensive results. The facts are detailed.[3]

---

the mountains about three weeks and were just about to cross, so I suppose they have reached the southern slope of the range by this time." [Seattle *Post-Intelligencer*, May 22, 1890]

Pierre Barnes made an erroneous conclusion about the region south of Lake Crescent. Had the expedition gone that way, the men would have found it necessary to cross, at right angles, the Soleduck, Hoh, and Queets canyons, and also to traverse Mount Olympus.

The May 22 issue of the *Post-Intelligencer* also contained an interesting but unrelated article entitled "Where Is Christie?" This told of a warrant for the arrest of one Clarence J. Christie, a "well known and rather eccentric real estate dealer" who allegedly had embezzled three thousand dollars. Two days later — coincidental with the arrival of the Press Exploring Expedition in Seattle — the *Post-Intelligencer* printed another item which indicated that Clarence J. Christie was still at large and had defrauded one R. H. Goldie of three hundred dollars. R. H. Goldie was, of course, the gentleman for whom James H. Christie and his companions had named Goldie River in the Olympics.

[3] Seattle *Press* (July 16, 1890), p. 20.

Indeed they were, and the *Press* was unstinting in its praise of the party's accomplishments and of the manner in which the men had endured the necessary hardships. They certainly had earned the praise, for it had been a memorable exploration, half a year "of rough work and wild adventure." The *Press* went on to assert that the men had never lost sight of "the real, substantial purpose" of the expedition — the finding, by actual investigation, of facts "about a vast area of the Northwest which, until now, was unknown to civilized and uncivilized man, and concerning which much curiosity had been excited by reports, chiefly fabulous, of the character of the country." [4]

Because the expedition had been undertaken by "experienced and reputable men" who were thoroughly equipped for the work, the *Press* did not hesitate to state its "entire confidence in the accuracy of the detailed report" published at this time.

> The path made by the PRESS explorers is indicated by indelible evidences that any one can see and follow. There are no assumptions. No attempt, either directly or by ambiguity of expression, is made to mislead the reader into believing that more was done than was actually accomplished. The full page topographical map indicates the configuration of the country, the courses of the rivers and many minor streams, the location of the more important mountain peaks and the valleys, together with much other detailed information, so accurately and distinctly, that future expeditions . . . will be enabled to escape many of the hardships incident to the original investigations . . . and also, to devote themselves to a more thorough investigation of particular districts. [5]

The main features of the country enclosed by the Olympic Mountains were now, the *Press* declared, known for the first time, and the illustrations drawn from expedition photographs would enable anyone traversing the interior of the peninsula in the future to recognize the "notable mountains and landmarks."

> The public generally is informed that in addition to the illustrations which appear in the issue, the PRESS has in its possession nearly two hundred photographs, which are available to anyone who desires to inspect them, or who believes that they will aid him in contributing additional

[4] *Ibid.*
[5] *Ibid.*

information to the public about a country that is now attracting general attention.[6]

The expedition's trip across the Olympic Mountains undoubtedly impressed the people living around Puget Sound at that time to the same degree that the successful assault of a Himalayan peak commands our respect today. "THE 'PRESS' PARTY WERE PATH-FINDERS," one headline proclaimed, while others indicated that the expedition found "no signs of white men ever having entered that district before," and that a good trail had been made for future explorers or prospectors.[7]

The Press explorers made many mistakes, of course, and arrived at several erroneous conclusions, but their experiences were tempered by a well-developed sense of humor, which made bearable the often comic, sometimes ludicrous, occasionally almost tragic situations which occurred. Of course, their blunders are easy to criticize, but one should remember that the Olympic topography is now thoroughly known and that well-kept trails crisscross the region, with excellent footbridges spanning even the smaller streams. The explorers were undeniably men of courage who did not hesitate to move into the very heart of a rugged, unknown mountain system and mark the way for future travelers. Not only was the interior of the peninsula unknown when they commenced their journey, but there were no trails other than misleading paths made by elk and deer.

Although not the first party to enter the Olympic Mountains, the Press Exploring Expedition was the first to cross from one side to the other. How much impact the expedition had upon later developments in the region is difficult to assess, for countless flakes of snow have fallen upon the high peaks since that historic cross-

[6] *Ibid.*

[7] On May 29, 1890, after the Press Expedition had returned to Seattle, a twenty-four-year-old Englishman, John Stothert, gatekeeper of the Grimshaw Street Mill in Preston, Lancashire, wrote to Edmond Meany. Stothert expressed a desire "to explore the dark and unknown land," and stated that he preferred to do so alone: ". . . if I enter the land at any point I will have no other motto but 'forward' as I am and would be determined to be either distinguished or extinguished." Edmond S. Meany Papers (MSS in the University of Washington Library, Seattle, Washington).

ing, one of the peninsula's momentous events. According to the *Press*, the map, the photographs, and the "trail" the men blazed through the wilderness were to be "of invaluable service to all future travelers in that region." The expedition's route across the mountains (except where the men departed from the Elwha and followed the Goldie) did become, in later years, approximately the Elwha and Quinault trails, which today lead troops of back-packers bent on their own "explorations" into the central wilderness of the Olympics.[8] In fact, the journey across the mountains by way of Low Divide is easily the most popular of many trail trips the Olympic National Park offers to the seasoned hiker. It cannot be said, however, that the Press Party actually "opened up" the Olympic country, because their route (again excluding the Goldie and Deception Divide) may have been the natural one determined by the configuration of the country — the one that subsequent adventurers would have followed in any event.

Together with competing explorers — the Gilmans, O'Neil, Wickersham, and others — the Press Expedition helped dispel the widespread ignorance then prevailing as to what really existed in the interior of the Olympic Peninsula. Yet the aura of mystery associated with the Olympic Mountains lingered for decades afterward and still has not been completely obliterated to this day. Provided that roads are not built across the interior of Olympic National Park, vestiges of that tradition of mystery will probably remain for many years to come.

Nevertheless, the men were trail blazers who marked the way across the mountains for others — the hunters, prospectors, mountaineers, and others seeking escape from the growing pressures of civilization crowding Puget Sound. Most of the Press Party's side trips and reconnaissance excursions occurred early in the journey, when the men were searching for a route across the mountains by way of the fabled "Elwha pass." Once the explorers reached the headwaters of the Quinault, however, the lateral explorations were abandoned, except for Barnes's ascent of Mount Seattle. By then the men were too footsore, too weary of rough outdoor living prolonged for many months, to linger.

[8] Currently the Boy Scouts of America are attempting to have the route of the expedition declared a National Historic Trail.

The Press explorers were the first to learn, of course, that the Olympic Mountains are not a "range" in the ordinary sense of that word, but a cluster of spurs and snowy peaks scattered helter-skelter. To the expedition must go the credit for naming the Bailey Range,[9] the "backbone of the Olympics," which — together with Mount Seattle and Mount Christie — divides the watershed of the Elwha from that of the Quinault and other streams flowing to the Pacific. "Around this backbone as a center the other ranges which constitute the whole lie with little regard to order. There seems to be something of the concentric in their general arrangement, but this is not very marked."[10]

The expedition's story of the crossing of these snow-clad peaks — covered in their lower levels with dense virgin forests — dispelled the vague rumors that the mountains encircled a great valley and lake, or a plateau of rolling grasslands, yet for years afterward the newspapers reported groups going into the "unknown Olympics." And although the men found evidence of former Indian habitations in the mountains, they did not encounter any savage cannibals.[11] They discovered no natural wonders that would lure the tourist who sought the unusual, except the Goblin Gates, and even that strange phenomenon on the Elwha has remained virtually unknown for decades. Today people living along the lower Elwha commonly refer to it as "the head of the canyon." In addition, the "geysers" the party heard — first on the Elwha and again on the Quinault, below the east fork — were nonexistent.

The Press explorers did, however, name many natural features

[9] The Press Expedition cannot actually be said to have "discovered" the Bailey Range, for Lieutenant O'Neil discerned it from a distance on his exploration of the northern Olympics in 1885. The members of the Press Party were the first, however, to view it close up and actually to traverse some of its spurs.

[10] Seattle *Press* (July 16, 1890), p. 5.

[11] The wild tales about cannibals in the Olympics may have stemmed, in part at least, from two incidents which occurred more than a century earlier. In 1775 Juan de la Bodega y Quadra landed a party of men at the mouth of the Hoh River to obtain fresh water and fuel. They were promptly killed by Indians. Twelve years later, in 1787, Charles William Barkley, commander of an East India Company ship, also sent a party ashore for fresh water at the same location, and his men met a similar fate at the hands of the natives residing along the coast.

in the Olympics — mountain peaks, rivers, lakes, and waterfalls — and in this respect probably made their greatest imprint on the region. Interestingly enough, feminine names were given to some of the streams, lakes, and waterfalls, but never to the mountain peaks, which were invariably honored with masculine names. Most of them, in fact, were named after newspaper editors. Three rivers — the Hayes, Sims, and Crumback — were named for members of the exploring group. Of these, however, only the Hayes retains the original name, for Sims River is called Promise Creek today, and Crumback River is the East Fork Quinault. Appropriately, Christie's name was given to a rough, weather-beaten mountain southeast of Low Divide, and Barnes was commemorated by another peak near Deception Divide. (See footnote, page 159.)

While some of the names the Press Party gave to natural features would be inappropriate today (such as Mount Bennett for Olympus), much of their nomenclature which has fallen into disuse through the years should properly be restored. In fact, a number of the peaks they named have no proper designations today.

Although from the standpoint of impact and attention the Seattle *Press* achieved what is commonly called a "scoop," the expedition's story was actually antedated by two accounts in the *Post-Intelligencer* of the Gilman explorations. The Press Exploring Expedition had barely returned to Seattle when the *Post-Intelligencer* printed on May 28 a short article by C. A. Gilman which pointed out that he and his son had, in the last three months of 1889, explored the Quinault, following the east fork to its headwaters; also they had traversed the country between the mountains and the sea, proving that there was "no foundation whatsoever for the interesting romance published last year regarding the lake and prairie and the wild Indians located in the Olympic mountains." [12]

The second article, which appeared on June 5, 1890, was considerably longer, and told of the Gilmans' trip up the Quinault and along the western margin of the peninsula. This account demonstrates that the Gilmans could have had the honor of the first

[12] Seattle *Post-Intelligencer* (May 28, 1890).

crossing of the Olympic Mountains had they elected to proceed on to Hood Canal when they reached the high country in the vicinity of Anderson Pass. They decided, however, to return by their route into the mountains, and thus the Press Party became the first actually to accomplish such a crossing.

When the story of the Press Exploring Expedition finally hit the newsstands in mid-July, 1890, the Olympics were swarming with explorers, prospectors, hunters, and timbermen. A large military expedition under Lieutenant O'Neil was busy hacking a mule path across the southern part of the mountains from Lake Cushman to Lake Quinault. A little to the north Judge Wickersham was leading another group on an extended excursion into the alpine region at the head of the Skokomish and Duckabush rivers. On June 16, exactly one month before the appearance of the Press story, a party of five prospectors left Hood Canal at the mouth of the Dosewallips, followed that stream to its source, crossed over the mountains, and descended the Elwha along part of the Press trail. During their trip the prospectors suffered hardships in some respects as severe as those endured by the Press explorers, despite the fact that it was summer, and they were half-starved when they arrived in Port Angeles. Nevertheless, the prospectors had been greatly impressed by the "fir-clothed, snow-capped and mist-veiled crags and peaks."

The Olympic Peninsula today is not the wilderness that faced the explorer of 1890. Then an almost unlimited expanse of virgin forest stretched from the salt-water beaches to the snows of the mountain peaks. The visitor today will find developments — particularly outside the mountains: farms, cities, and sawmills; roads and highways; and great areas of cutover land covered only with stumps and brush or with stands of second-growth timber.

Nor are the mountains themselves as wild as they once were. Few are the peaks that have not been explored by the mountaineer. The Olympic Mountains cover about three thousand square miles, and many of the foothills have been laced with logging roads and cut over, or are being logged. Fortunately, however, half the mountainous area has been preserved by the American people as the Olympic National Park. This constitutes the rugged core of the peninsula, and the terrain is still, for the most part, as wild and primitive as when Christie and his companions crossed the region.

Included within the national park is most of the Press Expedition's route — from Macdonald's Butte on the Elwha to Lake Quinault. However, that part of the Elwha where the men struggled with the ill-fated *Gertie* is outside the park boundaries and most of it lies beneath the waters of an artificial lake. Today automobiles pass swiftly along a modern highway not far from the point where the *Gertie* had to be portaged over a log jam at the mouth of Indian Creek.

Even within the national park, there have been developments. The river bottoms at the foot of the Devil's Backbone and where Wolf and Cat creeks entered the Elwha lie under the waters of Lake Mills, another reservoir created by a power dam constructed before the land came under the jurisdiction of the National Park Service. On the other end of the expedition route, the Quinault Indian Reservation, there is today much cutover land that was covered in 1890 by timber of such height and size that it caught the explorers' eyes, despite the fact that virgin forests were then commonplace in the Pacific Northwest.

Many years have passed since the Press Party crossed the Olympics. It is only natural to wonder what happened to the men after their return to civilization. They simply disappeared, each unknown outside his personal circle of family and friends. For decades, their later experiences were as obscure as the interior of the Olympics was to them at the start of their adventure. Today, however, some facts are known about their lives, although information about Crumback and Hayes is rather meager.

Though the Olympic Mountains are no longer unknown, one can still capture some of the spirit of mystery with which the region was long associated. Today's explorer has merely to depart from the well-traveled trails and pack into the back country, there to tramp through forest aisles or wander along fog-shrouded ridges. Then, lost in the enchantment evoked by imagination and the surroundings, he may find himself walking silently in the company of Christie, Barnes, Crumback, Sims, and Hayes; the dogs, Bud, Daisy, Tweed, and Dike; and the mules, Dollie and Jennie.

EPILOGUE

WHEN THE expedition returned to Seattle, the men undoubtedly met with the staff of the *Press*. Nothing indicates, however, that they ever held a reunion in later years to reminisce about their experiences together on the Olympic exploration. Nor do we have any evidence that the men ever saw Dr. Runnalls after their return to Seattle. At that time Runnalls was serving as physician to the Indian agency at Neah Bay on the Makah Reservation. He wrote to Edmond Meany on June 3, 1890, that "the boys are home again" and asked Meany to send him "the records of the trip."

On June 12, 1890, shortly after the conclusion of the Olympic expedition, Meany introduced Christie to Professor I. C. Russell, who was then organizing an exploration of Alaska in the vicinity of Mount St. Elias for the National Geographic Society. Christie joined the group, which reached the head of Yakutat Bay on June 28, and subsequently attempted to scale St. Elias, but before leaving Seattle he completed his narrative of the Press Exploring Expedition and submitted a bill for sixty dollars to the *Press* for his hotel expenses. "They generously returned me a check for $75," he wrote, "allowing me $15 for consideration of six months of damned hard labour for their benefit. So ho."

With that cryptic parting remark, Christie vanished into obscurity — at least so far as the Puget Sound country was concerned. Apparently, however, Meany — a member of the *Press* staff during the Olympic exploration — maintained contact with him in later years. In 1926, while a professor of history at the University of Washington, Meany wrote to Christie, who was then living near Vernon, British Columbia. In his reply, Christie said he wrote in response to Meany's "request to jog my memory of the original Press Expedition through the then mysterious Olympic Mountains, the reputed home of a tribe of cannibals."

Christie's letter was printed in the 1926 annual of The Mountaineers, an outdoor organization of which Edmond Meany was then president. The letter concluded:

> Of the comrades who tramped, packed, and climbed with me then, I believe that gallant Charlie Barnes rests somewhere down at Panama; Christopher O'Connell Hays [Hayes] I have met once since; Jack Sims, I heard of in Seattle; whilst Jack Crumlack [Crumback] accompanied me on the St. Elias expedition with Professor Russell the following year. But to the good friends if on top of the earth may they keep climbing, if below may they rest in peace.[1]

Nothing more was heard from James Halbold Christie until 1936, when Robert Hitchman, a Seattle resident, read the letter appearing in the 1926 *Mountaineer*. Hitchman thereupon dispatched a letter to the postmaster of Vernon, British Columbia, requesting that it be delivered to Christie's surviving relatives, if there be any, since presumably the leader of the Press Exploring Expedition was no longer living. Back came a terse note from Christie in his own handwriting: "Who the hell says I'm dead?"

Delighted to find the leader of the Press Party still alive, Hitchman went to British Columbia that summer. After questioning local residents, he located Christie residing in a remote area in a typical bachelor's cabin, a dog for his companion. At eighty-one, Christie still had a splendid physique, but he was mentally confused and could not relate a story with continuity. When asked about the Press Expedition — a brief interlude in his adventurous life — he tended to ramble, and confused it with other experiences, among them the Riel rebellion. He had also prospected for coal and gold in the Yukon, and hunted buffalo on the plains.

Christie resided in British Columbia more than forty years, dur-

[1] *The Mountaineer*, XIX, No. 1 (December, 1926), 37.

James H. Christie and Robert Hitchman near Vernon, B.C., August, 1937
(Courtesy Robert Hitchman)

210 / *Across the Olympic Mountains*

ing which time he became a self-appointed champion of the Indians. He carried on a controversy for years with the governments of Canada and British Columbia, to whom he became an irritating "gadfly," publishing a number of controversial pamphlets.

Robert Hitchman again visited Christie in the summer of 1937. Subsequently he received a communication from the Canadian government telling of Christie's death on June 15, 1942, at the age of eighty-seven years, six months. He died penniless and was buried in an unmarked grave. Twenty years later no one knew its location, but Mrs. Grace Worth of Vernon, British Columbia, who made a study of Christie's life, finally succeeded in locating it.

Charles Adams Barnes never married, and he lived only a few years after the conclusion of the Press Exploring Expedition. Following his service in the Navy and his days of mountain exploration, he went to South America. He located in Panama, where he engaged in mining operations. Later he was joined by a brother, Pierre, who contracted malaria. Charles Barnes then went to Colombia, where he, too, was stricken by the disease and died. Pierre buried him in Colombia in a grave beside the Rio Magdalena, four thousand miles from the Olympic wilderness.

Christie's right-hand man in the Press Exploring Expedition was the eldest child of William Horatio Barnes and Sarah Porter Barnes. His maternal grandfather, Charles Adams, was a cousin of John Quincy Adams. Charles Adams Barnes had one sister and several brothers. His father — who died when Charles was nineteen years old — had been a newspaperman in Washington, D.C., before the family moved to the west coast, and his mother was once commissioned by the White House to paint portraits of the presidents.

While Charles Barnes was in South America, his mother and one of his brothers, Paul, homesteaded on Lake Crescent, beside the creek which still bears their name. They were the first settlers on the lake. Nearby Marymere Falls was named for Charles Barnes's only sister, Mary Alice. Edward, another brother, later settled on the lake near Ovington. Other brothers were Pierre, for many years a patent attorney in Seattle, and Horace, a teacher. None are living today.

Dr. Harris B. Runnalls practiced medicine in England for ten years before he emigrated to the United States in 1888, then lived in Washington and Alaska until his death in 1913. In 1897, Runnalls was lured north by the Klondike gold rush. A pioneer of Skagway, he became the town's first postmaster and was closely identified with civic movements there.

Like Charles Barnes, Runnalls was also interested in mining, but he traveled only one fourth as far, and in the opposite direction, to find his fortune. Runnalls was one of the early stampeders in the Atlin, B.C., district, when gold was first discovered in that camp. There he helped in locating the "Discovery" and "Rock of Ages" claims on Pine Creek, which were rich in gold bearing quartz.

Runnalls returned to Washington in 1906. He died seven years later at the age of fifty-nine. On December 15, 1911, Runnalls wrote to his son: "The trails on this old sphere are many, and which one I'll choose I don't know, but it will be a new one . . . travelled by a man, sick of community conventionalities and hypocritical behavior."

John William Sims was the eldest of thirteen children. While he still lived in England he was married and fathered two children. After his discharge from the British Army, Sims came to North America in 1886 — first to Alberta, Canada, where he built a log cabin. Later he moved to the United States and became a naturalized citizen. His children and all his brothers and sisters (with the exception of one sister, Jennie) remained in England.

For several years after the Press Exploring Expedition, Sims lived in Seattle, and he is listed in the city directory as a carpenter. He then moved to Everett, Washington, and on June 1, 1909, Sims married Catherine E. (Williams) Wood. They had a daughter, Mary, and a son, Owen, who was killed in 1940. No one in the United States carries on Sims's name today, but several descendants of his first children live in England.

When he grew older, Sims no longer went into the mountains, but he often told his children stories of the Press Expedition's journey across the Olympics. When he retired, he moved to a small place in Yakima County, and lived there several years, until his death in the spring of 1943. He is buried in Marshland Cemetery, in the country near Snohomish.

Mary Sims Buell, his daughter, still possesses the tiny compass (in perfect working order) and the carved wooden whistle which her father carried across the Olympic Mountains.

On July 10, 1890, while John H. Crumback was on the Mount St. Elias expedition, his mother, Margaret Robinson, wrote to Edmond S. Meany from Galt, Ontario, stating that her son had not answered her letter, and indicating concern about his welfare. Although Crumback never perfected his squatter's claim in Geyser Valley, he did return to the Olympics. According to one source,[2] "Among the first to arrive [in the Quinault Valley] will be recalled . . . Jack Crumback, frontiersman, and with the Canadians against Louis Riel, in Riel's Rebellion."

As with Crumback, little is known of the subsequent life of Christopher O'Connell Hayes. In July, 1890, Hayes wrote to Meany from Kiona, Yakima County,[3] inquiring as to the whereabouts of Christie, who had not answered his letters, and asking the subscription price of the Seattle *Press*. A notation appears on the letter in Meany's handwriting: "7/25/90 ESM. Send wkly 1 yr. free." Here the trail vanishes.

It would be indeed interesting if the descendants of Crumback and Hayes could be located and some knowledge gained of their lives after 1890. Each passing year makes the task more formidable, however, and less likely of success.

[2] *Trails and Trials of the Pioneers of the Olympic Peninsula, State of Washington*, compiler Lucile Horr Cleland (Humptulips Pioneer Association, 1959), p. 171.

[3] Kiona, a post office on the Northern Pacific Railway, is located on a bend of the Yakima River, at the base of the Horse Heaven Hills. This area is now part of Benton County.

BIBLIOGRAPHY

THIS BOOK is based primarily on the July 16, 1890, issue of the Seattle *Press* (forerunner of today's Seattle *Times*), chief source of information about the Press Exploring Expedition. The story has been fortified, however, by additional material obtained elsewhere.

Most important were the notes I made when interviewing persons who had information to offer. A reference in *The Story of Port Angeles*, by G. M. Lauridsen and A. A. Smith (Seattle, Wash.: Lowman & Hanford, 1937), together with an article in the May 22, 1890, issue of the Seattle *Post-Intelligencer*, led me to Mrs. Pierre Barnes, who told of the life of Charles A. Barnes, her brother-in-law. Mrs. Shirley I. Fager made available the extensive file of personal papers and mementoes of her grandfather, Dr. Harris B. Runnalls, and I also relied on Mrs. Fager's excellent paper, "Doctor, Miner, Explorer: Dr. H. B. Runnalls." Mrs. Mary Buell and Mrs. Gladys Arnold reminisced about the life of their father and stepfather, John William Sims. Robert Hitchman related details of his 1936 and 1937 visits with James H. Christie in British Columbia, and also provided for my perusal Christie's scrapbook and other unpublished papers.

Bits of information were gleaned from the Edmond S. Meany Papers and Correspondence in the University of Washington Library; from Grace Worth's "Notes on the Life of James Halbold Christie" (a privately mimeographed paper); and from several articles in the Seattle *Post-Intelligencer*: "Bunchgrass on the Hills" (August 2, 1889), "The Promised Land" (May 22, 1890), "Farms in the Olympics" (May 28, 1890), and "Unknown No Longer" (June 5, 1890). Also, much of the information about Seattle in 1889–90 was found in the *Post-Intelligencer*.

Other helpful items included *Senate Document No. 59,* 54th Congress, 1st Session, U. S. Senate, "Report of Lt. Joseph O'Neil, Fourteenth Infantry, of his exploration of the Olympic Mountains, Washington, from June to October, 1890"; *The Mountaineer,* XIX, No. 1 (1926), which contains a letter from Christie to Meany; *Trails and Trials of the Pioneers of the Olympic Peninsula, State of Washington,* compiled by Lucile Horr Cleland (Humptulips Pioneer Association, 1959); the Tenth Census (1880) and Eleventh Census (1890) of the United States government; U. S. Weather Bureau records for four western Washington stations during the winter of 1889–90; and the book, *Washington: A Guide to the Evergreen State,* American Guide Series (Portland, Ore.: Binfords & Mort, 1941).

Several articles about the expedition, based on the Seattle *Press* account, could be termed "secondary sources." These included pages 151–56 of Ruby el Hult's *The Untamed Olympics* (Portland, Ore.: Binfords & Mort, 1954); Robert Hitchman's article, "Name Calling," in the *Mountaineer,* LII, No. 4 (1959); "The Land that Slept Late," by Preston P. Macy and Will Muller (*American Forests,* December, 1946); "The Wilderness Mountains," by Lois Crisler (in the book, *The Pacific Coast Ranges,* ed. Roderick Peattie [New York: Vanguard Press, 1946]); and Jerry Russell's three-part article, "An Exploration of the High Olympics," which appeared in the Seattle *Times's Charmed Land Magazine* on March 18 and 25 and April 1, 1962.

APPENDIX

NOMENCLATURE OF THE
PRESS EXPLORING EXPEDITION

The men of the Press Exploring Expedition named many of the natural features they observed in the Olympic Mountains. Some of the names have endured with the passage of time; others have not. Those marked with an asterisk (*) appear on today's maps.

RIVERS AND CREEKS

Alexander River: After Alexander Christie of Edinburgh, Scotland, apparently a relative of James H. Christie. (In Christie's scrapbook, there is a line drawn through "Edinburgh, Scotland," and written above, in Christie's handwriting, "Montreal, Quebec.") This stream is known today as Rustler Creek or The Rustler; on some older maps, The Rusher.

Belle River: Known today as Long Creek. The records do not disclose whom the name honored.

Crumback River: For John Crumback, a member of the expedition. This is the East Fork Quinault.

Godkin River: Known today as Godkin Creek; sometimes called The Godkin. Named for E. L. Godkin, editor of the New York *Post*.

* *Goldie River*: After R. H. Goldie of Seattle.

Hayes River: Perpetuates the name of Christopher O'Connell Hayes, a member of the expedition.

Lillian River: The records do not state for whom this stream was named.

Sims River: Known today as Promise Creek. Named after John W. Sims, a member of the expedition.

Six creeks were named: *Cat, Coldfeet, Kate, Jane, Louise,* and *Wolf.* Also a creek known today as Kimta was referred to as the *Lost Chord.*

Two waterfalls were named: *Adeline Cascade* and *Elizabeth Falls.*

VALLEYS

Chester Valley: Name given to portion of Quinault Valley west of Mount Lawson. The records do not indicate who Chester was.

*Geyser Valley: Name applied to bottomlands along the lower Elwha contiguous with confluence of Belle River (Long Creek). The name — which still prevails — was given because the men thought they heard geysers while camped there. The valley is sometimes called Geyser Basin. A few years after the expedition crossed the mountains, the valley was settled by homesteaders — the Humes, Michaels, Ludden, and Anderson families. In this valley the expedition erected the foundation of Crumback's "cabin."

*Press Valley: The upper Elwha Valley was named for the expedition. Today's maps show only that portion where the Hayes River joins the Elwha as being Press Valley, but the expedition intended the name to apply to the upper Elwha watershed from its headwaters in Elwha Basin to the juncture of the Goldie with the Elwha. Press Valley was described as being the largest valley on the Elwha, "30 miles long; 1 to 3 miles wide," and extending "to within a mile or two of the sources of the Quiniault and the Quillayute rivers." (The Hoh was mistaken for the Quillayute.)

MOUNTAIN RANGES

Three of the mountain ranges named by the expedition — the Bailey, Burke, and Holmes ranges — are rugged chains of peaks, snow-clad above timberline throughout the year.

Antrim Range: This forest-covered ridge north of Lake Quinault and west of Finley Creek was named for Frederick S. Antrim of Aberdeen, Washington, the first man the expedition members met as they emerged from the mountains.

*Bailey Range: After William E. Bailey, proprietor of the sponsoring newspaper, the Seattle *Press.* This range was considered the "backbone" of the Olympics. The name is well established.

Burke Range: "A succession of lofty and precipitous peaks," named for Judge Thomas Burke of Seattle, and bounded by the East Fork Quinault, Hayes River, and Godkin Creek. This name should be restored; the range is presently unnamed, and Burke was an important figure in western Washington at the time of the Press Exploring Expedition.

Deer Range: Name given to mountainsides bordering the Elwha on the east, between Devil's Backbone and Lillian River, because of many deer observed there.

Holmes Range: Constituted some of the peaks to the east, dominated by Mount Holmes, which was probably Mount Deception; contiguous with the Sound Range — by which name the peaks facing Hood Canal and Puget Sound were generally known at that time.

Kemp Range: After Alfred C. G. Kemp of Montesano, Washington; a forested ridge paralleling Lake Quinault on the south. Includes minor peaks such as Colonel Bob, Gibson Peak, and Mount O'Neil (not to be confused with the Mount O'Neil named by the Press Party).

MOUNTAIN PEAKS

Thirty-six mountain peaks were distinguished with names. Only nine, or 25 per cent, of the names appear on today's maps of the Olympics.

Mount Agnus: After General Felix Agnus of the Baltimore *American*. One of the high points on Happy Lake Ridge.

*Mount Barnes: Commemorates Captain Charles Adams Barnes of the expedition. See footnote on page 159.

Mount Bennett: Name given to Mount Olympus, after James Gordon Bennett of the New York *Herald*. Because the party mistook Mount Carrie for Olympus, they never realized that their Mount Bennett was the highest point in the Olympic Mountains.

Mount Brown: For Amos Brown of Seattle. Known today as Lost Cabin Mountain.

Mount Childs: A peak of the Bailey Range, named for George Washington Childs, proprietor of the Philadelphia *Ledger*. See footnote on page 159.

*Mount Christie: For James H. Christie, leader of the Press Exploring Expedition. It stands somewhat aloof from other peaks, as befits a leader.

*Mount Dana: After Charles A. Dana, editor and proprietor of the New York *Sun*. An outlier of the Bailey Range.

Mount De Young: For M. H. De Young, editor and proprietor of the San Francisco *Chronicle*. Known today as Muncaster Mountain, after a ranger of the United States Forest Service.

Mount Egan: Named for John G. Egan, city editor of the Seattle *Press*. Now known as Mount Norton.

Mount Eldridge: Named for William C. Eldridge of Washington, D.C. Known today as Hurricane Hill. At one time automobiles could be driven to the summit, but the road has been converted into a trail.

°*Mount Ferry*: Honors E. P. Ferry, governor of Washington in 1890.

Mount Fitten: For DuBose Fitten of Seattle. This peak may have been the mountain known today as Windfall Peak, but more likely was one of the unnamed high points on the ridge three or four miles to the northwest.

Mount Frazier: For S. R. Frazier, editor of the Seattle *Press*. High point on the Queets-Quinault divide near Lake Beauty, possibly the peak known today as Mount Kimta.

Mount Goodwin: For Judge C. C. Goodwin of the Salt Lake *Tribune*. This name does not appear on Barnes's map of the Olympics, and there is nothing to indicate its location.

Mount Grady: For the late Henry Grady, editor of the Atlanta *Constitution*. Known today as Mount Lawson, name given by Press Party to a different peak.

Mount Hearst: For W. R. Hearst, proprietor of the San Francisco *Examiner*. Known today as Mount Queets.

Mount Holmes: After John H. Holmes, editor of the Boston *Herald*. Probably Mount Deception.

Mount Hunt: For Leigh S. J. Hunt, proprietor of the Seattle *Post-Intelligencer*. Easternmost high point of Happy Lake Ridge.

Mount Jones: After George F. Jones, editor of the New York *Times*. This name does not appear on Barnes's map; therefore, its location is unknown.

°*Mount Lawson*: For Victor F. Lawson, editor of the Chicago *News*. In subsequent years the name was shifted to a peak one and one-half miles to the northeast, and the Press Party's Mount Lawson is presently unnamed.

Mount McClure: For Col. A. K. McClure of the Philadelphia *Times*. A high point on Happy Lake Ridge; probably Lizard Head Peak.

Mount McCullough: A peak in the Burke Range, named for J. B. McCullough of the St. Louis *Globe-Democrat*. Known today as Crystal Peak.

°*Mount Meany*: After Edmond S. Meany of the Seattle *Press*, later president of The Mountaineers and a professor of history at the University of Washington.

Mount Medill: Named for Joseph Medill of the Chicago *Tribune*. This is an unnamed peak today, in the Burke Range. A little to the northeast of Chimney Peak.

* *Mount Noyes*: After Crosby S. Noyes, of the Washington, D. C., *Evening Star.*

"*Old Snowback*": Term used, while the expedition was in the lower end of Press Valley, to designate the mountain known today as Chimney Peak.

Mount O'Neil: "after Lt. Joseph P. O'Niel, USA." The spelling in the text is erroneous, but correct on the map. The mountain was possibly Hoh Peak, or one of the unnamed peaks of the Mount Olympus Range southwest of Mount Olympus.

Mount Pulitzer: Name given to a prominent peak of the Bailey Range, after Joseph Pulitzer, proprietor of the New York *World*. Probably the peak called "Snagtooth" by fire lookout crews at the Dodger Point lookout. See footnote on page 159.

Mount Reid: Named for Whitelaw Reid, editor and proprietor of the New York *Tribune*. The present name is Mount Tom (after Tom Martin, former treasurer of the state of Washington).

*Mount Scott: For James W. Scott of the Chicago *Herald*.

*Mount Seattle: "in honor of the city of Seattle." From this peak Barnes made the observations which enabled him to complete his map of the Olympics.

Mount Squire: After Senator Watson C. Squire of the state of Washington. Later called Ludden Peak, for a Geyser Valley settler.

Mount Struve: After Judge H. G. Struve of Seattle. The peak is located slightly more than a mile southeast of the peak known today as Mount Lawson.

Mount Taylor: After Colonel Charles Taylor of the Boston *Globe*. High point on the ridge at the head of Buckinghorse Creek, three miles southeast of Mount Christie.

Mount Watterson: In the Burke Range, slightly southeast of Crystal Peak. This mountain, unnamed today, was named for Henry Watterson of the Louisville *Courier-Journal.*

Mount Zindorf: This peak is almost encircled by the Quinault, Promise Creek, and Kimta Creek. The men failed to disclose the source of this name, one of the last chosen by the expedition.

OTHER NAMES

Convulsion Canyon: Name given to the Elwha Canyon at the site of the great landslide south of the Lillian.

Deception Divide: The ridge running west from Mount Wilder toward Mount Barnes, where the expedition discovered that in following the Goldie it had been cutting a base line across a great curve of the Elwha.

Devil's Backbone: Not really Press Party terminology, this was the local settlers' name for the western spur of Mount Eldridge.

Difficulty Hill: Probably not meant as a permanent name; merely the designation for the mountainside above the Lillian Canyon.

Goblin Gates and *Goblin Canyon*: Names given to the most unusual phenomenon discovered by the expedition. Goblin Gates designates the place where the Elwha right angles into a cliff; Goblin Canyon the gorge below the gate.

Lakes Mary and Margaret: These were names given to the two small lakes at Low Divide, where the expedition finally departed from the Elwha watershed and crossed over to the Quinault.

Semple Plateau: For ex-Governor Eugene Semple of Washington Territory, because of the evidence of former Indian life found there, which reminded the explorers of the Governor's report in 1888 to the Secretary of the Interior. The "plateau" is actually a small bench above the Elwha just north of the confluence of Goldie River, where it emerges from its canyon. For unknown reasons the name has been applied to the southern part of the Bailey Range, near Bear Pass.

Thunder Canyon: The canyon on the Elwha near the present Elkhorn Ranger Station.